A Question of SPORT

QUIZ BOOK

ACKNOWLEDGEMENTS

With thanks to the BBC *A Question of Sport* production team who produced the book: Executive Producer Kieron Collins; Producer Carl Doran; Questions written and edited by Richard Morgale, Gareth Edwards and Dave Ball; Production Secretary Lucy Jones

The publishers would like to thank Empics and the following photographers for their kind permission to reproduce the pictures in this book:

Empics/Matthew Ashton, Sarah Bruntlett, Jon Buckle, Adam Davy, Mike Egerton, Tom Jenkins, Ross Kinnaird, Jed Leicester, John Marsh, Tony Marshall, Steve Mitchell, Don Morley, Phil O'Brien, Nick Potts, David Rawcliffe, Peter Robinson, Ross Setford, Michael Steele, Neal Simpson, Chris Turvey, Steve White.

Every effort has been made to acknowledge correctly and contact the source and/or copyright holder of each picture, and Carlton Books Limited apologises for any unintentional errors or omissions which will be corrected in future editions of this book.

First published by Carlton Books Limited in 2001
By arrangement with the BBC.

Reprinted 2005

A CIP catalogue for this book is available from the British Library.

ISBN 1 84442 275 5

Project Editor: Vanessa Daubney
Project Art Direction: Russell Porter
Picture Research: Debora Fioravanti
Production: Lisa French

Printed and bound in the United Kingdom

A Question of SPORT

QUIZ BOOK

CARLTON
BOOKS

contents

introduction

At 6.20 pm on Monday, 5 January 1970, David Vine launched television's longest-running sports quiz show — *A Question of Sport.* In the first programme captains Henry Cooper and Cliff Morgan were joined by sporting personalities George Best, Ray Illingworth, Lillian Board and Tom Finney. It's unlikely that George Best would have guessed then that he would return as a guest in a Sporting Greats edition of the show some thirty years later.

More than 1000 sporting stars have appeared on the programme in over 30 years, lead by 13 resident team captains. There have also been several guest team leaders including, in the early years, such football legends as Bobby Charlton and the late Bobby Moore. Surprisingly, only three main presenters have been asking the questions and keeping order. David Vine hosted the show for five years when the programme was first recorded in a converted church at the BBC North studios a few miles south of Manchester's city centre. He remained as question master for a further three years after the recordings were moved to Manchester's Oxford Road studios before making way for David Coleman in 1979.

Until that year the programme was a straightforward quiz show and David's brief was to 'loosen' it up. As one of the main voices of BBC Sport and host of *Sportsnight* and *Grandstand,* he was the ideal man for the job. During his reign the programme was consistently in the BBC's Top Ten. The audience averaged 8 million but, on the famous occasion when HRH The Princess Royal joined the guests for the 200th edition, the viewing figures hit 18 million.

In November 1997, after 376 programmes, David Coleman made way for the former British number 1 (at one time ranked number 4 in the world) tennis player Sue Barker. Then the captains were John Parrott and Ally McCoist. John gave way to jokey Frankie Dettori before the Wasps and England scrum-half, Matt Dawson, took over from him in 2004

The programme was given a makeover in the autumn of 1998, with a new television set and new opening titles and graphics. The quiz rounds though have changed little with the Mystery Guest, Picture Board and What Happened Next? rounds all proving as popular as ever. In 1999 and again in 2001, the programme won the prestigious Royal Television Society Sports Entertainment Programme of the Year Award.

So the award-winning *A Question of Sport* goes from strength to strength. And the millions of viewers who watch the show every week, can now find out what it's like to be in the hot seat — trying to answer some of the toughest sporting questions. All the favourite rounds from the shows have been included in 44 games which you can play with family or friends, or by yourself.

Good Luck!

game **1**

round one — name the year

The following events all happened in the same year, but which one?

1 Seve Ballesteros claims his first Open title.
Maurice Barnes and Rubstic are Grand National winners.
Michael Owen was born.
Bjorn Borg defeats Roscoe Tanner at Wimbledon.
Jim Watt becomes WBC Lightweight champion of the world.

1979

Now for the second year:

2 Rugby Union's 5 Nations is won by England.
Manchester United claim their third Premiership title.
A British driver wins the Formula One World Championship.
Steffi Graf beat Arantxa Sanchez-Vicario in the Wimbledon final.
Donovan Bailey breaks 100m World Record.

1998

SCOREBOARD

round two — picture board

Take a look at picture B on page 1 of Picture Board 1.

Who is it?

Take a look at picture A on page 6 of Picture Board 1.

Who is it?

~~Martin Johnson~~
Andrew Caddick

SCOREBOARD

round three — twenty sporting questions

20 questions on the history of the final stages of the football World Cup.

1 In which country was the first tournament staged?
2 Who were the winners in 1978?
3 Which former Arsenal player won the Golden Boot award at France '98?
4 Which was the first country to host the final stages twice?
5 In which year did Wales qualify for the first time?
6 Which country did Brazil defeat 4–1 to win the 1970 World Cup final?
7 Apart from Gary Lineker, who scored for England during the 1986 World Cup finals?
8 Which African nation played in the 1970 tournament?
9 Name the German who scored the only goal of the 1990 final.
10 How many goals did Just Fontaine score in 1958?
11 Which Irishman in 1982 became the youngest-ever player to appear in the tournament?
12 Which country appeared in the first 16 World Cups?
13 Which African nation upset the form-book in 1982 by beating West Germany 2–1?
14 Name the Cameroon striker who is the oldest player to appear in the final stages.
15 Which German midfielder has played in a record 25 matches in the final stages?
16 What World Cup 'first' occurred when the USA played Switzerland in 1994?
17 Jairzinho of Brazil in 1970 was the last player to do what?
18 How did Tofik Bakhramov achieve world-wide fame during the 1966 World Cup?
19 What links Pique in 1986, Willie in 1966 and Ciao in 1990?
20 Up to and including 1998, how many goals have England scored in the World Cup?

SCOREBOARD		

round four — sporting links

1 What connects record-breaking athlete Sir Roger Bannister, Welsh rugby legend JPR Williams and Olympic Modern Pentathlon gold medallist Stephanie Cook?

2 What connects Olympic rower Matt Pinsent, 1977 Wimbledon champion Virginia Wade and record-breaking triple-jumper Jonathan Edwards?

SCOREBOARD

round five — where am I?

From the following two clues you must work out which place is being described.

1 I have just left Bramall Lane and am on my way to watch the World Championship snooker at the Crucible. In which city am I?

Sheffield

2 The Dragons are playing cricket at Sophia Gardens, whilst the Bluebirds are playing football at Ninian Park. In which city am I?

Cardiff

SCOREBOARD

round six — what happened next?

All you have to do in this round is decide which of the three options is the correct answer.

Football. An international football friendly between Hong Kong and Macao. Referee Choi Kuok-kun has just shown Lee Kin-wo the red card. What happens next?

- **a** The player reacts badly and kicks the ball at the referee who in turn takes unkindly and a punch-up breaks out.
- **b** The manager disagrees with the decision and leads all his players off the field in protest.
- **c** 10 minutes later the referee realises he has sent the wrong player off and Lee Kin-wo is allowed back on the field.

Cricket from Bristol and a one-day international between Zimbabwe and the West Indies. Brian Lara is about to face a delivery. What happened next?

- **a** A snowstorm hits the ground and the match is abandoned.
- **b** Strong winds blow the stumps and sight-screens down and the players are forced from the field.
- **c** A swarm of bees invades the ground and players and spectators have to take evasive action.

SCOREBOARD		

round seven — home or away

football Who is the only British player to score a goal in an FA Cup final and a European Cup final?

rugby union	Which Welsh international holds the world record for most points in Tests?
cricket	Which Australian batsman has scored the most runs in Test history?
golf	At which course is the World Matchplay golf tournament held?

SCOREBOARD

round eight — captain's away

We're going to give each of you four people with the same names as fish, and you have to tell me whether they're genuine sports stars or simply made up!

1 Rugby Union – Was there a Scottish captain named David Sole?
2 True or false – a former World Indoor Bowls champion from Canada was Lisa Mackerel?
3 Ian Perch used to play full-back for the New Zealand Rugby League team?
4 True or false – Harry Haddock played football for Scotland?
5 The trainer of 1967 Grand National winner Foinavon was Geoff Trout?
6 England have had a Rugby Union international player named Jamie Salmon?
7 True or false – Winston Place played Test cricket for England?
8 True or false – a world lightweight boxing champion was called John 'Crispy' Cod?

SCOREBOARD

round nine — mystery guest

Can you guess the identity of these sporting stars from the four clues below? The more clues you need, the fewer points you get.

1 I was born in Singapore in 1958. (4 points)
I played for the same manager for club & country. (3 points)
I captained Ally McCoist to his first league title. (2 points)
I was bloodied but unbowed in Stockholm. (1 point)

2 I was born in Czechoslovakia in 1980. (4 points)
I was named after one of the great players in my sport. (3 points)
I was the youngest 20th-century winner at SW19. (2 points)
My nickname is "the Swiss Miss". (1 point)
Martina Hingis

SCOREBOARD

round ten — on the buzzer

The theme to this quick-fire round is venues. The next twenty questions are all to do with some of the world's most famous sporting arenas.

1 At which football league ground did Barry McGuigan win his featherweight world title in 1985?

2 What sport in England would you expect to see at Grace Road, Edgbaston and Headingley? Cricket

3 Which Spanish side play their home games at the Santiago Bernabeu stadium? Real Madrid

4 At which racecourse is the St. Leger run? Doncaster

5 Rugby Union – which side play their home games at Welford Road?

6 Where was the 2001 British Speedway Grand Prix held?

7 American Football – who play their home games at the Mile High Stadium?

8 In which British city would you find the football grounds of Ashton Gate and the Memorial Ground?

9 On which ground did Kenny Dalglish score to secure the 1986 League Championship?

10 In which city were the 1984 Winter Olympics held?

11 Where in Paris are the French Open tennis championships held?

12 On which course did John Daly win his only Open title?

13 In which city did Paul Gascoigne famously shed tears for England?

14 In which country would you find the world-famous Cresta Run bobsleigh course?

15 Which Rugby League team play their home games at the Jungle?

16 In which city would you find the Bislet Games, the home of the 'Dream Mile'?

17 Which American city has a basketball team named the Bulls, a baseball team called the Cubs and an American Football team called the Bears?

18 Cricket – At which Test venue would you find the Grace Gates and the Long Room?

19 Which Welsh rugby side play their home games at the Gnoll?

20 Which sport's world championships between 1979 and 1985 were held at Jollees nightclub in Stoke-on-Trent?

SCOREBOARD		

game **2**

round one — name the year

The following events all happened in the same year, but which one?

1 The Cricket World Cup final is held in Lahore.
Frank Bruno loses his World Title in Las Vegas.
The Dallas Cowboys win their second Super Bowl in three years, beating the Pittsburgh Steelers 27–17.
The favourite Rough Quest wins the Grand National.
The Olympic Games are held in Atlanta.

Now for the second year:

2 The Winter Olympics are held in Lillehammer.
Julio Cesar Chavez loses for the first time in 91 fights to Frankie Randall.
28-year-old Jose Marie Olazabal wins the Masters at Augusta.
Michael Schumacher wins the Formula One world title after colliding with Damon Hill in the final race of the season.
Manchester United do the double, beating Chelsea 4–0 in the FA Cup final.

SCOREBOARD

round two — picture board

Take a look at picture C on page 8 of Picture Board 2. Who is it?

Take a look at picture D on page 7 of Picture Board 1. Who is it?

SCOREBOARD

round three — twenty sporting questions

20 sporting questions with a Scottish connection.

1. Which player was World Snooker Champion in 1998?
2. Which football side play their home games at Easter Road?
3. Name the goalkeeper who, in 2001, was signed by Manchester United, three years after winning the last of his 43 caps?
4. Who won the World Darts title in 1982 and 1989?
5. Gavin Hamilton represented both Scotland and England at cricket during 1999 while he was with which county?
6. In which Scottish town do the Flyers play ice hockey?
7. Who was Olympic 100m gold medallist at the Moscow Olympics in 1980?
8. Name the flanker who captained the victorious 1989 British Lions in Australia?
9. At which club did Alan Hansen begin his professional career?
10. In 1991 who was the first British woman to win a world 10,000m gold medal?
11. What is the name of the NFL Europe team based in Scotland?
12. In which Olympic sport, popular in Scotland, would you try and put a quarter tonne of granite into a house?
13. Who are the only football side in either England or Scotland whose name contains a J?
14. Which athlete won the 400m at the 1924 Olympics and was immortalised in the film *Chariots of Fire*?
15. Who scored twice for Everton in the 1989 FA Cup final but still lost?
16. Golf – Who won the British Open in 1985?
17. Which player lifted the 1984 European Cup for Liverpool?
18. Which Scotsman played for Great Britain in Rugby League and the British Lions in Rugby Union during the 1990s?
19. Shirley Robertson won Olympic gold in which event at the Sydney Olympics?
20. On which course did Nick Faldo win the 1990 Open?

SCOREBOARD	

round four — sporting links

1 What links middle-distance runner Kelly Holmes, England Rugby Union forward Tim Rodber and former Aston Villa striker Guy Whittingham?

2 What links former Scotland goalkeeper Andy Goram, Welsh Rugby Union international Nigel Walker and former Liverpool and Scotland defender Alan Hansen?

SCOREBOARD

round five — where am I?

From the following two clues you must work out which place is being described.

1 In 1976 I watched Sue Barker win the French Open and five years later saw Alan Kennedy score the winning goal in a European Cup Final. In which city am I?

2 You could watch cricket at the Gabba, or watch the Broncos play Rugby League in this city, but which one?

SCOREBOARD

round six — what happened next?

All you have to do in this round is decide which of the three options is the correct answer.

USPGA Golf from New Orleans, and Paraguay's Carlos Franco has just hit his approach shot on to the green. What happened next?

- **a** A seagull flies down and steals the ball.
- **b** A turtle is on the green, Franco picks it up and it relieves itself over him.
- **c** He plays the wrong ball on the green and the two-shot penalty results in him finishing the tournament in second place.

Cricket. Lancashire versus Glamorgan at Blackpool in July 1999. Mike Atherton hits Robert Croft through the covers and Steve Watkin gives chase. What happened next?

- **a** A dog runs on the field and stops the ball reaching the boundary.
- **b** The batsman run three, then the ball is thrown in but hits a fielding helmet and five penalty runs are added – a total of eight is scored.
- **c** Watkin tries to stop the ball with his boot but only manages to stick a spike through the ball and gets it stuck on the bottom of his shoe.

SCOREBOARD		

round seven — home or away

fooball Name the current England international who has won FA Cup winners' medals in the last three decades?

boxing	Can you name the other future world champion whom Lennox Lewis beat to win his Olympic gold in 1988?
athletics	Who is the only British athlete to win track and field medals at the last three Olympics?
tennis	Since Pat Cash's Wimbledon victory in 1987, who is the only other Australian to have won a Grand Slam singles title?

SCOREBOARD

round eight — captain's away

Here are two riddles from the often unusual world of sport. Can you tell me...

1 In 1999 why did a Randy Duck fly home from Dallas to Guard the Towers of London?
2 Where would you find Magnolia, Flowering Peaks and Carolina Cherry?

SCOREBOARD

round nine — mystery guest

Can you guess the identity of these sporting stars from the four clues below? The more clues you need, the fewer points you get.

1 I was born in Hammersmith in 1972 but am a Welshman. (4 points)
I turned professional in 1993 and was World Champion by 1997. (3 points)
My father's name is Enzo. (2 points)
I retained my World title in April 2001 with a first-round knockout. (1 point)

2 I was born in Zimbabwe in 1966 and played in the 1983 World Cup. (4 points)
I won my first county cap in 1986 and made my England debut in 1991. (3 points)
I was the second youngest player ever to make 100 centuries. (2 points)
I made 405 not out for Worcestershire in 1988. (1 point)

SCOREBOARD		

round ten — on the buzzer

A look back at the Sydney Olympics, and the first letter of each answer will spell out the words 'OLYMPIC GAMES.' In the case of a person's name, this means the surname.

1 Which former World Champion took silver in the women's 5000m at Sydney?
2 In which event did Ivan Pedroso win gold at Sydney?
3 Which country claimed bronze in men's Water Polo?

4 Briton Kate Allenby won Olympic bronze on the last day of the Games in which event?

5 Which female athlete failed to defend her 200m and 400m titles in Sydney?

6 Which country won its only gold medal of the games in the Badminton men's doubles?

7 In which event did Paul Ratcliffe win silver for Great Britain?

8 Which American sprinter anchored his team to 4 x 100m relay gold in Sydney?

9 In which city will the Olympics be held in 2004?

10 From which country does Olympic 800m champion Maria Mutola come from?

11 In which sport did Briton's Pippa Funnell and Ian Stark compete in Sydney?

12 Which country did Cameroon defeat on penalties to take the men's football gold medal?

SCOREBOARD		

game 3

round one — name the year

The following events all happened in the same year, but which one?

1 Three British athletes win world titles.
Chris Eubank and Nigel Benn draw in Manchester.
Nigel Mansell wins the Indy Car Championship driving for Newman-Hass, the team part-owned by the actor Paul Newman.
The Grand National, the 150th to be run, is turned into a farce.
Manchester United win the first-ever Premiership title.

Now for the second year:

2 Steve Elkington wins a play-off with Colin Montgomerie to claim the US PGA title.
England achieve another Grand Slam, but captain Will Carling is disciplined after calling the RFU an organisation run by 'old farts'.
Spain's Miguel Indurain, 31, wins a record fifth consecutive Tour de France.
Arsenal reach the Cup Winners' Cup Final but are unable to retain the trophy.
Paul Rideout scores the only goal in the FA Cup Final.

SCOREBOARD		

round two — picture board

Take a look at picture F on page 5 of Picture Board 1. Who is it?

Take a look at picture A on page 1 of Picture Board 2. Who is it?

SCOREBOARD		

round three — twenty sporting questions

20 questions on sport in the 1980s.

1 Which team appeared in four FA Cup Finals but only managed to win once?
2 In which city were the 1984 Olympics held?
3 Eddie 'the Eagle' Edwards became a household name in which sport?
4 Which boxer won the World Featherweight title at Loftus Road in 1985?
5 In 1981 Aldaniti won the Grand National in a fairy-tale story, but who rode him?
6 Name the Dutchman who scored a hat-trick against England during Euro '88?
7 Which Spaniard won the Open in both 1984 and '88?
8 Which famous race was won by Britons Charlie Spedding in 1984 and Steve Jones in 1985?
9 At which ground did Ian Botham score a century and Bob Willis take eight wickets to record a famous victory over Australia in 1981?
10 Which partnership won Gold in the ice dancing at the 1984 Olympics?
11 Which country won the inaugural Rugby World Cup in 1987?
12 In which sport was Jahangir Khan world champion six times during the '80s?
13 Which team did the League and FA Cup double in 1986?
14 Which famous horse-race was won by Nashwan, Slip Anchor and Reference Point during the decade?
15 Who captained England Rugby Union to the Grand Slam in 1980?
16 Which German won Wimbledon aged 17 in 1985?
17 Clive Lloyd and Viv Richards captained which side to series victories in England in 1984 and 1988?
18 Lawrie Sanchez scored the only goal of the 1988 FA Cup final to help which side defeat Liverpool?
19 In which sport did Neil Adams become a world champion in 1981?
20 Who scored a goal with the final kick of the 1989 season to win the League Championship for Arsenal?

SCOREBOARD		

round four — sporting links

1 What connects jockey Paul Carberry, footballer Eidur Gudjohnsen and snooker player Neil Foulds?

2 What connects Welsh international footballer Barry Horne, Olympic boxing champion Audley Harrison and former Manchester United and England winger Steve Coppell?

SCOREBOARD

round five — where am I?

From the following two clues you must work out which place is being described.

1 In this country you could watch a league football match between Afan Lido and Connahs Quay Nomads, or play first division Rugby Union at the Eugene Cross Park or Sardis Road. Name the country.

2 If you were watching Malmo playing football or saw Magnus Norman play a home match in the Davis Cup, in which country would you be?

SCOREBOARD

round six — what happened next?

All you have to do in this round is decide which of the three options is the correct answer.

Motor racing from the 1999 Le Mans 24 Hours. Mercedes' Peter Dumbreck is about to overtake. What happened next?

- **a** He passes the car in front but then takes the practice lane instead of the correct race track and is disqualified.
- **b** The car stalls and all other cars overtake him.
- **c** Dumbreck's car flies into the air, flips over and over before landing off the track. Amazingly Dumbreck was completely unhurt.

Football from the 1999 Copa America and a match between Argentina and Colombia. The referee awards a penalty to Argentina. What happened next?

- **a** Argentina's Martin Palermo misses his third penalty of the match. There were five penalties awarded in the match… and four were missed.
- **b** The Colombian team are incensed and argue furiously with the referee and six of their players are eventually sent off.
- **c** Argentinean goalkeeper Roa takes it, but it is saved by Higuita who in turn kicks the ball the length of the field and scores into an empty net.

SCOREBOARD		

round seven — home or away

golf During the 1990s two Europeans twice claimed the Green Jacket at the US Masters. Nick Faldo was one but can you name the other?

football Who is the only player to have won caps for England whilst playing for both Everton and Liverpool?

cricket Who, by taking a hat-trick against the West Indies in December 2000, became only the third Australian in history to take over 300 wickets?

athletics Who is the only British female athlete to win an Olympic 10,000m medal?

SCOREBOARD

round eight — captain's away

Here are two riddles from the often unusual world of sport. Can you tell me...

1 Horse racing – Who doesn't exist, but won a major race of 1964?

2 Football – What was unique about Ivan Robinson's goal for Barrow against Plymouth in 1968?

SCOREBOARD

round nine — mystery guest

Can you guess the identity of these sporting stars from the four clues below? The more clues you need the fewer points you get.

1 I was born in 1960 and played in two World Cup finals. (4 points)
I made my international debut in 1977. (3 points)
I have used all parts of my anatomy to score goals. (2 points)
I lifted the World Cup in 1986. (1 point)

2 I was born in Sidcup in 1969 and have competed in three Olympics. (4 points)
I set three world records in the '90s but never won Olympic gold. (3 points)
I was the first British man to set a world record in the javelin. (2 points)
My main competitor is Jan Zelezny. (1 point)

SCOREBOARD		

round ten — on the buzzer

We'll be creating a chain where the surname of the first answer forms the Christian name of the next, and so on. Here's the first chain of nine:

1 Cricket – Name the Worcestershire opening batsman who played five Tests for England in the late 1980s.
2 Which Liverpool athlete reached the 800m Olympic final in 1992?
3 Rugby Union – Name the former England outside-half who is now director of rugby at Newcastle.

4 Which Scottish snooker player knocked Mark King out of the 2000 World Championship?

5 Which Bradford Bulls player took the Man of the Match award at the 2000 Challenge Cup final?

6 Football – Name the former West Ham and Spurs midfielder who played alongside cousin Clive in the 1987 FA Cup final.

7 Who resigned as chairman of Tottenham Hotspur in 2001?

8 Boxing – Which former Olympic champion has held world titles at five different weights?

9 Name the snooker referee whose nickname is Ballcrusher.

And here's the second chain: there are ten answers in this one.

10 Football – Which Aston Villa defender's Premiership debut was in 1998 when he was aged only 17?

11 Rugby Union – Which famous Wales and Lions fly-half was nicknamed 'the King?'

12 Football – Which legendary Welshman joined Juventus in 1957 from Leeds United, was nicknamed 'the Gentle Giant' and could play equally well in either defence or attack?

13 Football – Who scored the winning goal in the 1971 FA Cup final for Arsenal, and later joined Derby?

14 Which Scotland prop has the same name as a former Arsenal and Spurs boss?

15 Rugby Union – Name the New Zealander who coaches both Wales and the British Lions.

16 Rugby League – Which New Zealander plays alongside his brother Robbie for the Bradford Bulls?

17 Golf – Name the Scotsman who won the 1999 Open.

18 Football – Name the Wycombe Wanderers manager who scored Wimbledon's winning goal in the 1988 FA Cup final.

19 Tennis – Name the Spanish woman who's won three French Opens.

SCOREBOARD		

game 4

round one — name the year

The following events all happened in the same year, but which one?

1 Daniel Amokachi leads his country to Olympic gold.
Steffi Graf wins her seventh Wimbledon, beating Arantxa Sanchez Vicario in the final.
Wasim Akram smashes a record 12 sixes in a Test innings of 257.
Damon Hill emulates the success of his father Graham by winning the World Drivers' Championship title.
Jurgen Klinsmann leads Germany to European Championship success.

Now for the second year:

2 Liz McColgan wins a World Championship gold medal in Tokyo.
At 42 years, George Foreman returns to challenge Evander Holyfield for the World Heavyweight title but loses on points.
Ayrton Senna wins his third World Drivers' Championship title.
Australia beat England 12–6 to win the World Rugby Union title.
Alex Ferguson wins the Cup Winners' Cup with Manchester United, eight years after winning it with Aberdeen.

SCOREBOARD

round two — picture board

Take a look at picture F on page 1 of Picture Board 1. Who is it?

Take a look at picture C on page 6 of Picture Board 1. Who is it?

SCOREBOARD

round three — twenty sporting questions

20 questions on sports stars who are called Smith or Jones.

1. Whose goal won the European Cup Winners' Cup final against Parma in 1994?
2. Which British Lions scrum-half won 54 caps for Wales between 1986–95?
3. Tennis – Which British lady won the 1969 Wimbledon singles title?
4. Name the Hampshire and England batsman who is known as 'the Judge'.
5. Which Australian won the Formula 1 Drivers' Championship for Williams in 1980?
6. Name the Liverpool defender who scored in the 1977 European Cup final win?
7. Which boxer who won Olympic silver in 1988 later went on to become light-heavyweight champion of the world?
8. Which Australian batsman scored over 6,000 runs in 164 One-Day Internationals?
9. The 1996 US Open was won by which American?
10. Which Irish swimmer won the Olympic 400 metres freestyle gold medal in 1996 and later changed her surname to de Bruin?
11. Name the American sprinter who was 200m World Champion in 1983 and 1987?
12. England Under-21 striker Alan Smith helped which club to the Champions League semi-final in 2001?
13. Name the Scotland and British Lions prop forward who scored a crucial try in his country's Six Nations draw against Wales in 2001?
14. Which female athlete won five Olympic medals in Sydney – three of them gold?
15. Gorilla Jones was World Champion during the 1930s in which sport?
16. Rugby Union – which New Zealand lock forward with 79 caps retired in 2001?
17. USA international Cobi Jones played in the Premiership for which club?
18. Who broke Dalton Grant's British high-jump record in 1992?
19. Name the former Liverpool defender who played in the 1996 FA Cup final and won eight caps for England before injury cut his career short?
20. 'And Smith must score…' was a famous commentary line about Gordon Smith in the 1983 FA Cup final, but for which club was he playing?

SCOREBOARD		

round four — sporting links

1 What connects former Coventry goalkeeper Steve Ogrizovic, ex-England lock forward Wade Dooley and Welsh snooker world champion Ray Reardon?

2 What connects former England striker Trevor Francis, the 1976 French Open winner Sue Barker – and that famous sailor Sir Francis Drake?

SCOREBOARD

round five — where am I?

From the following two clues you must work out which place is being described.

1 You can see the Jets play basketball in this city, and in 1979 Ian Rush began his career with the city's home club. Where?

2 In this English city you would find a Rugby Union club called the Saints and a cricket side known as the Steelbacks. Where?

SCOREBOARD

round six — what happened next?

All you have to do in this round is decide which of the three options is the correct answer.

Baseball from New York, and the Mets versus the Yankees in 1999. Mets batter Ordonez hits the ball back towards Yankees pitcher Elduke. What happened next?

- **a** Ordonez slips as he sets off for a run; as he gets back to his feet he loses his bearings and begins to run the wrong way round the bases.
- **b** Elduke fields the ball but it gets stuck in his glove – so he throws his glove to first base and runs Ordonez out.
- **c** The ball hits the pitcher's mound and rebounds to a vacant left-field allowing Ordonez to complete a home run.

Cycling. The 1999 Tour de France. Italian Guiseppe Guerini is just half a mile from victory in Stage Ten. What happened next?

- **a** A spectator runs out in front of Guerini to take his picture, they collide and the Italian falls off. Guerini manages to get back up and wins the stage.
- **b** Guerini gets a puncture, but carries his bike over the line to win the stage.
- **c** Guerini thinks he has crossed the finish line 200 yards too early, celebrates and gets off his bike. The rest of the peleton pass him and Guerini finishes last.

SCOREBOARD		

round seven — home or away

darts Who is the only darts player in history to have won world titles in three decades?

athletics	Which sprinter broke the 100m World Record twice during the 1990s but failed to win a major individual title?
horse racing	Name the eight-times National Hunt champion jockey who rode in the Grand National 13 times but never managed to finish higher than third?
football	Which Irish international played in five FA Cup finals during the 1990s, with two different clubs?

SCOREBOARD

round eight — captain's away

Here are two riddles from the often unusual world of sport. Can you tell me...

1 Where did Sunderland midfielder Stefan Schwarz's contract prevent him from moving to in 2002?

2 Every year, in which event do competitors from all over the world cover 140.6 miles on a land and sea course; the record finishing time is just over eight hours?

SCOREBOARD

round nine — mystery guest

Can you guess the identity of these sporting stars from the four clues below? The more clues you need, the fewer points you get.

1 I was born in Madras in 1968. (4 points)
I have a Natural Sciences degree from Durham University. (3 points)
I made my test debut in 1990 in a victory over the West Indies. (2 points)
I captained England to a series win over Sri Lanka in 2001. (1 point)

2 I was born in Surinam in September 1962. (4 points)
I made my international debut in 1981 for Holland. (3 points)
I captained my country to victory at Euro '88, scoring in the final. (2 points)
I have managed Chelsea and Newcastle to the FA Cup final, playing some 'sexy football' on the way. (1 point)

SCOREBOARD		

round ten — on the buzzer

The last letter of the surname will provide the first letter of the next Christian name (eg. Sue Barker would be followed by Roger Black).

1 Which British cyclist took Olympic gold in the 4000m Individual Pursuit in 1992?

2 Which boxer was known as 'the Dark Destroyer'?

3 Football – Name the England Under-21 goalkeeper who plays for Manchester City?

4 Boxing – Name the 1988 Olympic light-middleweight silver medallist who went on to win the WBC, WBA and IBF light-heavyweight belts?

5 Athletics – Name the only British woman to win World and Olympic titles?

6 Cycling – Who won the Tour de France in 1999 and 2000?

7 Which Italian scored the winning goal for Chelsea in the 1998 European Cup Winners' Cup final?

8 Which Scottish sprinter took Olympic gold in the 1980 100 metres?

9 Name the Irish boxer who was undefeated as WBO super-middleweight champion?

10 Snooker – Which player won six world titles in the 1980s?

11 Which Australian spinner played for Hampshire in 2000?

12 Name the England international striker who moved from Leicester to Liverpool for £11 million in 2000.

13 Which British athlete took the European 3000 metres title in 1990?

14 Name the tennis player who captained his country to victory in the Davis Cup and won the 1983 French Open.

15 Which cricketer played with Yorkshire and Leicestershire and went on to umpire a record number of Test matches?

16 Name the Briton who won the first of his two decathlon gold medals at the 1980 Olympics in Moscow.

17 Motor racing – name the Brazilian driver who was Formula One world champion in 1981, 1983 and 1987.

18 Who scored the first of Manchester United's two goals in their Champions League final against Bayern Munich in 1999?

19 Name the former undisputed middleweight boxing champion of the world who later went on to star in a movie called *Indio*.

20 Which snooker player won his first world championship at the Crucible in 2001?

SCOREBOARD		

game **5**

round one — name the year

The following events all happened in the same year, but which one?

1 Dundee United, under the management of Jim McLean, reach the UEFA Cup final.
Mike Tyson beats Tony Tucker to become undisputed world Heavyweight Champion.
New Zealand win the very first World Rugby Union Cup.
Jeremy Bates and Jo Durie of Britain win the Wimbledon Mixed Doubles title.
Keith Houchen scores with a magnificent header at Wembley.

Now for the second year:

2 Norwich's Herbie Hide beats Michael Bentt to becomes WBO Heavyweight Champion.
Jimmy White loses in the snooker world final for the fifth successive year.
Aston Villa defeats Manchester United in the League Cup Final.
Brian Lara reaches a Test record score of 375.
Roberto Baggio misses a penalty in the World Cup Final.

SCOREBOARD		

round two — picture board

Take a look at picture C on page 8 of Picture Board 1. Who is it?

Take a look at picture A on page 5 of Picture Board 1. Who is it?

SCOREBOARD		

round three — twenty sporting questions

20 questions on the history of the FA Cup

1 During the 20th century, which club won the most FA Cups?
2 Which Italian player scored after only 42 seconds for Chelsea in the 1997 final?
3 Which non-league team knocked Newcastle United out of the cup in 1972?
4 In 1986 the winning team had no English-qualified players. Which team was it?
5 In 1980, West Ham won the Cup thanks to a goal by which BBC soccer pundit?
6 Which Welsh international scored five goals in FA Cup finals for Liverpool?
7 In 1985, Man United's Kevin Moran was the first to do what in an FA Cup final?
8 Which club during the 1980s won consecutive finals both after a replay?
9 In 1988 whose penalty did Dave Beasant save, the first miss in a Wembley final?
10 Which England international defender scored an own goal in the 1991 final to help Spurs defeat Nottingham Forest?
11 Which stadium hosted the semi-final between Liverpool and Wycombe in 2001?
12 Who scored the only goal of the 1995 Cup final?
13 Who came from 3–0 down against Southampton to win 4–3 in the 2001 FA Cup?
14 Elton John was chairman of which defeated finalists during the 1980s?
15 Which ex-England winger played in five FA Cup finals with three different clubs during the 1980s and '90s?
16 Who are the only team from outside of England to win the FA Cup?
17 Name the Frenchman who scored the only goal of the 1996 final?
18 Which non-league club hold the record for the most League scalps?
19 How many different teams have won the FA Cup to complete the 'double'?
20 Which club's only success came in the 1987 FA Cup when they beat Spurs 3–2 ?

SCOREBOARD		

round four — sporting links

1 What connects former England cricket captain Mike Gatting and England international footballers Glenn Hoddle and Peter Reid?

2 What connects David O'Leary's only appearance in the World Cup finals, Jeremy Guscott's first England try and Bjorn Borg's first Wimbledon men's singles final ?

SCOREBOARD

round five — where am I?

From the following two clues you must work out which place is being described.

1 If you had just watched football at Pride Park and you had seen cricket where the Scorpions were playing at home, in which city would you be ?

2 In 1954 Roger Bannister ran the first sub-four minute mile at Iffley Road in this city, and today you could see the Cheetahs compete in Speedway's Elite League. Where?

SCOREBOARD

round six — what happened next ?

All you have to do in this round is decide which of the three options is the correct answer.

Tennis. Seniors' doubles, Wimbledon, 1999; Kevin Curren and Johan Kriek face Henri Leconte and Mansour Bahrami. Leconte is about to serve. What happened next?

- **a** The ball hits the net post and ricochets back into Bahrami who is standing near the net.
- **b** Leconte serves and it hits Bahrami on the head. Leconte collapses in hysterics, and the crowd erupts in laughter.
- **c** Curren returns the serve, but Bahrami puts another ball into play and a two-ball rally develops.

Golf from the 1999 Open at Carnoustie. Derek Cooper is about to hit his approach shot to the 18th green. What happened next?

- **a** The club head flies off and actually lands nearer the hole than the ball.
- **b** His shot is about to enter a bunker when it hits a rake and ends up on the green.
- **c** Cooper's ball flies into the Barry Burn, hits the wall, bounces straight back out again and lands on the fairway.

SCOREBOARD		

round seven — home or away

horse racing Who in 2000 became the first British-born champion jockey on the flat for 17 years, the last being Willie Carson in 1983 ?

football Ian Rush's five League Cup winners' medals are a record, but can you name the Welshman who holds the record for FA Cup winners' medals at Wembley ?

cricket Who in December 2000 became the first player from his country to take 300 Test wickets, and only the third spinner in history to reach this milestone?

golf At which course is the World Matchplay Golf tournament held ?

SCOREBOARD		

round eight — captain's away

Here are two riddles from the often unusual world of sport. Can you tell me...

1 In which sport might you split the pile, grind it out or muff?

2 In which sport can you throw some heat, go round the horn or hit a blooper?

SCOREBOARD		

round nine — mystery guest

Can you guess the identity of these sporting stars from the four clues below ? The more clues you need the fewer points you get.

1	I was born in 1976 but have had my recent career interrupted by injury.	(4 points)
	I won Olympic bronze in 1996.	(3 points)
	I played under an Englishman at PSV Eindhoven.	(2 points)
	I played for Brazil in the 1998 World Cup final after an injury scare.	(1 point)
2	I was born in 1963 and made my test debut the same day as Nasser Hussain.	(4 points)
	I followed in my father's footsteps into the Surrey and England sides.	(3 points)
	In 1994 I became the first Englishman to score centuries in both innings of a match against the West Indies.	(2 points)
	My father Mickey was coach of England for a time.	(1 point)

SCOREBOARD		

round ten — on the buzzer

You have to finish off these famous quotes – here are the first lines of some well-known phrases which you have to complete.

1 Steve Redgrave: 'If anyone sees me near a boat again…'
2 Bill Shankly: 'There are two teams on Merseyside; Liverpool and…'
3 George Best: 'I spent a lot of money on birds, booze and fast cars…'

4 Muhammad Ali: 'I float like a butterfly…'

5 Kevin Keegan: 'They've got to go to Middlesborough and get a result and I'll tell you what…'

6 Eric Cantona: 'When the seagulls are following the trawler it is because…'

7 Paul Gascoigne: 'Coping with the language in Italy shouldn't be a problem because…'

8 John Motson: 'For those of you watching in black and white…'

9 Brian Clough: 'If I catch spectators on my pitch in the future I know exactly what I'll do. They'll get…'

SCOREBOARD		

game **6**

round one — name the year

The following events all happened in the same year, but which one?

1 The Buffalo Bills reach the Super Bowl for the second year running but lose 37–24 to the Washington Redskins.
Martin Offiah moves from Widnes to Wigan for £440,000.
Derek Warwick, Mark Blundell and Yannick Dalmas win the Le Mans 24-Hour race.
Sunderland become the first side since the war to reach two FA Cup Finals while playing in the Second Division.
Denmark win the European Championships beating Germany 2-0 in the final.

Now for the second year:

2 In April Bernhard Langer becomes the first German player to win the US Masters.
Last Suspect wins the Grand National at odds of 50–1.
Ravi Shastri hits six sixes from a six-ball over – only the second player to do so.
Barry McGuigan defeats Eusebio Pedroza to win the World Featherweight crown.
Norman Whiteside scores Manchester United's FA Cup final winner against Everton.

SCOREBOARD		

round two — picture board

Take a look at picture B on page 7 of Picture Board 1. Who is it?

Take a look at picture A on page 1 of Picture Board 1. Who is it?

SCOREBOARD		

round three — twenty sporting questions

20 questions on sporting connections with the Republic of Ireland.

1 Which cyclist won the 1987 Tour de France?
2 Who captained Manchester United to the Premiership title in 2001?
3 At which stadium do Ireland's Rugby Union side play their home matches?
4 Who won the 1997 World Snooker Championship?
5 Which boxer claimed the WBO World Welterweight Championship in 1993?
6 Which golfer who finished third at the 1985 Open played in two Ryder Cups, following in the footsteps of his father, who played ten times?
7 Who won the 5000 metres gold medal at the 1983 World Championships?
8 Michael Carruth won Olympic gold in 1992 in which event?
9 Name the Irish international who scored twice in the 1982 League Cup final and again the following year to help Liverpool win the trophy on both occasions?
10 Football – Who led Ireland to the World Cup finals in 1990 and 1994?
11 Name the Ireland and British Lions hooker who scored four tries against the USA during the 1999 World Cup.
12 Which team has won the All-Ireland Gaelic Football championship most often?
13 Who won the 1995 World Championship women's 5000 metres title?
14 Which team has won the Irish football league on the most occasions?
15 Name the former Arsenal and Leeds defender who scored a penalty against Romania in 1990 which helped Ireland to the quarter-finals of the World Cup?
16 Who rode Papillon to victory in the 2000 Grand National?
17 Which ex-Liverpool midfielder's header helped knock England out of Euro '88?
18 Which ex-Manchester United and Aston Villa defender was voted 1993's PFA Player of the Year?
19 At which racecourse is the Irish Gold Cup run?
20 Name the university graduate who scored in two FA Cup finals for Liverpool and won 34 caps for the Republic of Ireland?

SCOREBOARD		

round four — sporting links

1 What connects Republic of Ireland manager Mick McCarthy, England fast bowler Darren Gough and European indoor athletics champion Jon Mayock?

2 What connects Spurs' match with Bristol Rovers in 1976, Yugoslavia against Zaire at the 1974 World Cup and Manchester United versus Ipswich Town in 1995?

SCOREBOARD

round five — where am I?

From the following two clues you must work out which place is being described.

1 In which country would you be if you were at the home of the first Modern Olympics and watching Nicolas Dabizas playing a home international?

2 If you were watching Lance Klusener bowling at Port Elizabeth and Ernie Els was playing golf at the Houghton Golf Club in Johannesburg, in which country would you be?

SCOREBOARD

round six — what happened next ?

All you have to do in this round is decide which of the three options is the correct answer.

Cricket from the 1999 World Cup – the West Indies against Bangladesh. Sherwin Campbell attempts a quick single. What happened next?

- **a** Shahriar Hossain tries to run out Sherwin Campbell, but only succeeds in under-arming the ball over everyone all the way to the boundary for four runs.
- **b** Campbell, Shahriar Hossain and umpire Darrell Hair all collide and end up in one big heap.
- **c** A direct hit from Shahriar Hossain results in Campbell being given run-out by the third umpire – the first time in World Cup history.

Boxing. A bout between Clayton Stewart and Paul Carr has just ended. What happened next?

- **a** The result is a tie, which neither boxer is happy with, and the fight re-starts.
- **b** Stewart is so excited with his first win in ten years that he tries to do a flying somersault in the ring and almost knocks himself out.
- **c** Carr is announced as the victor but Stewart's incensed mother runs into the ring and begins to hit him with her handbag.

SCOREBOARD		

round seven — home or away

tennis Which Frenchman was defeated by Pete Sampras in the US Open singles final in 1993 and the Wimbledon final in 1997?

golf	At the 1999 Ryder Cup, who became the first teenager to play for either side in the competition's 72-year history?
motor racing	Michael Schumacher's World Drivers' Championship for Ferrari in 2000 was their first for over two decades – who was their last world champion?
football	Name the cousins who were both in England's 1998 World Cup squad.

SCOREBOARD

round eight — captain's away

Here are two riddles from the often unusual world of sport. Can you tell me...

1 In which sport would you find a Garbage Man, a Cherry Picker and a Wingman who double-pumps and alley-oops?

2 In which sport can you have a chop with a sandwich?

SCOREBOARD

round nine — mystery guest

Can you guess the identity of these sporting stars from the four clues below? The more clues you need, the fewer points you get.

1 I was born in Coatbridge, Scotland in 1944. (4 points)
I made my international debut in 1972 while I was playing for Arsenal. (3 points)
My nickname as a player was 'Stroller'. (2 points)
I have managed Arsenal, Tottenham and Leeds United. (1 point)

2 I was born in Frimley in 1979. (4 points)
I made my England debut in 1998 aged 18 years and 301 days. (3 points)
I have played at both centre-half and outside-half. (2 points)
I am now England's leading points scorer of all time. (1 point)

SCOREBOARD

round ten — on the buzzer

A numerical theme to this buzzer round. Every answer will be a number in some form.

1 Golf – What is shouted as a warning following a wayward shot on a golf course?
2 How many league appearances did Ally McCoist make for Kilmarnock in the 1999–2000 season?
3 How many points are awarded for a drop-goal in Rugby League?
4 What age was Sue Barker when she reached the Wimbledon semi-final in 1977?

5 Name the French international footballer who played for Aston Villa during the 1980s.
6 Athletics – How many competitors in an Olympic 100m final?
7 How many points are awarded for a Formula 1 Grand Prix victory?
8 How many frames in total has John Parrott won in his two World Championship finals?
9 Football – How many goals did England score at Euro 2000?
10 Which boxer lost to Muhammad Ali in the 'Rumble in the Jungle'?
11 How many goals did Michael Owen score in the 2001 FA Cup final?
12 What age was Boris Becker when he won his first Wimbledon singles title?
13 How many times did Gérard Houllier and Arsène Wenger play for France?
14 In snooker, how many points would you be awarded for potting the yellow?
15 How many players would you find in a netball team?
16 Horse racing: in the 2001 Grand National at Aintree, how many horses finished the race?

SCOREBOARD		

game **7**

round one — name the year

The following events all happened in the same year, but which one?

1 Nick Faldo beats Scott Hoch to win the Masters after a play-off.
Frank Bruno challenges Mike Tyson for the World Heavyweight Championship.
Ginny Leng wins individual and team three-day events in the European Championships.
Luton reach the final of the League Cup for the second year running.
Liverpool beat Everton in the FA Cup final.

Now for the second year:

2 Jack Nicklaus at 46 years wins his sixth US Masters title.
Graeme Souness moves from Sampdoria to join Glasgow Rangers.
Viv Richards hits 100 in just 56 balls against England.
Dancing Brave dominates the Flat Season, culminating in victory in the Prix de L'Arc de Triomphe.
Maradona performs his 'Hand of God'.

SCOREBOARD		

round two — picture board

Take a look at picture D on page 2 of Picture Board 1. Who is it?

Take a look at picture C on page 3 of Picture Board 2. Who is it?

SCOREBOARD		

round three — twenty sporting questions

20 questions on the Summer Olympics.

1. Which city hosted the games in 1968?
2. Cycling – Name the Briton who won the 1km time-trial at the Sydney Olympics?
3. Which country has won most Olympic medals?
4. Which Canadian broke the Olympic record for the 100m to win gold in 1996?
5. Which team won football gold at the Sydney Olympics?
6. Which Olympic games is the Oscar winning film *Chariots of Fire* based upon?
7. In which sport did Paul Ratcliffe win Olympic silver at the Sydney Games?
8. Which US diver won double gold medals at both the 1984 and 1988 Olympics?
9. Which Cuban boxer won the Heavyweight gold medal at the last three Games?
10. Bob Beamon set a World Record at the 1968 Olympics which stood for 23 years – in which event?
11. At which Olympics did Mark Spitz win a record seven gold medals?
12. Who was the first British sprinter for 56 years to win gold in the 100 metres – doing so in 1980?
13. Which former gold medallist lit the flame to start the Atlanta games in 1996?
14. What nationality was 1996 1500m gold medallist Noureddine Morceli?
15. Six-times world pole-vault champion Sergey Bubka won how many Olympic titles?
16. Who partnered Steve Redgrave to the first of his three Olympic gold medals in the coxless pairs?
17. In which event did Dick Fosbury win Olympic gold in 1968?
18. Which Australian claimed gold in the 400 metres on her home soil at the 2000 Games?
19. Who won four consecutive Olympic long-jump gold medals between 1984 and 1996?
20. In what year did London last host the Olympic Games?

SCOREBOARD		

round four — sporting links

1 How old were: Ian Botham, when he 'couldn't get his leg over' and was out hit wicket at the Oval; Heike Drechsler when she won her second Olympic long-jump gold medal; and Ally McCoist in his final game for Rangers?

2 How old were: Martina Hingis the first time she won the ladies' singles at Wimbledon; Justin Rose when he played in the Amateur Championships; and John Parrott when he made the highest break on Junior Pot Black to win... a set of snooker balls?

SCOREBOARD		

round five — where am I?

From the following two clues you must work out which place is being described.

1 In which English city is the highest Football League ground above sea-level, where the Saddlers might meet the Villans in a local derby?

2 In which Scottish city would you see the Heriot's FP play rugby union and football taking place at Easter Road ?

SCOREBOARD		

round six — what happened next ?

All you have to do in this round is decide which of the three options is the correct answer.

Motorcycling. Valentino Rossi has just crossed the finishing line of the Spanish 250cc Grand Prix in first place. What happened next?

- **a** On his lap of honour Rossi stops to visit a Portaloo.
- **b** Fans run on to the track and steal his bike.
- **c** He pulls a wheelie but is over-zealous and does a somersault.

Rugby Union. A league match is taking place between Cardiff and Newport. Gareth Thomas scores a try for Cardiff, and Paul Burke steps up to kick the conversion; what happened next?

- **a** The Newport players run out in an attempt to charge down Burke's kick, but it hits Newport's Rod Snow on the head and goes over the bar.
- **b** The ball hits both posts and the crossbar before eventually creeping over for the two extra points.
- **c** A spectator runs on to the field and takes the kick, but narrowly misses and is escorted from the field by the referee Mr Whitehouse.

SCOREBOARD		

round seven — home or away

cricket Which Worcestershire and England batsman in 1998 became only the 24th player in history to score 100 first-class centuries?

rowing Can you name the only sisters to win an Olympic rowing medal for Great Britain ?

boxing Before Audley Harrison's victory in Sydney, which middleweight was the last British fighter to win an Olympic medal, doing so in 1992?

football Name the England player who scored four international goals in a 12-month period in 1987–88 but didn't score his fifth until a match in 2000 against the Ukraine ?

SCOREBOARD

round eight — captain's away

Here are two riddles from the often unusual world of sport. Can you tell me...

1 Which sport's original rules, written in the 19th century by John Sholto Douglas, prohibited competitors from hugging and biting or from having springs on the soles of their boots?

2 In which sport do two teams in snorkels and goggles chase a squid into a gully?

SCOREBOARD

round nine — mystery guest

Can you guess the identity of these sporting stars from the four clues below? The more clues you need, the fewer points you get.

1 Born in Kensington in 1966, I have spent all my career in London. (4 points)
I made my England debut in 1991 scoring against Turkey. (3 points)
I was stripped of the club captaincy by Glenn Hoddle after being sent off in 1993. (2 points)
I won my first FA Cup with the Crazy Gang in 1988 and then two more with Chelsea in 1997 and 2000. (1 point)

2
I was born in Bath in 1965 and am a qualified bricklayer. (4 points)
I scored a hat-trick against Romania on my international debut. (3 points)
I was called up for the British Lions in 1989, replacing the injured Will Carling, and scored the winning try in the second Test. (2 points)
I won 65 caps in the centre for England. (1 point)

SCOREBOARD		

round ten — on the buzzer

These answers are all in alphabetical order - if it's a person's name, it's the surname that counts. We start with 'A.'

1 Athletics – Name the British athlete who ran the final leg for the victorious 4 x 400m relay at the 1991 World Championships?

2 Name the Manchester United midfielder who captained England for the first time against Italy in November 2000.

3 Rugby Union – Which Australian holds the record for most tries in international rugby ?

4 Football – Which Scottish team play their home games at Tannadice ?

5 Snooker – Who claimed his first ranking title for three years by beating Jimmy White in the 2000 British Open ?

6 Who won Australia's only track and field gold medal at the Sydney Olympics, doing so in the 400m?

7 In which sport might you see Kerry play Dublin in the All-Ireland championship?

8 Name the New Zealander who coached the British Lions on their 2001 tour of Australia?

9 The San Marino Grand Prix is held at which track?

10 Which American athlete won five track and field medals at the Sydney Olympics, three of them gold?

11 Which Scottish football club play their home games at Rugby Park?

12 In cricket, where do Middlesex play their home matches?

13 Stephanie Cook is best known for competing in which sport?

14 Bjorn Borg won his first Wimbledon singles title in 1976. Whom did he beat?

15 Name the home of Barnsley Football Club.

16 Who partnered Sir Steve Redgrave to gold in the 1992 Olympics?

17 Which football club finished runners-up in the 1982 FA Cup and were coached by Terry Venables?

18 In which sport would you find Richard Burns competing?

19 Who managed Blackburn Rovers back to the Premiership in 2001?

SCOREBOARD		

game **8**

round one — name the year

The following events all happened in the same year, but which one?

1

Niki Lauda takes the World Championship by half a point.
Secreto is a surprise winner of the Derby, beating hot favourite El Gran Senor.
John McEnroe destroys Jimmy Connors in the Wimbledon Singles Final.
Zola Budd fails to win Olympic Gold.
France win the European Championships, with Michel Platini their inspiration.

Now for the second year:

2 New Zealand's Richard Hadlee is the first bowler to take 400 Test wickets.
James 'Buster' Douglas knocks out Mike Tyson in the tenth round in Tokyo.
Trained by Sirrel Griffiths and ridden by Graham McCourt, the 100–1 outsider Norton's Coin wins the Cheltenham Gold Cup.
Palace destroy Liverpool's hopes of retaining the FA Cup by beating them 4–3 in the semi-final.
Germany beats Argentina 1–0 to win the World Cup.

SCOREBOARD		

round two — picture board

Take a look at picture D on page 8 of Picture Board 1. Who is it?

Take a look at picture E on page 2 of Picture Board 2. Who is it?

SCOREBOARD		

round three — twenty sporting questions

20 questions on sport during the 1990s

1 Which team won the FA Cup four times during the decade?
2 Where were the 1996 Olympic games held?
3 Which lady took her first Grand Slam title by winning the 1997 Australian Open in 1997?
4 Which jockey won the Grand National twice during the '90s, on Party Politics in 1992 and Earth Summit in '98?
5 Which batsman scored a world-record 501 not out for Warwickshire against Durham in 1994?
6 Who defeated England to win the 1991 Rugby Union World Cup?
7 Who was world snooker champion in 1991?
8 Which British driver won the Formula One Drivers' Championship in 1996?
9 Name the English golfer who won the US Masters twice during the 1990s.
10 Which Scottish side won the Premier league title every season from 1990–97?
11 Maurice Greene won which event at the 1997 World Championships?
12 Which boxer became WBA heavyweight champion in 1994 – 21 years after he first became champion of the world?
13 Who were runners-up at the 1994 World Cup?
14 Which team did Manchester United defeat to win 1999's Champions League?
15 In which sport did Rodney Eyles of Australia become World Champion in 1997?
16 Rugby League – Which team won the Challenge Cup six times in the 1990s?
17 The Bills lost four consecutive Superbowls during the '90s: from which city do they come?
18 Who was leading scorer at Euro '96?
19 On which course did Paul Lawrie win his first Open title in 1999?
20 Which Indian bowler became only the second player in history to take all ten wickets in an innings during 1999?

SCOREBOARD		

round four — sporting links

1 How old were: Eddie Hemmings when Kapil Dev hit four sixes in a row off his bowling at Lord's; Mark O'Meara when he won the Open; and Pat Jennings when he made his final international appearance against Brazil?

2 How old were: David Beckham when he scored against Colombia in the World Cup; Ieuan Evans when his try against Scotland helped Wales to the Triple Crown; and Michael Schumacher when he won his first Grand Prix?

SCOREBOARD		

round five — where am I?

From the following two clues you must work out which place is being described.

1 After watching the Knicks play some basketball, you could stay in this city and watch the US Open tennis. Where ?

2 In 1985 Everton beat Rapid Vienna to win the European Cup Winners' Cup and a golden goal helped France win the European Championships in this city.

SCOREBOARD		

round six — what happened next?

All you have to do in this round is decide which of the three options is the correct answer.

Boxing from Bethnal Green, and the start of a fight between Daniel James and Steve Tucket. What happened next?

- **a** They both run from their corners but clash heads in the middle of the ring and are both knocked out, and the fight abandoned.
- **b** James knocks Tucket out with the first punch. The fight officially lasted 13 seconds.
- **c** The bell sounds and they start fighting before the judges realise that the referee is yet to enter the ring.

Football from South Africa, and the Orlando Pirates have a corner. What happened next?

- **a** The Pirates' Bashan Mishlango completely misses the ball and kicks the corner-flag instead.
- **b** The corner is crossed into the box, hits the referee on the back of the head and goes into the top corner for a goal.
- **c** The Pirates' goalkeeper comes up into the box on the attack and scores a remarkable overhead kick to win the game for the Pirates.

SCOREBOARD		

round seven — home or away

tennis Who won his fifth Wimbledon men's doubles title in 1992, partnered by Michael Stich?

figure-skating Which female figure-skater won four individual World titles and two Olympic golds in the 80s?

football Who in 1998 became the first player to appear in losing Cup finals for three different clubs?

cricket Can you name the only player to appear in each of the first six Cricket World Cups?

SCOREBOARD		

round eight — captain's away

Here are two riddles from the often unusual world of sport. Can you tell me...

1 Name the five English Premiership and Football League teams that begin and end with the same letter.

2 Name the five Football League teams that have an 'X' in their names.

SCOREBOARD		

round nine — mystery guest

Can you guess the identity of these sporting stars from the four clues below? The more clues you need, the fewer points you get.

1 Born in Italy in 1964, I made my name as a goalscorer. (4 points)
I have won winners' medals in all three of the major European competitions. (3 points)
I helped Chelsea win the 1997 FA Cup as a substitute. (2 points)
I replaced Ruud Gullit as a player-manager in 1998. (1 point)

2 I was born in 1960 in Stoke-on-Trent, but didn't start playing my sport until I was 26. (4 points)
I started playing at the Crafty Cockney Pub. (3 points)
I won my first world title in 1990. (2 points)
Known as 'The Power', I am the most successful player ever. (1 point)

SCOREBOARD

round ten — on the buzzer

A look back at the year 2000 and some of the more memorable sporting moments. So starting with…

1 January – Name the American who defeated Yevgeny Kafelnikov to claim his second Australian Open title.

2 February – Which side defeated Scotland for only the second time, and recorded their first-ever Six Nations victory?

3 March – Which university, after seven consecutive defeats, won the 146th Boat Race?

4 April – Which Irish snooker player beat John Parrott en route to his first World Championship semi-final?

5 May – Which Italian scored his second FA Cup final goal for Chelsea to defeat Aston Villa?

6 June – By a margin of how many strokes did Tiger Woods win the US Open?

7 July – Which American claimed his second consecutive Tour de France victory?

8 August – Which Ipswich midfielder with an out-of-this-world surname scored the first goal of the new Premiership season?

9 September – Name the Australian 400m runner who lit the flame to open the Sydney Olympic Games?

10 October - Name the former European Golden Boot winner who has now gone 12 months without scoring a league goal in the Scottish Premiership?

11 November – Which side captained by Brad Fittler won the Rugby League World Cup?

12 December – Which player beat Mark Williams to win the UK Snooker Championships?

SCOREBOARD

game 9

round one — name the year

The following events all happened in the same year, but which one?

1 Initially a reserve for the tournament, John Daly wins the USPGA title.
Mike Powell breaks Bob Beamon's 23-year-old world long-jump record.
The USA beats Britain by a single point to win the Ryder Cup at Kiawah Island.
Manchester United win the Cup Winners' Cup in Rotterdam.
Brian Clough tastes defeat in his only FA Cup final.

Now for the second year:

2 England beat France 31–13 in the Parc des Princes after Gregoire Lascube and Vincent Moscato are sent off.
Kevin Young breaks Ed Moses's world 400 metres hurdles record.
Ossie Ardiles is sacked by Newcastle and Kevin Keegan is appointed.
Tom Kite finally wins a major – the US Open at Pebble Beach.
Liverpool win the FA Cup with goals from Ian Rush and Michael Thomas.

SCOREBOARD		

round two — picture board

Take a look at picture A on page 3 of Picture Board 2. Who is it?

Take a look at picture C on page 6 of Picture Board 2. Who is it?

SCOREBOARD		

round three — twenty sporting questions

20 questions on sport with a connection to London.

1 Who play their home games at Stamford Bridge?
2 Who defeated Bruges at Wembley to win the 1978 European Cup?
3 How many times did 'Crafty Cockney' Eric Bristow win the world darts championship?
4 What is the name of the basketball team from London who play in the British premier league?
5 At which cricket ground would you find the Grace Gates?
6 Which team defeated Wasps to win the 1998 Tetley Bitter Cup?
7 Which famous race takes place between Putney and Mortlake bridges?
8 What sporting event takes place in SW19?
9 Which football club's nickname is the Addicks?
10 Who scored a last-minute try at Wembley in 1999 to help Wales defeat England in the last Five Nations match?
11 Who scored Arsenal's only goal in the 2001 FA Cup final?
12 Rugby Union – Which famous exile club play their home games at Old Deer Park?
13 Which football club's home ground has the postcode N17?
14 Which team defeated Wigan at Wembley in 1998 to win the Rugby League Challenge Cup?
15 Name the Dutchman who won the Wimbledon singles title in 1996.
16 Which snooker player is known as 'the Whirlwind of Old London Town'?
17 Which Sri Lankan bowler took 9–65 against England at the Oval in 1998?
18 Which race has Tanni Grey-Thompson won a record five times?
19 Which London venue is known as 'Billy Williams' Cabbage Patch'?
20 Which football club play their home games at the Boleyn Ground?

SCOREBOARD		

round four — sporting links

Put these sporting events in chronological order.

1 (a) Ian Botham's 149 not out against Australia at Headingley (b) Ernie Hunt's 'donkey kick' goal against Everton (c) Seb Coe setting three world records in 41 days (d) Gareth Edwards' try for the Barbarians vs.the All Blacks in Cardiff.

2 (a) Alan Shearer's first international goal (b) Graham Gooch's 333 for England against India (c) Steffi Graf and Boris Becker winning Wimbledon singles titles (d) Kriss Akabusi anchoring Great Britain to world 4x400 metres relay gold.

SCOREBOARD		

round five — where am I?

From the following two clues you must work out which place is being described.

1 The birthplace of Bryan Robson and the home of Durham County Cricket Club will lead you to this million-pound town in the North-East of England.

2 If you were watching the St. Leger being run or you were at the Belle Vue Ground to see the home side drop out of the Football League in 1998, where would you be ?

SCOREBOARD		

round six — what happened next ?

All you have to do in this round is decide which of the three options is the correct answer.

Football from the Premiership, and a match between Coventry and Leicester City from November 1999. A free-kick is awarded. What happened next?

- **a** Muzzy Izzet of Leicester blasts the ball on target but it hits the frame in the back of the goal and rebounds out, and the goal is not awarded.
- **b** As he is running back towards the half-way line, referee Stephen Lodge attempts to back-heel the ball but only manages to trip over it.
- **c** A dog runs on to the field as Matt Elliot is about to take the kick and steals the ball away from the defender's toes.

Tennis from Chicago, and John McEnroe is at match point against his brother Patrick in a final. What happened next?

- **a** A mobile phone rings in the crowd, and John quips: 'Tell Mom we're busy!'
- **b** John serves what he thinks is an ace to win the match, only for a judge to call 'foot fault'. John then launches into a 'You cannot be serious' tantrum.
- **c** John serves a double fault and in a temper smashes his racquet on the floor, only to realise he has no spares and is forced to forfeit the match.

SCOREBOARD		

round seven — home or away

fooball On which ground did England first play under the management of Sven-Göran Eriksson ?

athletics	Which British athlete set six personal bests at the 1999 World Championships in Seville?
golf	Name the European whose record run of 11 Cup appearances ended when he wasn't selected in 1999 ?
tennis	Who is the only woman to have won the Wimbledon singles title representing two different countries?

SCOREBOARD

round eight — captain's away

Here are two riddles from the often unusual world of sport. Can you tell me...

1. How did Richard Stokes witness Test cricket history as a 10-year-old at Old Trafford in 1956, and again while on business in New Delhi in 1999?
2. In which Olympic sport have the governing body announced that women's shorts can only be six centimetres wide, while men's shorts have to stop at least 20 centimetres above the knee?

SCOREBOARD

round nine — mystery guest

Can you guess the identity of these sporting stars from the 4 clues below? The more clues you need the fewer points you get.

1 I was born in Newcastle in 1970. (4 points)
I made my England debut in 1992 against France. (3 points)
I have broken the British transfer record on two occasions. (2 points)
I helped Blackburn to the 1995 Premiership title. (1 point)

2 I was born in Portsmouth in 1966 and have won medals on my own and as part of a team. (4 points)
I won a European and Commonwealth gold medal in 1986. (3 points)
In 1996 I won Olympic silver in both the 400 metres and relay. (2 points)
I am now a BBC presenter and am more colourful than my name suggests. (1 point)

SCOREBOARD		

round ten — on the buzzer

This buzzer round is a progression of numbers. The answer to the first question will contain one letter, the second will have two letters and so on – though the very last one has 26! In the case of someone's name, it will be the surname that counts.

1 From which area on a snooker table must you always break?
2 Name the snooker star from Hong Kong who reached the world top 16 in the year 2000?

3 Which Newcastle midfielder played for England during the 1998 World Cup?

4 Cricket – which West Indian batsman holds the record for the highest test score with 375?

5 After winning the US Masters in April 2001 which golfer held all 4 major titles?

6 Name the Liverpool and England striker who is nicknamed 'Bruno'.

7 At which racecourse would you find the Canal Turn and the Chair?

8 Name the Lancashire batsman who captained England 52 times.

9 Which team defeated Liverpool to win the 1988 FA Cup final?

10 Dominic Cork, Phil DeFreitas, Kim Barnett, Devon Malcolm and Chris Adams have all played first-class cricket for which county?

11 Which woman won her first Wimbledon singles title in 1983?

12 Which golfer won the 1989 Open at Royal Troon ?

13 Which Scottish first division club caused a major shock by knocking Celtic out of the 2000 Scottish Cup?

SCOREBOARD		

game 10

round one — name the year

The following events all happened in the same year, but which one?

1 Nigel Mansell returns to Formula One racing with McLaren, but can't start the first two races as he is too big for the car.
The West Indies lose to Australia, their first series defeat at home since 1973.
Wigan's run of successive Challenge Cup wins is extended to eight.
Eric Cantona is involved in a 'kung fu' incident at Crystal Palace.
Blackburn win the Premiership title.

Now for the second year:

2 Having begun his baseball career in 1963, Peter Rose finally retires from the sport.
Daley Thompson wins the European Decathlon title.
Mike Tyson takes the WBC World Heavyweight title from Trevor Berbick.
Maradona lifts the World Cup.
Liverpool complete the League and Cup double.

SCOREBOARD		

round two — picture board

Take a look at picture B on page 5 of Picture Board 2. Who is it?

Take a look at picture B on page 2 of Picture Board 1. Who is it?

SCOREBOARD		

round three — twenty sporting questions

20 questions with a Spanish connection.

1 Which golfer won the US Masters in 1999?
2 Which football team won the first five European Cups?
3 Miguel Indurain won which race five times during the 1990s?
4 In which city were the 1992 Olympics staged?
5 Name the Spaniard who won the 1994 ladies singles title at Wimbledon?
6 Against which South American side did Spain lose 27–15 during the 1999 Rugby Union World Cup?
7 Which English side knocked Barcelona out of the 2001 UEFA Cup?
8 In which sport was Carlos Sainz World Champion in 1990 and '92?
9 Which event was won by Fermin Cacho at the Barcelona Olympics?
10 Which former Liverpool and Wales striker has had spells as manager of Real Madrid and Real Sociedad?
11 At which course was the 1997 Ryder Cup held?
12 Who in 1998 beat Alex Corretja in an all-Spanish French Open final?
13 Name the England international who scored for Real Madrid in the 2000 European Cup Final?
14 Pelota is an Olympic sport. True or false?
15 Golf – Which Spaniard won the Open for the third time in 1988?
16 In which city were the 1999 Athletics World Championships held?
17 Name the Spanish international who played for Barcelona in the 1992 and '94 European Cup finals and later moved to Chelsea?
18 Who in 1999 became the youngest player to represent Europe in the Ryder Cup competitions?
19 Name the cyclist who won the 1988 Tour de France.
20 Which club play their home games at the Vicente Calderon stadium?

SCOREBOARD		

round four — sporting links

These sports stars all have interesting nicknames: what are they?

1 Australian cricket captain Steve Waugh; former world boxing champion Nigel Benn; 2000 world darts champion Ted Hankey; 1976 French Open winner Sue Barker.

2 1982 Masters golf champion Craig Stadler; snooker star Joe Swail; Olympic 100 metres champion Maurice Greene; Ally McCoist, when he first joined Rangers.

SCOREBOARD		

round five — where am I?

From the following two clues you must work out which place is being described.

1 If you were watching a league match between the Grasshoppers and the Young Boys, you'd be in the country which is home to the Cresta Run.

2 If former World Champion Juha Kankkunen was rallying on home soil and Sami Hyypia was playing a home international, you would be in this country.

SCOREBOARD		

round six — what happened next?

All you have to do in this round is decide which of the 3 options is the correct answer.

World Indoor Bowls in Norfolk, and David Gourlay is playing Les Saunders. They're about to start another end. What happened next?

- **a** 22-year-old Tracy Sergeant runs naked on to the rink and kisses both players.
- **b** David Gourlay drops a bowl on his foot and retires injured.
- **c** Les Saunders plays his first bowl with such pace that he splits the jack in two.

Snooker from the 1999 UK Championships. Joe Swail is playing Matthew Stevens. He has a tricky shot with the white positioned awkwardly behind a cluster of reds. What happened next?

- **a** Swail hits the ball with such power that five reds all go in.
- **b** Swail uses the rest but as he tries to play the shot his cue gets stuck in the spider and needs the referee's assistance to remove it.
- **c** As Swail tries to get into a comfortable position to play the shot, with one leg resting on the table, his trousers rip.

SCOREBOARD		

round seven — home or away

tennis Which American tennis player won her first Grand Slam tournament at this year's Australian Open?

cycling	Which cyclist added Olympic bronze at Sydney 2000 to the two Tour de France victories he had previously claimed?
rugby league	Which current Wigan player scored the winning try in the 1992 World Cup final?
boxing	Which boxer has won a record six world titles at five different weights, his latest coming in June 1991 against Virgil Hill to claim the WBA Light-Heavyweight belt?

SCOREBOARD

round eight — captain's away

Here are two riddles from the often unusual world of sport. Can you tell me...

1 Football – There are six Scottish teams with names that contain a double 'E'. Name five.

2 Cricket – Name the five first class counties that don't end in 'S-E-X', such as Middlesex, or 'SHIRE', as in Yorkshire.

SCOREBOARD

round nine — mystery guest

Can you guess the identity of these sporting stars from the 4 clues below? The more clues you need, the fewer points you get.

1 I was born in the North-East of England in 1957. (4 points)
I captained my club to three FA Cup wins. (3 points)
I was captain of my country and won 90 caps. (2 points)
As a player I was nicknamed 'Captain Marvel' (1 point)

2 I was born in 1970 in the rugby heartland of Mid-Glamorgan. (4 points)
My international debut was in 1996, wearing the No. 9 shirt. (3 points)
I was picked for the British Lions tour of 1997 but had to return home with an injured shoulder. (2 points)
I have captained my country and have spent much of my career with Neil Jenkins beside me. (1 point)

SCOREBOARD		

round ten — on the buzzer

The theme to this buzzer round is Occupations. All the answers have a job title somewhere in the name.

1 Name the former Ipswich and Rangers defender who won 77 caps for England.
2 Golf – Which Australian won the Open in 1991?
3 Which forward, then with Sheffield Wednesday, represented Belgium during Euro 2000?

4 Which British athlete took Olympic gold in the Modern Pentathlon in Sydney?

5 Who won his seventh consecutive World Darts title in 2001, his ninth in total?

6 Which Ajax midfielder played for Holland in both the 1974 and '78 World Cup finals and scored the winning goal in the '73 European Cup?

7 Snooker – Which Leeds-based player won the 1998 Regal Welsh Open, beating John Higgins in the final?

8 Which Australian scored two tries and was named Man of the Match during the 2000 Rugby League World Cup final?

9 Which Irish Ryder Cup player was runner-up at the 1997 Open?

10 Who played in goal for Oxford United at the 1986 League Cup final?

11 Which former Zimbabwe international is the coach of the England cricket team?

12 Name the England goalkeeper at Euro '96.

SCOREBOARD		

game **11**

round one — name the year

The following events all happened in the same year, but which one?

1 21-year-old Graeme Hick scores 405 not out for Worcestershire.
Aged 22, Harlequins centre Will Carling is appointed England captain.
David Jenkins, the 1971 European 400 metres champion, is sentenced to seven years in jail.
Sandy Lyle becomes the first British golfer to win the Masters.
John Aldridge misses a penalty in the FA Cup Final.

Now for the second year:

2 Lennox Lewis becomes World Champion after beating Tony Tucker.
In the middle of the Ashes series, Mike Atherton is named England captain.
Zimbabwe-born Graeme Hick becomes the youngest batsman to score more than 20,000 runs in first-class cricket.
Andy Linighan scores a last-minute winner in the FA Cup Final.
The British Lions, led by Gavin Hastings, lose 2–1 to New Zealand in the Test.

SCOREBOARD

round two — picture board

Take a look at picture B on page 2 of Picture Board 2. Who is it?

Take a look at picture E on page 6 of Picture Board 2. Who is it?

SCOREBOARD

round three — twenty sporting questions

20 questions on sport in the 1970s.

1 Which British player won the ladies' singles title at Wimbledon in 1977?
2 Football – Who won the 1974 World Cup?
3 Name the Welsh scrum-half who played in 53 consecutive matches for his country, scoring 20 tries, and retired in 1978.
4 How many World Cups did England qualify for during the 1970s?
5 Who won his first Open in 1979?
6 Name the Briton who won the Formula One Drivers' Championship in 1976.
7 Which all-rounder made his England debut in 1977 against Australia and went on to take 383 test wickets?
8 Which famous horse won the Grand National three times during the 1970s?
9 In which city were the 1976 Olympics held?
10 Which club defeated Manchester United 3–2 in the 1979 FA Cup final thanks to a late goal from Alan Sunderland?
11 In which sport was John Curry an Olympic champion in 1976?
12 Name the Irish hurricane who won his first World Snooker title in 1972.
13 Which horse ridden by Lester Piggott won the English Triple Crown in 1970?
14 Who did Muhammad Ali fight in the 'Rumble in the Jungle' in 1974?
15 Mario Kempes scored twice for which country in the 1978 World Cup final?
16 Who won the inaugural cricket World Cup in 1975?
17 Name the Swede who won the first of five Wimbledon singles titles in 1976.
18 What nationality was Lasse Viren, who won four Olympic golds during the 1970s?
19 Name the Scotsman who won gold in the 200m breaststroke at the 1976 Olympics.
20 Which player, nicknamed 'Crazy Horse', lifted the European Cup as captain of Liverpool in 1977 and '78?

SCOREBOARD		

round four — sporting links

These sportspeople all have unusual middle names. What are they?

1 England striker Emile Heskey; Wasps, England and Lions forward Laurence Dallaglio; former Manchester United goalkeeper Peter Schmeichel; ex-England fast bowler Bob Willis.

2 Former England winger Mark Walters; snooker star Ronnie O'Sullivan; 1990 European 400 metres hurdles champion Kriss Akabusi; former Scotland striker Ally McCoist.

SCOREBOARD		

round five — where am I?

From the following two clues you must work out which place is being described.

1 The venue of the 1952 Winter Olympics will lead you to a home international for Ole Gunnar Solskjaer.

2 Walter Payton helped the Bears to the 1986 Superbowl for this city where you would also find a basketball team called the Bulls.

SCOREBOARD		

round six — what happened next ?

All you have to do in this round is decide which of the three options is the correct answer.

Golf. The AT&T National Pro-Am tournament from Pebble Beach in America. Ray Romano has hit his drive on to the beach alongside the fairway and is contemplating his second shot. What happened next?

- **a** The ball is plugged so deeply in the wet sand that as he tries to play his shot, his club stops and bends the shaft.
- **b** A dog from the crowd runs on and picks the ball up and runs away.
- **c** Romano tries to get some steady stance but slips on a big pile of seaweed.

Golf. And still the AT&T National Pro-Am tournament from Pebble Beach. Poor old Ray Romano is still on the beach. What happened to him next?

- **a** The tide comes in, washing the ball away, and everyone runs for cover.
- **b** He manages to get his shot on to the green and incredibly it runs into the hole for a birdie three.
- **c** He slices the ball once again and it sails into the ocean, forcing him to quit the hole.

SCOREBOARD		

round seven — home or away

rugby union Which Welshman during 2001 became the first player to score over 1,000 points in international rugby?

football Only two English born managers won the FA Cup in the 90s. Joe Royle with Everton in 1995 was one; who was the other?

horse racing Which jockey won the Grand National twice in the 1990s – on both occasions as a substitute for another rider?

hockey Alyson Annan scored in the 2000 Olympic hockey final for which country?

SCOREBOARD		

round eight — captain's away

Here are two riddles from the often unusual world of sport. Can you tell me...

1 Horse racing – Name the four English race courses that end in a 'T'.

2 Name the four Football League teams that end with an 'E'.

SCOREBOARD		

round nine — mystery guest

Can you guess the identity of these sporting stars from the four clues below? The more clues you need, the fewer points you get.

1 I was born in 1963 in Rotherham. (4 points)
I made my international debut against Saudi Arabia in 1988. (3 points)
I moved to Arsenal after spells with Birmingham and QPR. (2 points)
I saved penalties during Euro '96. (1 point)

2 I was born in 1958 in Hereford and won for the first time 20 years later. (4 points)
I was outright champion in my sport on seven occasions. (3 points)
My father was also a jockey but, unlike me, he did ride a Grand National winner. (2 points)
I retired after riding 1,677 winners and am known as 'Scu'. (1 point)

SCOREBOARD		

round ten — on the buzzer

In this buzzer round all the answers are in alphabetical order – backwards!

1 In which country did Muhammad Ali defeat George Foreman in the 'Rumble in the Jungle?'
2 What colour jersey does the leader of the tour de France wear?
3 What links the finals of the World Cups of 1966, 1978 and 1994?

4. Who won the 2001 Embassy World Darts?
5. Which Premiership coach in the 2000–2001 season won two caps for England under Sir Alf Ramsey?
6. Athletics – Which country is six times world pole-vault champion Sergey Bubka from?
7. Desmond Douglas is a former British number one in which sport?
8. In which Olympic sport did Ben Ainslie win gold at the Sydney Olympics?
9. Colin McRae is the only Briton to become world champion in which sport?
10. Football – Which club play their home games at Hampden Park?
11. Cricket – Which country won the 1992 World Cup ?
12. In football, the 1986 League Cup was won by which club ?

SCOREBOARD		

game **12**

round one — name the year

The following events all happened in the same year, but which one?

1 George Foreman wins the World Heavyweight title, beating Joe Frazier.
Gareth Edwards scores his most famous try for the Barbarians against the All-Blacks.
Wilt Chamberlain retires from professional basketball.
Red Rum pips Crisp to win his first Grand National.
Sunderland famously beat Leeds to win the FA Cup.

Now for the second year:

2 Chris Evert-Lloyd wins Wimbledon for the third time: John McEnroe wins it for the first time.
The USA wins the Ryder Cup 18–9.
Ian Botham brings off an Ashes Test victory at Headingley.
Sea Pigeon, ridden by John Francome, wins a second Champion Hurdle.
Steve Davis wins his first world title, beating Doug Mountjoy.

SCOREBOARD

round two — picture board

Take a look at picture A on page 7 of Picture Board 1. Who is it?

Take a look at picture D on page 8 of Picture Board 2. Who is it?

SCOREBOARD

round three — twenty sporting questions

20 questions on the 2000–01 football season.

1 Name the Ipswich player who scored the first goal of the Premiership season.
2 On which ground did England play Spain in February 2001?
3 Which second division club reached the semi-final of the FA Cup before losing to Liverpool?
4 Which Leeds striker scored four times in a match against Liverpool?
5 Who was named as Football Writers' Player of the Year?
6 Which Celtic striker scored over 50 goals during the season?
7 Which team knocked Manchester United out of the Champions League?
8 Which club were relegated from the Football League on the last day of the season?
9 Name the Scottish midfielder who scored a 40-yard free-kick in the last minute of the Merseyside derby to claim victory for Liverpool?
10 Darren Purse scored in the League Cup final against Liverpool for which club?
11 From which club did Robbie Keane join Leeds in December 2000?
12 Who managed Fulham to the First Division championship?
13 Who resigned as manager of West Ham United after seven years?
14 Which former England manager joined Middlesborough in a coaching capacity during the season?
15 Who scored the winning goal for England in their game against Finland at Anfield in March?
16 Who was voted as the players' choice for Young Player of the Year?
17 Which Spanish club knocked both Leeds and Arsenal out of the Champions League?
18 Which Charlton defender made his England debut aged 31 against Spain?
19 Which team won the Scottish League Cup?
20 How many goals did Fulham score in winning the first division?

SCOREBOARD		

round four — sporting links

These sports stars all have interesting nicknames: what are they?

1 Six-times world snooker champion Ray Reardon; French World Cup captain Didier Deschamps; nine-times Derby winner Lester Piggott; Sumo wrestler Konishiki.

2 Snooker star Anthony Hamilton; England footballer Darren Anderton; 1997 Wimbledon ladies' singles champion Martina Hingis; former West Indies fast bowler Joel Garner.

SCOREBOARD		

round five — where am I?

From the following two clues you must work out which place is being described.

1 The home of the Robins at Ashton Gate will lead you to Rugby Union at the Memorial Ground.

2 The Witches from Speedway's Elite League will give you a clue as to the home of Portman Road.

SCOREBOARD		

round six — what happened next?

All you have to do in this round is decide which of the three options is the correct answer.

Athletics. A 100-kilometre athletics race from Belgium; Jean-Paul Praet of Belgium and Charles Mattheus of South Africa are leading. What happened next?

- **a** Praet thinks that Mattheus has taken a short cut and he and his manager, who is on the side of the track, begin to hit Mattheus.
- **b** Russian athlete Konstantin Santalov in third place trips up both runners and goes on to win the race.
- **c** Jean-Paul Praet goes on to win the race but is later disqualified when it is found out that his twin brother had actually run the first 60 kilometres.

Football. A German league match between Borussia Dortmund and TSV Munich is in full swing. What happened next?

- **a** The referee whistles for a free-kick but the half-time entertainment band and dancers think it is their cue and all run on to the field.
- **b** A parachutist lands on the field and the game is held up.
- **c** An eagle flies down on to the field and perches on the Dortmund crossbar and is unable to be moved for five minutes.

SCOREBOARD		

round seven — home or away

athletics Which female sprinter won five world titles in the '90s in three different events – the most recent in 1999?

tennis	Who in 2000 won his first Grand Slam tournament and became the youngest-ever world number one?
snooker	Which player won the 2001 Regal Scottish Masters?
football	Who in the 1980s became the only player to captain a side in four FA Cup finals?

SCOREBOARD

round eight — captain's away

Here are two riddles from the often unusual world of sport. Can you tell me...

1 Cricket - Who never took a wicket in his county career, but managed a hat-trick for England?

2 In 1999 sheep, goats, cows, 27 steers and his wife's camel delayed which World Cup winner's move to a British Super League team?

SCOREBOARD

round nine — mystery guest

Can you guess the identity of these sporting stars from the four clues below? The more clues you need, the fewer points you get.

1 I was born in Scotland and have been a professional since 1970. (4 points)
I've played in over 600 tournaments on the European Tour. (3 points)
I clinched the Ryder Cup for Europe in 1985 with a putt to beat Andy North. (2 points)
I captained the Ryder Cup team in 2001. (1 point)

2 I was born in Sheffield in February 1974. (4 points)
I 'Walked Like A Champion' on *Top of the Pops.* (3 points)
Despite my name, I do not come from royalty. (2 points)
I lost my world title in 2001 – the first defeat of my career. (1 point)

SCOREBOARD		

round ten — on the buzzer

All the answers to this buzzer round will begin and end with the same letter.

1 Cricket – Name the Essex batsman who captained England to series victories over Zimbabwe, West Indies and Pakistan in 2000.
2 Which Spanish golfer won the Open in 1979, 1984 and 1988?
3 Which Scottish League side formed in 1869 and won the league title in 1965?

4 Who was Commonwealth 110m hurdles champion in 1998?

5 Which former world champion boxer is the cousin of England footballer Paul Ince?

6 From which South American country does golfer Eduardo Romero hail?

7 Which Liverpool striker holds the record for the fastest-ever Premiership hat-trick?

8 Which famous horse won the 1989 Cheltenham Gold Cup?

9 In which sport was Briton George Lee three times a world champion?

10 Name the Birchfield Harrier who won Commonwealth discus gold medal at the 1998 games.

11 How is the cricket umpire who stood in 66 Test matches, and whose first name is Harold, better known?

12 Which American female tennis player won the 2000 Wimbledon doubles title with her sister Venus?

13 Which Stoke newsagent won Olympic hockey gold for Great Britain in 1988?

14 For which American Football side was quarter-back Joe Montana playing when they won the Superbowl in 1989 and 1990?

15 Which English football club won the European Cup in 1984?

SCOREBOARD		

game 13

round one — name the year

The following events all happened in the same year, but which one?

1 QPR are the first side to play on a plastic pitch in Britain.
The Grand National winner, Dick Saunders on Grittar, is aged over 50.
Bryan Robson scores a World Cup goal in just 27 seconds.
Jimmy Connors wins Wimbledon, eight years after his first victory.
The World Cup Finals are held in Spain.

Now for the second year:

2 Lynn Davies adds the European long-jump title to the Olympic title he won two years previously.
Mohammed Ali defeats Henry Cooper to retain his World Heavyweight title.
Liverpool win the League and neighbours Everton win the FA Cup.
The Jules Rimet Trophy, the World Cup, is stolen.
England's greatest hour came at Wembley on July 30.

SCOREBOARD		

round two — picture board

Take a look at picture A on page 2 of Picture Board 1. Who is it?

Take a look at picture D on page 2 of Picture Board 2. Who is it?

SCOREBOARD		

round three — twenty sporting questions

20 questions on sports men and women whose surname begins with a vowel.

1 Which American tennis star won the Wimbledon men's singles title in 1992?
2 Who is the British triple-jumper who claimed Olympic gold in Sydney?
3 Who is the English midfielder nicknamed 'the Guvnor'?
4 Which American golfer won the Masters and the Open in 1998?
5 Who was the French striker who scored for Arsenal in the 1998 FA Cup final?
6 Whose record points total for England did Jonny Wilkinson overtake in 2001?
7 Name the former Worcestershire spin bowler who took a wicket with his first ball in Test cricket for England in 1991?
8 Snooker – Who became World Champion for the first time in 2001?
9 Which striker scored the first goal of the 1989 FA Cup final and later went on to manage Tranmere Rovers?
10 Which rugby league player holds the record for most career tries by an Englishman?
11 Which former English bowler, nicknamed 'Deadly', took 297 Test wickets?
12 Who was the Liverpool striker who scored two goals in the 1998 World Cup for England when aged 18?
13 Which snooker player was runner-up to Steven Hendry at the 1996 World Championship?
14 Which manager guided Manchester United to success in the 1985 FA Cup?
15 Which Wigan scrum-half won a record nine rugby league Challenge Cups?
16 Who broke David Hemery's British record for the 400m hurdles in 1990?
17 Which West Indian fast bowler, taker of 405 Test wickets, retired in 2000?
18 Which Swede won the Wimbledon men's singles title in 1988 and 1990?
19 Which British man won a sailing gold medal in the Laser class at the Sydney Olympics?
20 Name the French driver who won the 1995 Canadian Grand Prix?

SCOREBOARD		

round four — sporting links

1 What connects Manchester United and England striker Andy Cole, boxer Prince Naseem Hamed and tennis star Jo Durie?

2 What connects these three England internationals: rugby union centre Will Greenwood, former Nottingham Forest striker Nigel Clough and Surrey batsman Mark Butcher?

SCOREBOARD		

round five — where am I?

From the following two clues you must work out which place is being described.

1 In this place, the Royals play at the Madjeski Stadium and there's snooker at the Hexagon. Where is this?

2 Here, the Sharks play rugby league at the Boulevard, and at Boothferry Park the Tigers play football. But where are we talking about?

SCOREBOARD		

round six — what happened next?

All you have to do in this round is decide which of the three options is the correct answer.

Ice Hockey, and the siren signals the end of the 2000 Challenge Cup final between the Sheffield Steelers and the Nottingham Panthers, with Sheffield winning 2–1. What happened next?

- **a** Referee Andy Carson decides there are three seconds to go, but the fireworks and ticker-tape go off, covering the rink. Carson decides to finish the game there and then. Sheffield won 2–1.
- **b** The players and officials don't hear the final siren, the game continues and the Panthers equalise – but to their dismay the goal does not stand.
- **c** The organisers release balloons and streamers in the Panthers' colours and play the Nottingham victory song even though it is Sheffield who have won.

Cycling. The Tour of Italy; Daniel Schneider of Switzerland leads. What happened next?

- **a** A horse runs across the road, causing Daniel to swerve violently and end up through a hedge and in a field.
- **b** In trying to pick up a bottle from a water-station he loses balance and wipes out the entire station.
- **c** One of the motorbike stewards drives past him and accidentally knocks him off his bike.

SCOREBOARD		

round seven — home or away

athletics Which field athlete at the Sydney games gained his fourth successive Olympic medal, the last three being a hat-trick of golds?

rugby union Will Greenwood's three tries against Wales in 2001 was the second time an England player had scored a Six Nations hat-trick. Who was the first, in the previous season?

motor sport Which Frenchman won the World Rally Championship in 1994?

horse racing What connects the National wins of Lovely Cottage in 1946, Jay Trump in 1965, Ben Nevis in 1980, Grittar in 1982 and Mr Frisk in 1990?

SCOREBOARD

round eight — captain's away

This question has 12 answers and you each have six goes for one point each (if you are playing on your own, you need to name all 12)

1 The question is: name the twelve Olympic sports that use a ball.

SCOREBOARD

round nine — mystery guest

Can you guess the identity of these sporting stars from the four clues below? The more clues you need, the fewer points you get.

1 I was born in Bloemfontein in 1966. (4 points)
I played for Warwickshire between 1987 and 1995. (3 points)
I was the first South African to take 300 Test wickets. (2 points)
My nickname is 'White Lightning'. (1 point)

2 I was born in Northern Ireland in 1952 and moved to Nottingham Forest in October 1971. (4 points)
I won many honours at Forest including the European Cup. (3 points)
I was in management with Grantham, Wycombe and Leicester. (2 points)
I am now Celtic's manager. (1 point)

SCOREBOARD		

round ten — on the buzzer

This buzzer round is on the memorable events of the year 2001

1 Which American defeated Arnaud Clement to win his third Australian Open title?

2 Which striker scored a hat-trick for Rangers in the Auld Firm Challenge Cup match in January?

3 Rugby League – Which team did St Helens beat to win the World Club Challenge?

4 Who became the youngest woman ever to sail around the world single-handed during the Vendée Globe Challenge?

5 Which Ipswich player scored the first Premiership goal of 2001?

6 Which female athlete set a British and Commonwealth 400m record at the Birmingham Indoor Grand Prix?

7 In January John 'Boy' Walton became World Champion in which sport?

8 Which non-league side came within minutes of knocking Premiership side Charlton out of the FA Cup?

9 Against which former World Champion did Dave Harold come back from 5–1 down in the quarter-finals of the B&H Masters?

10 Which team defeated the New York Giants to win the Superbowl?

11 Name the British swimmer who broke the 50m short-course freestyle world record in Paris during January?

12 Snooker – Which 22-year-old beat Fergal O'Brien to win the B&H Masters?

13 Football – Who won promotion to the Premiership as champions of the First Division?

14 Who won Rugby League's Challenge Cup?

15 Who managed Celtic to the Scottish Premier League title?

16 Who won the 2001 US Masters?

SCOREBOARD		

game **14**

round one — name the year

The following events all happened in the same year, but which one?

1 Irishman Steve Collins ends Chris Eubank's 43-fight unbeaten record and becomes WBO Super-Middleweight Champion of the World.
Rob Andrew joins Newcastle as Rugby Development Director.
Cardiff bring Jonathan Davies back to Rugby Union from Warrington RLFC.
Nayim scores a winner in the Cup Winners' Cup Final against Arsenal.
Liverpool beat Bolton to win the League Cup Final.

Now for the second year:

2 Tony Jacklin adds the US Open title to the British Open he won the previous year.
Roger Taylor of Britain ends Rod Laver's reign as Wimbledon champion.
The Commonwealth Games are held in Edinburgh.
Leeds lose to Chelsea in the FA Cup Final replay at Old Trafford.
England lose to West Germany in the World Cup quarter-final.

SCOREBOARD		

round two — picture board

Take a look at picture E on page 3 of Picture Board 1. Who is it?

Take a look at picture F on page 5 of Picture Board 2. Who is it?

SCOREBOARD		

round three — twenty sporting questions

20 sports questions with a Welsh connection.

1 Who was world snooker champion in 2000?
2 Hywel Davies rode which horse to win the 1985 Grand National?
3 Golf - Who was US Masters champion in 1991?
4 Which team play their home games at the Vetch Field?
5 Who was the 110m hurdles world champion in 1999?
6 Which Welshman scored for Manchester United in the 1994 FA Cup final?
7 Which side beat Wales in the 2000 Rugby League World Cup semi-final?
8 At which racecourse is the Welsh Grand National run?
9 Who was BDO World Darts champion in 1995?
10 Which former Welsh outside-half was nicknamed 'the King'?
11 Who captained Glamorgan to the 1997 County Championship title?
12 Who was Commonwealth 400m champion in 1998?
13 Wrexham had a giant-killing victory over which club in the 1992 FA Cup?
14 Lynn Davies won Olympic gold in 1964 in which event?
15 Who defeated Mario Veit in 2001 to retain his WBO Super-Middleweight belt for the eighth time?
16 Who is the Welsh Rugby Union full-back, capped 55 times, who was a qualified doctor and also competed at junior Wimbledon?
17 Which player holds the record for most FA Cup final goals during the 20th century?
18 Who was world snooker champion in 1979?
19 In which sport have the Cardiff Devils competed?
20 Which Rugby Union side play their home games at Stradey Park?

SCOREBOARD		

round four — sporting links

Three of these four sports stars have something in common, but one is the odd one out. Can you spot which one?

1 John Parrott; Nigel Mansell; Liz McColgan; David Campese.

2 Steve Backley; Mark Williams; Phil Mickelson; John McEnroe.

SCOREBOARD		

round five — where am I?

From the following two clues you must work out which place is being described.

1 If you had attended the 1968 Olympics, then you would have been in the country which is home to champion boxer Julio Cesar Chavez. Which country?

2 If you had been watching the 1998 Winter Olympics or seeing Gary Lineker play football for Grampus Eight, in which country would you have been?

SCOREBOARD		

round six — what happened next?

All you have to do in this round is decide which of the three options is the correct answer.

Horse racing from Punchestown in Ireland, and it's the Harristown Hurdle. Only three horses are left in the race. Miss Lyme and Idiot's Venture are well clear of Loaves and Fishes in third. What happened next?

- **a** Miss Lyme and Idiot's Venture both fell, leaving Loaves and Fishes to come through and win.
- **b** All three horses fell and the race was void.
- **c** The race was a three-way tie – for the first time in racing history.

Motor racing from Bathurst in Australia. Dwayne Bewley is about to finish the race. What happened next?

- **a** A kangaroo runs in front of the car, causing Bewley to swerve off the road and not complete the course.
- **b** Dwayne Bewley breaks down a few yards from the chequered flag and is forced to push his car to the line.
- **c** Due to the torrential rain Bewley does a complete spin and actually finishes the race reversing over the line.

SCOREBOARD		

round seven — home or away

cricket Which Indian bowler did Courtney Walsh overtake to become the leading wicket-taker in Test cricket?

squash Who in 1998 became the first British winner of the British Open for 25 years?

rugby Which player overtook Rob Andrew during the 2001 Six Nations Championship to become England's all-time leading point-scorer?

football Which Premiership manager played in FA Cup finals in the 1970s, '80s and '90s?

SCOREBOARD

round eight — captain's away

It's odd one out. Of the four names below, which is the misfit?

1 Which of these horses has not won the Grand National?
Ally Sloper.
Tipperary Tim.
Wild Man From Borneo.
Doorknocker.

2 Which of these boxers have not held the World Middleweight title?
Gorilla Jones.
George Chip.
Max Baer.
Dick Tiger.

SCOREBOARD

round nine — mystery guest

Can you guess the identity of these sporting stars from the four clues below? The more clues you need, the fewer points you get.

1	I was born in 1974 and come from a family of tennis players.	(4 points)
	My grandmother was the first lady to serve overarm at Wimbledon.	(3 points)
	I split with my long-time coach David Felgate in 2001.	(2 points)
	I reached the Wimbledon semi-finals in 1998 and '99 when the crowd enjoyed 'Henmania'.	(1 point)
2	I was born in 1963 and my middle name is Boleslaw.	(4 points)
	I helped my country to win the European Championships in 1992.	(3 points)
	I won the FA Cup three times with Manchester United.	(2 points)
	In 1999 I left to take over the No. 1 shirt at Sporting Lisbon.	(1 point)

SCOREBOARD

round ten — on the buzzer

All the answers to this buzzer round will end in a double letter.

1 Which former England midfielder became manager of first division Nottingham Forest in July 1999?

2 Name the British female athlete who won Olympic gold in 1992 in the 400 metres hurdles?

3 Which British boxer defeated Sugar Boy Malinga in 1998 to claim the WBC Super-Middleweight title?

4 Name the Bath and England centre who won his 50th international cap against Italy in 2001.

5 Fir Park is home to which Scottish League side?

6 Which snooker player captained England to victory in the 2000 Nations' Cup?

7 Which former Ryder Cup player has been the BBC's 'Voice of Golf' for more than 20 years?

8 Which jockey holds the record for most Derby winners, with nine victories?

9 In which sport were Croatia the male Olympic gold medallists in 1996?

10 Which England cricketer is nicknamed 'The Cat'?

11 Name the British sprinter who claimed a silver medal in the 200 metres at the Sydney Olympics.

12 Name the Premiership footballer who joined Liverpool from Bournemouth and whose father managed West Ham.

13 Sir Steve Redgrave, Tim Foster, Matt Pinsent and which other rower won gold in the coxless fours at the Sydney Olympics?

14 Name the former Derbyshire captain who helped Gloucestershire to one-day glory in 2000.

SCOREBOARD		

game **15**

round one — name the year

The following events all happened in the same year, but which one?

1 Mick Fitzgerald wins the Grand National.
Rangers take their eighth League title in succession.
Sri Lanka win cricket's World Cup final.
Michael Johnson wins the Olympic 200m x 400m.
Despite leading the Premiership by 12 points in January, the Geordies of Newcastle United are 'out-psyched' by Manchester United.

Now for the second year:

2 Kevin Keegan resigns as manager of Newcastle United.
Tiger Woods becomes the youngest winner of the Masters.
Irish player Ken Doherty wins the World Snooker Championship, beating Stephen Hendry in his seventh final in eight years.
The Grand National is postponed due to a bomb threat.
Chelsea's Robert di Matteo scores an FA Cup final goal after 43 seconds.

SCOREBOARD		

round two — picture board

Take a look at picture B on page 6 of Picture Board 2. Who is it?

Take a look at picture D on page 1 of Picture Board 1. Who is it?

SCOREBOARD		

round three — twenty sporting questions

20 questions on football goal scorers.

1 Apart from Geoff Hurst, who scored for England in the 1966 World Cup final?
2 Which Manchester City player scored at both ends in the 1981 FA Cup final?
3 Which goalkeeper scored in the last minute of the last game of the 1998–99 season to save Carlisle from relegation?
4 Allan Nielsen's last-minute header against Leicester secured the 1999 Worthington Cup for which club?
5 Who scored for Everton in the 3–1 defeat by Liverpool in the '86 FA Cup final?
6 Which German striker scored 14 goals during the World Cups of 1970 and '74?
7 Who scored two goals against Scotland to see England qualify for Euro 2000?
8 Which former Spurs player scored from the half-way line for Real Zaragoza in the last minute of the 1995 European Cup Winners' Cup final to beat Arsenal?
9 Who scored 49 goals in 1986–87 although his club, Spurs, won no trophies?
10 Who scored Scotland's only goal during Euro '96?
11 Against which country did Andy Cole score his first international goal?
12 Sunderland did it in 1979 and Villa did it in 1981, but who did it in 1980?
13 Who scored two goals in the 1998 World Cup final for France?
14 Name the Scottish international forward who scored in the 1984 FA Cup final and the 1985 European Cup Winners Cup final for Everton.
15 For which Italian club did Dutchman Frank Rijkaard score the only goal of the 1990 European Cup final?
16 Which Frenchman scored three goals in FA Cup finals in the 1990s?
17 Who was Premiership top scorer in 1999–2000 with 30 goals for Sunderland?
18 Who scored a back-heel for Manchester City to help relegate Manchester United from the first division in 1974?
19 Which goalkeeper scored for Manchester United in a European tie in 1995?
20 For which club did Dixie Dean score 60 goals in a season during the 1920s?

SCOREBOARD		

round four — sporting links

1 George Headley, his son Ron, and his son Dean have all played Test cricket – the only instance of this happening. Which is the odd one out, and why?

2 Jamie Redknapp, his father Harry, his brother-in-law Frank Lampard and his son Frank junior have all played League football. Which of them hasn't been capped for England?

SCOREBOARD

round five — where am I?

From the following two clues you must work out which place is being described.

1 In which county would you be if you were celebrating with the winners of the 1976 FA Cup and watching the start of the Round the World Yacht Race?

2 If you were watching cricket and the Phoenix were playing a home match, then you'd be in the county which is home to rugby league's Rhinos. Name the county.

SCOREBOARD

round six — what happened next ?

All you have to do in this round is decide which of the three options is the correct answer.

Football from 1998, and a match between Bristol City and Wolves. The game is five minutes from kick-off. What happened next?

- **a** The officials realise one of the buses carrying some of the Wolves team has not arrived, and coaches and physiotherapists are called upon to get changed ready to play.
- **b** The Wolves mascot 'Wolfie' has a fight with one of the Three Little Pigs who are the Bristol mascots.
- **c** The balls are found to be under-inflated but there is no pump in the stadium.

Tennis from the 1998 Australian Open. Venus Williams serving at break point against Lindsay Davenport. What happened next?

- **a** Some beads fell out of Williams' hair, and the umpire penalised her a point costing her the game.
- **b** Williams serves underarm and wins the point, but Davenport complains because she claims she wasn't given prior warning and the point is replayed.
- **c** As Williams is about to serve, a member of the crowd sneezes loudly and she serves a double-fault and loses the game.

SCOREBOARD		

round seven — home or away

boxing Who in 1975 in Kuala Lumpur became the only British boxer ever to take Muhammad Ali the distance in a World title bout ?

football Who is the only player to have played in the Manchester, Liverpool and Glasgow derby matches ?

horse racing How many horses finished the 2001 Grand National ?

baseball Why was the World Series of 1994 not completed, for the first time in its 90-year history?

SCOREBOARD

round eight — captain's away

Here are two riddles from the often unusual world of sport. Can you tell me...

1 Name the major sporting event which was held in Britain in 1999, whose qualifying competition began with Latvia beating Norway in 1996.

2 Richard Raskind played in the men's singles at the 1960 US Open. Renee Richards reached the final of the ladies' doubles at the 1977 US Open. What do Richard and Renee have in common?

SCOREBOARD

round nine — mystery guest

Can you guess the identity of these sporting stars from the four clues below? The more clues you need, the fewer points you get.

1	I was born in London in 1965 but brought up elsewhere.	(4 points)
	I was an Olympic gold medallist in 1988.	(3 points)
	I won my first British title in 1991.	(2 points)
	I lost my World Heavyweight title to Hasim Rahman in 2001.	(1 point)
2	I was born in England in 1962 and turned professional in 1980.	(4 points)
	Although I reached six world finals I was unable to win one.	(3 points)
	Stephen Hendry defeated me in four of those finals.	(2 points)
	I am often referred to as 'The Whirlwind'.	(1 point)

SCOREBOARD

round ten — on the buzzer

This buzzer round will test your knowledge of sporting arenas and venues.

1 At which football league ground would you find the Stretford End?
2 What sport would you expect to see at Grace Road, Edgbaston and Headingley?
3 In which Italian city would you find the Guiseppe Meazza stadium?
4 On which ground did Ally McCoist score his first English league goal?

5 Rugby Union – Which side play their home games at Welford Road?
6 Where was the 2001 British Speedway Grand Prix held?
7 At which racecourse is the St. Leger run?
8 American Football – Who play their home games at Soldier Field?
9 In which city did England lose to Germany in the 1990 football World Cup?
10 Speedway – In which English town would you find the Knights?
11 Football – Who would you be watching playing in a home match at the Priestfield Stadium?
12 The 1970 and 1986 Commonwealth Games were held in which British city?
13 In the 2000–01 season, Watford shared their football ground with which rugby union side?
14 Name the city which staged the 2001 FA Cup final.
15 In 1979 Seve Ballesteros won his first Open title. Where?
16 Cricket – On which Test venue do Nottingham play their home games?

SCOREBOARD		

game **16**

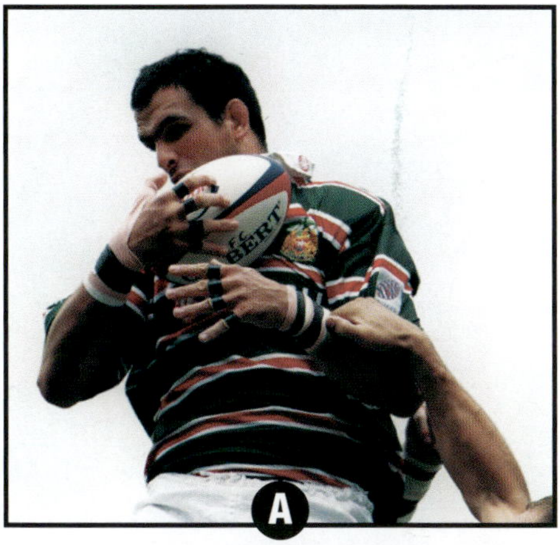

A

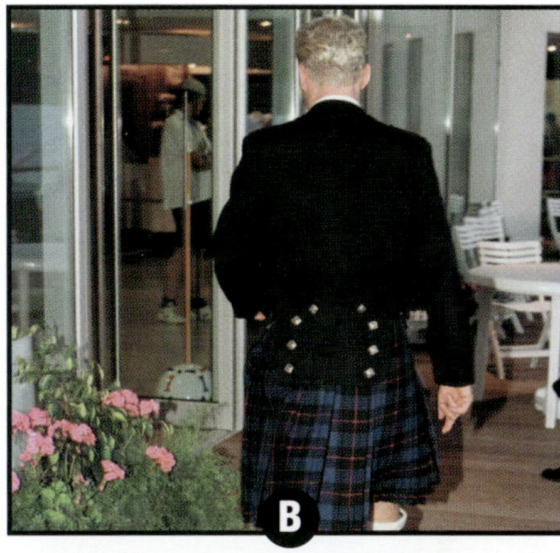

B

C

D

E

F

A

B

C

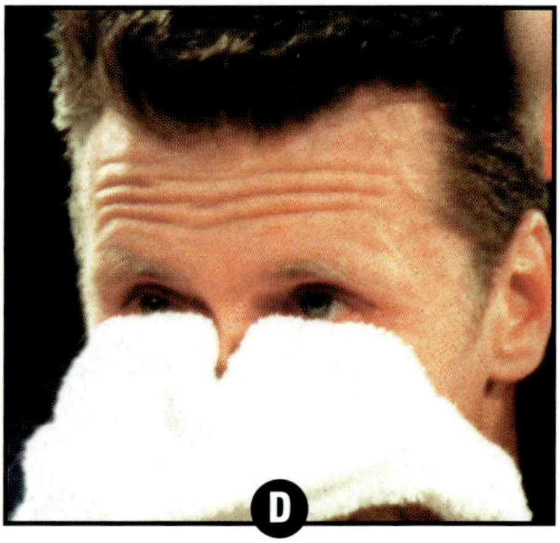
D

E

F

A

B

C

D

E

F

A

B

C

D

E

F

A

B

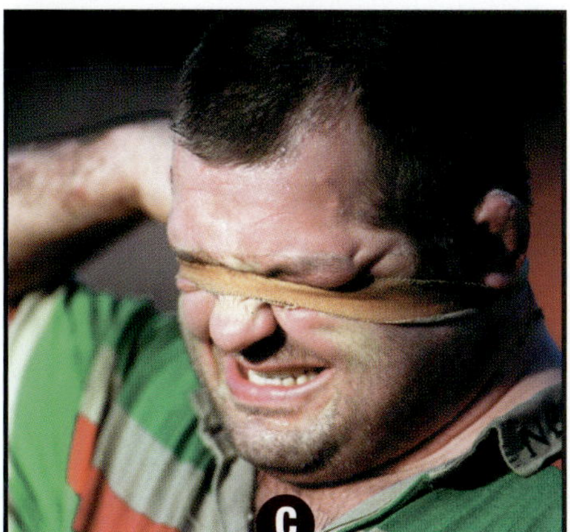
C

D

E

F

A

B

C

D

E

F

A

B

C

D

A

B

C

D

round one — name the year

The following events all happened in the same year, but which one?

1 In an exciting Super Bowl, the New York Giants beat the Buffalo Bills 20–19.
Bryan Robson retires from international football after 26 goals in 90 appearances.
Kriss Akabusi leads Great Britain to victory in the World 4 x 400m relay.
The Rugby Union World Cup final is held at Twickenham.
Stuart Pearce scores in the FA Cup semi-final and final.

Now for the second year:

2 Rangers make it nine Championships in succession.
Lord Gyllene wins the Grand National on a Monday.
Britain's Greg Rusedski and Tim Henman both reach the quarter-finals at Wimbledon.
Glamorgan, captained by Matthew Maynard, win the County Cricket championship.
Middlesbrough lose in both the FA Cup and League Cup finals.

SCOREBOARD		

round two — picture board

Take a look at picture C on page 3 of Picture Board 1. Who is it?

Take a look at picture A on page 5 of Picture Board 2. Who is it?

SCOREBOARD		

round three — twenty sporting questions

20 questions on general sporting knowledge.

1 Which football team play their home games at Glanford Park?
2 In which sport have Britons Gary Havelock and Michael Lee been world champions?
3 What nationality is three-time French Open champion Mats Wilander?
4 In which county did Gary Sobers hit six sixes in an over against Glamorgan?
5 Which country won the 1995 Rugby Union World Cup?
6 What is the surname of the eight-times champion jockey who won the 1993 Champion Hurdles on Granville Again?
7 How many caps did Ray Clemence win for England?
8 Hockey – What is the surname of Britain's all-time leading female scorer?
9 In which city were the 1988 Olympics held?
10 What is the surname of the Englishman who was the 1977 world snooker champion?
11 Football – Who is England's most-capped goalkeeper of all-time?
12 In which English city would you find Hillsborough?
13 In which sport was Jonah Barrington a former British champion?
14 Cricket – Which team won the County Championship in 2000?
15 Boxing – What is the surname of the American brothers who have both held versions of the World Heavyweight title?
16 In which country was the 1958 World Cup final held?
17 Rugby Union – For which country did the Hastings brothers win 126 caps between them?
18 Which team won the 1987 Scottish FA Cup final?
19 Which Grand Prix is held at Imola?
20 Which team were beaten by Liverpool in the 1992 FA Cup final?

SCOREBOARD		

round four — sporting links

One of these events and personalities is the odd one out. But which?

1 Gwen Torrence winning the 1995 world championships 200 metres; Esha Ness finishing first in the 1993 Grand National; Marc Overmars' winning goal for Arsenal against Sheffield United in the 1999 FA Cup fifth round; Phil Edmonds catching Greg Ritchie in the third Ashes Test in 1985.

2 Somerset and England bowler Andrew Caddick; Liverpool and England striker Michael Owen; World indoor triple jump record holder Ashia Hansen; England cricket captain Nasser Hussain.

SCOREBOARD		

round five — where am I?

From the following two clues you must work out which place is being described.

1 If you were standing in the Racecourse watching Mark Hughes playing in an international in his place of birth, where would you be ?

2 The 2001 PDC World Darts Champion Phil Taylor should lead you to the home of the Potters. Where ?

SCOREBOARD		

round six — what happened next ?

All you have to do in this round is decide which of the three options is the correct answer.

Football. A match between Walsall and Chesterfield. Martyn O'Connor of Walsall is injured after a tackle. What happened next?

- **a** As he is laid out on the floor one of his team-mates shoots for goal. The shot is going well wide until it hits O'Connor on the head and is re-directed into the goal.
- **b** O'Connor is stretchered off the field, but unfortunately the St John's ambulance men drop him.
- **c** A Chesterfield defender attempts a back-pass only for O'Connor to jump to his feet, collect the ball and score easily.

Golf from the Players' Championship in Sawgrass. Fred Couples drives into the water at the par 3 17th. What happened next?

- **a** Fred takes a penalty stroke and tees off again; this time he puts it straight in the hole for a most unusual par three.
- **b** He takes off his shoes, wades into the water and chips the ball to the green.
- **c** He takes the drive again, and drives into the water again. This happens seven times and he eventually ends up with a 17 – 14 over par.

SCOREBOARD		

round seven — home or away

football What was introduced in the severe winter of 1963, and is still with us today?

tennis	Which Croatian player won her first Grand Slam tournament at the 1997 French Open ?
boxing	Who did Marco Antonio Barrera defeat in 2001 to claim the IBO World Featherweight Championship ?
motor racing	Which Grand Prix driver finished in the top three eight times in 1998, but didn't win a race?

SCOREBOARD

round eight — captain's away

True or false? Can you tell which of these famous pairings are genuine sports stars and which have been made up?

1 Cannon and Ball both played football for Darlington.
2 Banger and Mash have both played football for Southampton.
3 Marks and Spencer have played cricket for Somerset.
4 Tate and Lyle have both fought for the World Heavyweight title.
5 Emerson, Lake and Palmer have all played football in the Premiership.
6 Stock, Aitken and Waterman have all won rugby union caps for Scotland. (Jim Aitken captained Scotland, but not the other two!)
7 Bride and Groom won the Wimbledon men's doubles in 1921.
8 Mills and Boone both play Major League Baseball.

SCOREBOARD

round nine — mystery guest

Can you guess the identity of these sporting stars from the four clues below? The more clues you need, the fewer points you get.

1 I was born in Germany in 1969 and turned professional in 1982. (4 points)
I won all four major titles and an Olympic gold medal in 1988. (3 points)
In 1996 I won my seventh Wimbledon singles, which was my 100th career singles title. (2 points)
I lost to Lindsay Davenport in the 1999 Wimbledon Final. (1 point)

2 I was born in 1970 in the same place as Dickie Bird. (4 points)
I once wrote a book entitled *My Guide To Your Success.* (3 points)
I was England's Player of the Year in 1994. (2 points)
I took a Test hat-trick in 1999 and my nicknames include 'Dazzler'. (1 point)

SCOREBOARD

round ten — on the buzzer

This buzzer round has something of a Scouse flavour and will test your knowledge of sport on Merseyside and further afield.

1 Which Wirral-born cyclist set a world one-hour record in 2001?
2 Which club did Everton defeat to win the 1985 European Cup Winners' Cup final?
3 Which horse, ridden by Carl Llewellyn, won the Grand National at Aintree in the General Election year of 1992?

4 Name the Wallasey-born rugby union star who scored England's first ever Six Nations hat-trick in the match against Italy in 2000.

5 Scotland defeated which side 2–0 at Anfield to qualify for the '78 World Cup?

6 Comedian Freddie Starr was part-owner of which Grand National winner?

7 On which golf course in 1967 did Argentinean Roberto di Vicenzo win his only Open title?

8 Which Liverpool-born manager led Sheffield Wednesday to success in the 1991 League Cup?

9 Which British boxer held the WBC light-heavyweight title in 1974?

10 Which rugby union side play their home games at St. Anthony's Road, Liverpool?

11 Who broke Dalton Grant's British high-jump record?

12 What is Everton's club nickname?

13 Who won the World Snooker Championship in 1991?

14 What day of the week did Tony Dobbin win the 1997 Grand National on?

15 Who managed Liverpool before Gérard Houllier?

16 In which sport in the 1990s would you have been watching world champion Paul Hodkinson?

17 Tranmere Rovers knocked out which Premiership club in the fourth round of the 2001 FA Cup competition?

SCOREBOARD		

game 17

round one — name the year

The following events all happened in the same year, but which one?

1 Sue Barker becomes the first English player since Ann Jones in 1966 to win the French Singles title.
John Stracey made his first defence of the WBC World Welterweight title.
James Hunt wins his only World Drivers' Championship.
The Olympic Games are held in Montreal.
Southampton of Division Two defeat Manchester United in the FA Cup final.

Now for the second year:

2 Nottingham Forest make their third successive League Cup final appearance.
Seve Ballesteros becomes the youngest winner of the US Masters.
Evonne Goolagong-Cawley wins Wimbledon, nine years after her first singles success.
Alan Wells, Steve Ovett, Daley Thompson and Seb Coe win Olympic Gold.
The USSR hosts the Olympic Games, but the USA boycotts them.

SCOREBOARD

round two — picture board

Take a look at picture A on page 4 of Picture Board 2. Who is it?

Take a look at picture A on page 7 of Picture Board 2. Who is it?

SCOREBOARD

round three — twenty sporting questions

20 questions on American sport.

1 American Football – From which city do the 49ers come?
2 Golf – Who won the 2001 US Masters?
3 Which American scored for Sheffield Wednesday in the 1993 League Cup final?
4 How many medals did Jesse Owens win at the 1936 Olympics?
5 Which boxer won Olympic bronze in 1984 and later went on to become World Heavyweight champion?
6 Who won the Tour de France in 1999 and 2000?
7 In which sport are Ty Cobb and Willie Mays all-time greats?
8 What are the basketball team from Dallas known as?
9 Which golfer won the Open in 1997?
10 Which American jockey rode Slip Anchor to victory in the 1985 Derby?
11 Who was Formula One World Champion in 1978?
12 Bill Johnson and Tommy Moe were Olympic champions in which winter sport?
13 Which swimmer won 50m and 100m freestyle Olympic gold medals in 1988?
14 Who won the 2000 Wimbledon ladies' singles championship?
15 Name the American striker who played in the 1989 League Cup final for Luton.
16 Who won the gold medal in the men's 400 metres at the Sydney Olympics?
17 In which American city would you find an American Football team called the Dolphins?
18 Who won his sixth US Masters title in 1986 aged 46?
19 In which sport are Charles Barkley and Shaquille O'Neal famous names?
20 Who won his first Wimbledon singles title in 1974?

SCOREBOARD		

round four — sporting links

1 What connects Northants cricketer David Steele, swimmer Anita Lonsborough, Her Royal Highness Princess Anne and Paul Gascoigne (apart from all having appeared on *A Question Of Sport* – though not at the same time!)?

2 What connects World War II hero Sir Douglas Bader, Nobel Prize-winning author Samuel Beckett, former Prime Minister Sir Alex Douglas-Home and Julius Caesar?

SCOREBOARD

round five — where am I?

From the following two clues you must work out which place is being described.

1 The birthplace of England cricketer Ted Dexter will lead you to the home of the San Siro. Name the city.

2 The home of football's Shaymen is the same as Rugby League's Blue Sox. But where in England is it?

SCOREBOARD

round six — what happened next?

All you have to do in this round is decide which of the three options is the correct answer.

Golf. American Dottie Pepper has just won the Nabisco Dinah Shore in Palm Springs. What happened next?

- **a** She jumps on her caddie to celebrate but they topple over and she sprains her elbow.
- **b** She lifts the trophy in the air, but it falls to pieces in her hand.
- **c** Dottie and her caddy jump into the water beside the 18th green as is tradition for the winner.

Football. Carlisle vs Plymouth in the last game of the 1998–99 season. Five minutes of injury time have been played and Carlisle have a corner. What happened next?

- **a** Carlisle keeper Jimmy Glass comes up for a corner and scores, giving Carlisle the win and meaning they avoid relegation to the Conference.
- **b** The referee blows his whistle and the crowd think the game has finished, but it hasn't. It take 20 minutes to clear the pitch and repair the frame of the goal.
- **c** The corner is headed in for the winning goal but the referee disallows it, saying that he had already blown his whistle.

SCOREBOARD		

round seven — home or away

cricket Which country defeated Australia in March 2001 to end their unbeaten streak of 16 Test matches?

boxing Which British boxer fought twice for the world heavyweight title, losing on both occasions to two of the greatest fighters of all time: Floyd Patterson and Muhammad Ali?

golf Which Irishman became the oldest-ever winner on the European Tour by winning the Madeira Island Open in March 2001, aged 48 years and 34 days?

rubgy union Who in 2001 became the first Frenchman ever to score a try in all five matches of a Six Nations Championship?

SCOREBOARD		

round eight — captain's away

Here are two riddles from the often unusual world of sport. Can you tell me...

1 In July of 1997, a New York broker paid $11,000 for which small but significant piece of sporting memorabilia that originally cost a famous sportsman $3 million?

2 What cost $9 in April 1998, travelled 370 feet in September, and was sold for $3.2 million in January 1999?

SCOREBOARD		

round nine — mystery guest

Can you guess the identity of these sporting stars from the 4 clues below? The more clues you need the fewer points you get.

1 I was born in 1960 and joined my local club in 1977. (4 points)
I've played cricket for the MCC and snooker with Willie Thorne. (3 points)
I won my first England cap in 1984 and scored a World Cup hat-trick two years later. (2 points)
I am now one of the BBC's main sports presenters. (1 point)

2 I was born in Las Vegas in 1970, but my father competed for Iran in the Olympic Games. (4 points)
I am a born-again Christian, collect cars and as a child suffered from the bone disease Osgood-Schlatter. (3 points)
I won the Olympic tennis gold medal in 1996. (2 points)
I won my first Wimbledon singles title in 1992 and have won all four of the Grand Slam tournaments. (1 point)

SCOREBOARD		

round ten — on the buzzer

It's fun with the alphabet for this buzzer round. The first answer will have the initials AB, the second CD and so on.

1 Squash – Name the Egyptian who was runner-up in the 1999 World Open.
2 Which horse ridden by Andrew Thornton won the '98 Cheltenham Gold Cup?

3 Formula One – Which Brazilian won the drivers' championship twice during the 1970s?

4 Name the England batsman who scored 405 not out for Worcestershire in 1988.

5 Which Swede in 1959 defeated Floyd Patterson to become heavyweight champion of the world?

6 Name the Wasps and Scotland winger who has won over 50 caps for his country.

7 Tennis – Name the Swede who was runner-up at the 2000 French Open.

8 Which Frenchman won the 1996 Monaco Grand Prix?

SCOREBOARD		

game **18**

round one — name the year

The following events all happened in the same year, but which one?

1 In Rugby Union the try is now worth four points instead of three.
Non-league Hereford famously knock first division Newcastle out of the FA Cup.
Mary Peters wins Olympic gold.
Australia and England tie the Ashes series 2–2.
In the first all-English European final, Tottenham Hotspur beat Wolverhampton Wanderers on aggregate.

Now for the second year:

2 Paul Ringer is the first player to be sent off at Twickenham since 1925.
Ian Botham becomes the first cricketer to score a century and take ten wickets in a Test match.
Robin Cousins beats Jan Hoffman to claim the Olympic ice skating gold medal.
Arsenal lose to Valencia in the European Cup Winners' Cup final.
Bill Beaumont leads England to rugby union's Grand Slam.

SCOREBOARD		

round two — picture board

Take a look at picture D on page 6 of Picture Board 1. Who is it?

Take a look at picture E on page 1 of Picture Board 2. Who is it?

SCOREBOARD		

round three — twenty sporting questions

20 questions on women in sport.

1. Which British athlete won Olympic gold in 1992 in the 400 metres hurdles?
2. Golf – Who in 1987 became the first Briton to win the US Women's Open?
3. In which sport at the Sydney Olympics did Yvonne McGregor win bronze?
4. Which Spaniard won the 1994 Wimbledon ladies' singles title?
5. Which team won the 2001 Women's FA Cup?
6. Which German won six swimming gold medals at the 1988 Olympic Games?
7. Geraldine Rees was the first woman to complete which famous race in 1982?
8. Which Jamaican sprinter won gold in the 200 metres at both the 1993 and 1995 World Championships?
9. In which sport were Lucinda Green and Virginia Leng both world champions during the 1980s?
10. Which country won the 2000 Women's Cricket World Cup?
11. In which indoor sport have Martine le Moignan and Susan Devoy both been world champions?
12. Who, with Corbière in 1983, became the first woman to train a Grand National winner?
13. Which tennis player won the last of nine Wimbledon singles titles in 1990?
14. In December 2000 Canadian Gayl King became the first woman to compete in which sportsmen's world championship?
15. Katarina Witt was Olympic champion in 1984 and 1988 in which sport?
16. Which Romanian gymnast won overall gold at the 1976 Olympics, including seven perfect 10 scores?
17. Who in 2000 was the first British woman to win the Olympic Heptathlon?
18. Hockey – Which country won Olympic gold in 2000?
19. In which sport do Europe and America compete for the Solheim Cup?
20. Who won the Women's Modern Pentathlon gold at the Sydney Olympics?

SCOREBOARD		

round four — sporting links

1 What connects Welsh rugby legend Gareth Edwards, New Zealand cricketer John Reid and England footballer Neil Franklin?

2 What's the link between Welsh midfielder David Phillips, American tennis legend John McEnroe and England second row Paul Ackford?

SCOREBOARD		

round five — where am I?

From the following two clues you must work out which place is being described.

1 Despite missing out on hosting the 2000 Olympics, this city could boast the country's Premier league champions five times during the 1990s. Where?

2 This American state hosted the 1996 Olympics and is home to the US Masters every year. But which state is it?

SCOREBOARD		

round six — what happened next ?

All you have to do in this round is decide which of the three options is the correct answer.

Football. Newcastle vs Celtic in Peter Beardsley's testimonial match. Newcastle are awarded a throw-in. What happened next?

- **a** Steve Watson throws the ball for a world-record 52 yards.
- **b** Newcastle's Steve Watson does a somersault as he takes it.
- **c** The ball goes directly into the net and the referee allows the goal to stand, seeing as it was Beardsley who took it.

Baseball. Game One of the 1996 American League championship series between the New York Yankees and the Baltimore Orioles. The ball is hit into the outfield and the Orioles' Tony Tarasco is about to field it. What happened next?

- **a** A Yankees fan catches the ball before Tarasco can catch it.
- **b** Tarasco fields the ball and throws it back to home plate, but his glove also comes off and both end up with the catcher.
- **c** Tarasco catches the ball but runs straight through an advertising hoarding.

SCOREBOARD		

round seven — home or away

speedway In 2000, Mark Loram became only the third Briton since 1980 to become World Individual Speedway Champion. Michael Lee won the title 20 years before but who was the only British champion during the 1990s?

cricket	Name the international captain who in December 2000 became the youngest man from his country to take 200 test wickets.
football	Which goalkeeper played in his fifth Scottish FA Cup final in 2000, 18 years after his first?
horse racing	Before Red Marauder in 2001, what was the last horse with a colour in its name to win the Grand National?

SCOREBOARD

round eight — captain's away

For this round, here are two questions about unusual items which have found their way into sportsmen's kit bags. So can you tell me...

1 What unusual piece of kit did French Rugby Union star Andre Behoteguy wear during his 19 internationals in the '20s?

2 What unusual attire did England goalkeeper James Mitchell wear during his one and only international at Goodison Park in 1924?

SCOREBOARD

round nine — mystery guest

Can you guess the identity of these sporting stars from the four clues below? The more clues you need, the fewer points you get.

1	I was born in 1964 in Germany.	(4 points)
	I was voted Footballer of the Year in England in 1995.	(3 points)
	I won the World Cup and European Championships with Germany.	(2 points)
	I had two spells with Spurs and was often seen diving in celebration.	(1 point)
2	I was born in Liverpool in 1964 and turned professional in 1969.	(4 points)
	I won my only World Championship in 1991.	(3 points)
	I am a supporter of Everton, but snooker's the game I play.	(2 points)
	I enjoy getting the better of Ally McCoist on *A Question Of Sport.*	(1 point)

SCOREBOARD		

round ten — on the buzzer

This buzzer round has an alphabetical and boxing theme. The first letter of every answer will spell out the word KNOCKOUT. In the case of a person's name, it's the first letter of the surname that counts.

1 Who was the only player from the United Kingdom or Ireland to start this season in Series A?

2 Who was the only Australian to win the Open during the 1990s ?

3 Rugby Union – How many times has a British side reached the World Cup final?

4 Name the Arsenal defender who made his debut for England in Albania in 2001.

5 What nationality is former Olympic 800m champion Paul Ereng?

6 Which manager won the League cups of England and then Scotland in consecutive seasons?

7 Basketball – In which American city do the Jazz play?

8 In which sport do you get turkeys, strikes and bedposts ?

SCOREBOARD		

game **19**

round one — name the year

The following events all happened in the same year, but which one?

1 Derek Bell and Jackie Ickx win Le Mans for a second successive year.
The Formula One World Champion is Keke Rosberg, despite having only won one Grand Prix in the season, the Swiss.
Australia beat England in the third Test, taking seven wickets for 35 runs in some 15 overs between lunch and tea.
Tottenham beat QPR in the FA Cup final after a 1–0 win in the replay.
Kevin Keegan makes his last bow for England in the World Cup finals.

Now for the second year:

2 An injured Darren Gough returns home early from England's tour of Australia.
Francois Pienaar leads South Africa to victory in the rugby World Cup final.
Jonathan Edwards breaks the Triple Jump World Record in Salamanca.
Prince Naseem defeats Steve Robinson to take the WBO Featherweight title.
Jenny Pitman's Royal Athlete wins the Grand National at 40–1.

SCOREBOARD		

round two — picture board

Take a look at picture A on page 3 of Picture Board 1. Who is it?

Take a look at picture D on page 7 of Picture Board 2. Who is it?

SCOREBOARD		

round three — twenty sporting questions

20 questions on the sporting highlights of a single year – 1996.

1. Which Englishman won the US Masters?
2. Cricket – Which country beat Australia to win the 1996 World Cup?
3. Which former Millwall and Manchester City defender was named as manager of the Republic of Ireland?
4. Who won their fourth boat race in a row in 1996?
5. Which Wigan player became England's youngest-ever Rugby League captain?
6. Which Italian club beat Ajax 4–2 on penalties to win the European Cup?
7. Which Russian won his first Grand Slam by beating Michael Stich in the French Open final?
8. Which former Lion turned out for the Scottish Claymores in the World Bowl?
9. Which umpire stood in his 66th and final test during 1996?
10. Which Swiss player, aged 15, partnered Helena Sukova to the Wimbledon women's doubles title?
11. Who won cricket's county championship for only the second time?
12. Which team beat Bradford Bulls 40–32 to win Rugby League's Challenge Cup?
13. Which team completed their second League and FA Cup double?
14. Which African country upset the form-book to beat the West Indies by 73 runs during the Cricket World Cup?
15. Who rode Rough Quest to victory in the Grand National?
16. Which brothers became the first siblings to represent England together since Bobby and Jackie Charlton?
17. Tom Lehman of the USA won the Open on which course?
18. Which city's Cowboys beat the Pittsburgh Steelers to win the Superbowl?
19. Which Newcastle United striker was named as PFA Player of the Year?
20. Who broke the 400m Olympic record in taking the gold medal at Atlanta?

SCOREBOARD		

round four — sporting links

1 What links Gabriel Batistuta, Linford Christie and Sir Garfield Sobers?

2 What connects Arsenal's Brian Marwood, Harlequins' Andrew Harriman and Yorkshire's Arnie Sidebottom?

SCOREBOARD		

round five — where am I?

From the following two clues you must work out which place is being described.

1 The football team in this city play in black and white stripes and Susan Rolph has competed for their swimming team. But where in England?

2 The 1987 FA Cup winners and the England's Rugby Union Challenge Cup winners in 1973 and '74 will lead you to this Midlands city.

SCOREBOARD		

round six — what happened next

All you have to do in this round is decide which of the three options is the correct answer.

Football from the League of Wales and Ton Pentre against Mold Alexander. Jason Watkins of Ton Pentre is about to take a corner. What happened next?

- **a** A cow runs on to the field and starts chewing at the net.
- **b** A flock of ducks lands on the centre circle.
- **c** Jason Watkins is attacked by a dog while taking the corner.

Tennis from Olympia. Mansour Bahrami in action in a Seniors match. What happened next?

- **a** Bahrami jumps over the net and plays a rally with himself.
- **b** Bahrami starts playing with two balls and plays each shot with alternate hands.
- **c** Bahrami starts using his head and feet instead of his racquet.

SCOREBOARD		

round seven — home or away

rugby league Who, in 1998, became the first man ever to score tries in six successive Test matches?

golf Laura Davies has won more points in the Solheim Cup than any other European. But can you name the American with the same distinction?

football How did Laurent Blanc's goal against Paraguay in France '98 make World Cup history?

snooker Name the 1995 World Championship semi-finalist who in 2001 prevented Steve Davis from competing at the Worlds for the first time since 1979.

SCOREBOARD

round eight — captain's away

Here are two riddles from the often unusual world of sport. Can you tell me...

1 Leeds got theirs from Real Madrid, Arsenal's used to belong to Nottingham Forest, Tottenham Hotspur's was originally Preston North End's and Juventus got theirs from Notts County. What are we talking about?

2 How have Holland and Bramble of Ipswich, Izzet of Leicester and Ginola of Aston Villa all won outside of the Premiership over the past three years?

SCOREBOARD

round nine — mystery guest

Can you guess the identity of these sporting stars from the 4 clues below? The more clues you need the fewer points you get.

1 I was born in 1968 in Manchester and attended Cambridge University. (4 points)
I scored over 1,000 runs in my debut season in 1987. (3 points)
I was appointed England captain in 1993 and went on to lead them in 52 Tests. (2 points)
I won my 100th cap the same day as Alec Stewart. (1 point)

2 I was born in 1976 and wear a number 9 shirt. (4 points)
I am rated the best hooker in the world, playing for my home-town club. (3 points)
I was the only Great Britain player to be named in *Rugby League World* magazine's World XIII in 1999. (2 points)
I play for Wales in League and have attracted much attention from Union clubs, especially Swansea in 2001. (1 point)

SCOREBOARD		

round ten — on the buzzer

These answers are all numbers.

1 How many players would you find on a basketball team?
2 Football – How many goals did Ally McCoist score in Euro 96?

3 Swimming – How many different strokes do you swim in an individual medley race?

4 Golf – What record score did Darren Clarke shoot in the second round of the 1999 European Open?

5 Snooker – What is John Parrott's highest-ever break at the Crucible?

6 What is the minimum number of points you need to win a set in table tennis?

7 Football – How many substitutes can a team use in a Premiership match?

8 Tennis – How old was Sue Barker when she won the French Open in 1976?

9 How many players would you find in a hockey team?

10 Boxing – What's the maximum number of rounds in a professional bout?

11 Golf – At St Andrews, which is the Road Hole?

12 Horse racing – How many fences do they jump in the Grand National?

13 Snooker – In how many World Championship finals has Jimmy White played?

14 Athletics –To the nearest mile, how long is a marathon?

15 Football – How many goals did Bobby Charlton score for England?

16 Horse racing – How many Classics are there in England's flat-racing season?

17 Boxing – In South Africa, Lennox Lewis was beaten in which round against Hasim Rahman?

18 Snooker – How many frames does the world champion need to win in the final at the Crucible?

19 Athletics – To the nearest mile, how far is the Great North Run?

SCOREBOARD		

game 20

round one — name the year

The following events all happened in the same year, but which one?

1 Chris Evert and her fiancée Jimmy Connors both win singles titles at Wimbledon.
The British Lions sensationally win a series in South Africa.
John Conteh beats Jorge Ahumada to win the World Light-heavyweight title.
Liverpool defeat Newcastle 3–0 in a one-sided FA Cup final.
Tottenham lose to Feyenoord in the UEFA Cup final.

Now for the second year:

2 The first professional American Football match staged in Britain is held at Wembley Stadium.
India wins cricket's World Cup.
John McEnroe wins Wimbledon for the second time, beating New Zealand's Chris Lewis.
Brighton hold Manchester United to a 2–2 draw in the FA Cup final.
Liverpool beat Manchester United 2–1 in the League Cup final.

SCOREBOARD		

round two — picture board

Take a look at picture E on page 4 of Picture Board 1. Who is it?

Take a look at picture C on page 1 of Picture Board 1. Who is it?

SCOREBOARD		

round three — twenty sporting questions

20 questions with a French connection.

1 Which Frenchman finished joint runner-up at the 1999 Open at Carnoustie?
2 Who did France beat to win Euro 2000?
3 Which French woman won Olympic gold at the 1992 and '96 Olympics over 400 metres?
4 Who managed Arsenal to the League and FA Cup double in 1998?
5 Tennis – Who was runner-up to Mats Wilander at the 1988 French Open?
6 Rugby Union – Name the flamboyant French full-back who scored 38 tries during 93 appearances for his country.
7 At which stadium was the 1998 World Cup Final held?
8 Bernard Hinault won which race five times between 1978 and 1986 ?
9 Which French jockey rode High-Rise to win the 1998 Derby ?
10 France were the inaugural winners of which Olympic sport in 1900?
11 For which French club did Chris Waddle play in a European Cup final?
12 Who in 2001 arrived in Les Sables d'Olonne in Western France to become the youngest woman ever to sail around the world?
13 Where were the 1992 Winter Olympics held?
14 Which driver won a record 51 Formula One races between 1980 and 1993?
15 Which Frenchman scored the penalty for Juventus against Liverpool to win the 1985 European Cup final?
16 Stephane Diagana was World Championship gold medallist in 1997 in which track event?
17 At which racecourse is the Prix de l'Arc de Triomphe run?
18 Who scored the golden goal to help France win Euro 2000?
19 Who did France beat in the semi-final of the 1999 Rugby Union World Cup?
20 Which manager led Liverpool to three Cup finals in 2001?

SCOREBOARD		

round four — sporting links

1 What links Pele, Muhammad Ali and...1977 US Open women's doubles runner-up Renee Richards?

2 What links Pele, Kazimierz Deyna of Poland and Paul van Himst of Belgium?

SCOREBOARD

round five — where am I?

From the following two clues you must work out which place is being described.

1 In this city you will find the Test match ground Trent Bridge and the oldest club in the football league.

2 Where in Scotland would you find the racecourse with the shortest name in the country and the Honest Men playing at Somerset Park?

SCOREBOARD

round six — what happened next?

All you have to do in this round is decide which of the three options is the correct answer.

Football, and a match between Linfield and Glentoran from the Irish league. The Glentoran defence have just cleared the ball into touch. What happened next?

- **a** The ball gets stuck on the roof of the stand and the game is held up for five minutes.
- **b** The ball goes into the stands – no one is sitting there, so it doesn't come back. They can't find a replacement ball, so the game is held up for five minutes.
- **c** The ball lands on a bottle in the crowd and it bursts, causing the game to be held up for five minutes.

Greyhound racing from Monmore Green; Lissarda Kate has just won the race. What happened next?

- **a** Lissarda Kate won't return to her handler after the race, and spends the next half-hour running round the infield of the track.
- **b** Lissarda Kate picks up the hare and makes off with it in her mouth.
- **c** All the dogs – led by Lissarda Kate – decide that they don't think the race should end and continue for another lap.

SCOREBOARD		

round seven — home or away

horse racing	Istabraq won three consecutive Champion Hurdles at Cheltenham, but which horse was runner-up to him three times in the late 1990s?

swimming	Who in 1999 won her ninth and tenth European Championship medals in Istanbul – all of them the same colour?
cricket	Name the Yorkshire player capped by England against Australia in 1985, who also helped Manchester United to the Second Division title in 1975?
motor racing	Carl Fogarty's 59 career victories make him by far the most successful Superbiker of all time but who, by winning 17 races in 1991, holds the record for most wins in a season ?

SCOREBOARD

round eight — captain's away

Here are two riddles from the often unusual world of sport. Can you tell me...

1 In which sport would you perform an Adolph, or do a randy on a bed?

2 In which sport can you be penalised for standing up or holding the ball with both hands, unless you're playing in goal?

SCOREBOARD

round nine — mystery guest

Can you guess the identity of these sporting stars from the four clues below? The more clues you need the fewer points you get.

1 I was born in 1967 and have played in three different countries. (4 points)
In 1990 I was voted BBC Sports Personality of the Year. (3 points)
I suffered a bad leg injury in an FA Cup final. (2 points)
I'm often remembered for crying in Turin. (1 point)

2 I was born in 1962 and won my first Olympic gold medal in 1984. (4 points)
My first two gold medals were won alongside Andrew Holmes. (3 points)
I was unbeaten in major finals from 1991 until I retired. (2 points)
I have won a record five Olympic gold medals. (1 point)

SCOREBOARD		

round ten — on the buzzer

In this buzzer round the answers all have some connection with the world of work – so they include the names of different occupations.

1. Snooker – He could make you a suit and he won the world title in 1985.
2. Football – You might find him in the Navy, and he plays for Arsenal and England.
3. Athletics – This green-fingered British sprinter broke the 10-second barrier over 100 metres in Lausanne in 1999.

4 Golf – He might be found in a cake shop, and won three out of his four matches for Europe in the 1993 Ryder Cup.

5 Cricket – This Test umpire could look after a flock of sheep, but he hops around when the score reaches 111.

6 Boxing – His surname is a person who makes barrels, and he won three Lonsdale Belts.

7 Motor racing – He might work as a cobbler, and was Formula 1 World Champion in 1994, '95 and 2000.

8 Athletics – She would be handy in the kitchen and still holds British records at 100, 200 and 400 metres.

9 Boxing – He may be found on a building site, and was world heavyweight champion aged 45.

10 Tennis – This American could deliver you a package and won the French Open in 1991 and '92.

11 Cricket – He could have worked on the railways and kept wicket for Lancashire and India in the '70s.

12 Football – He could also be handy with sheep, and won 63 caps for England.

13 Rugby League – You might find him on a yacht, and he scored in the 2000 World Cup final for Australia ?

SCOREBOARD		

game **21**

round one — name the year

The following events all happened in the same year, but which one?

1 Gary Sobers hits six sixes in an over.
Black Power salutes are given by athletes at the Olympics.
Bob Beamon leaps to a world record 29' 2½" and remains the record-holder until 1991.
The Olympics are held in Mexico City.
Manchester United become the first English club to win the European Cup.

Now for the second year:

2 45-year-old Ray Reardon wins his sixth and final World Snooker Championship.
David Gower makes his England Test debut and hits his first ball for four.
England travel to Australia under the captaincy of Mike Brearley to defend the Ashes.
Liverpool win the European Cup for the second time.
Argentina win the World Cup.

SCOREBOARD		

round two — picture board

Take a look at picture A on page 6 of Picture Board 2. Who is it?

Take a look at picture B on page 5 of Picture Board 1. Who is it?

SCOREBOARD		

round three — twenty sporting questions

20 questions where the answers all begin with R. In the case of a person's name, then it will be the surname.

1 Which Brazilian striker was named World Footballer of the Year in 1996?
2 Which Scottish club play their home games at Ibrox?
3 In which Olympic sport has Agostino Abagnale been a gold medallist?
4 Which Finnish driver won the Formula One World Championship in 1982?
5 What is the nationality of footballer Georghe Hagi?
6 What is the name of the American Football team from Washington which won the 1992 Superbowl?
7 Which horse won the 2001 Grand National?
8 In which sport was Tommi Makinen World Champion in 1996 and 1997?
9 Where were the 1960 Summer Olympics held?
10 Which Yugoslavian team beat Marseille to win the 1991 European Cup?
11 Tennis – Which Australian won the 1997 and '98 US Open titles?
12 Which Football League side play their home games at Millmoor?
13 Who in 1993 became the first Italian to play in the Ryder Cup?
14 Who scored the winning goal in the 1995 FA Cup final?
15 Which boxer defeated Lennox Lewis for the World Heavyweight title in April 2001?
16 Which Liverpool midfielder scored his first international goal for England in a friendly against Belgium in 1999?
17 What nationality is Olympic swimming gold medal winner Aleksandr Popov?
18 Who lost to Bayern Munich in the semi-final of the 2001 Champions League?
19 Which Welshman was World snooker champion six times during the 1970s?
20 Name the former Wigan Rugby League winger who crossed codes and made his England Rugby Union debut in 2001.

SCOREBOARD		

round four — sporting links

1 What links England centre Jeremy Guscott, Australian cricketer Damien Fleming and Great Britain Rugby League winger Henderson Gill?

2 What links Derby County Football Club, Steve and Mark Waugh and the 1979 UK Snooker Champion?

SCOREBOARD

round five — where am I?

From the following two clues you must work out which place is being described.

1 The venue of the 1976 Olympics will lead you to the birthplace of the 1995 Australian Open ladies' champion. Where is it?

2 In the city which hosted the 1984 Olympics you will also find teams called the Lakers and the Dodgers. Where?

SCOREBOARD

round six — what happened next

All you have to do in this round is decide which of the three options is the correct answer.

Cricket. West Indies vs Zimbabwe in March 2000. Courtney Walsh is bowling to Henry Olonga. What happened next?

- **a** Olonga is caught by Wavell Hinds and Walsh breaks Kapil Dev's record for the number of wickets taken in Test matches.
- **b** Olonga hits six sixes off the over – the first time ever in Test history.
- **c** Walsh bowls Olonga to take all 10 wickets – only the third time in Test history.

Ice skating from the 2001 World Championships. Alexandre Malkov and Alissa de Charbonnet are competing in the ice dance. What happened next?

- **a** Malkov gets his skates tied together.
- **b** Both skaters trip and fall into the audience.
- **c** The CD playing the music sticks, ruining their routine.

SCOREBOARD		

round seven — home or away

golf Who was the last European to win the Open before Paul Lawrie's success in 1999?

swimming	Name the American who set an Olympic Record in the 100 metres freestyle while claiming the gold medal at the 1988 Olympics.
football	Why was Torquay's Worthington Cup game with Portsmouth in August 1999 postponed?
horse racing	At which racecourse is the Derby run?

SCOREBOARD

round eight — captain's away

Here are two riddles from the often unusual world of sport. Can you tell me...

1 In which Olympic event is the gold medal usually won by the biggest jerk?

2 In which sport did the players' pimples get shorter in July 1999?

SCOREBOARD

round nine — mystery guest

Can you guess the identity of these sporting stars from the four clues below? The more clues you need, the fewer points you get.

1	I was born in 1973 and represented England Boys.	(4 points)
	I made my league debut against Everton in 1991 and was soon to become Wales's youngest player.	(3 points)
	I was the PFA Young Player of the year in 1992 and 1993.	(2 points)
	I've spent my whole career at Old Trafford.	(1 point)
2	I was born in Cardiff in 1967.	(4 points)
	I won a world title and set a world record in 1993.	(3 points)
	I was unbeaten in 44 successive races from 1993–95.	(2 points)
	I am Britain's greatest-ever 110 metres hurdler.	(1 point)

SCOREBOARD		

round ten — on the buzzer

These answers all include place-names – some a long way away!

1. Football – Name the Dutch winger who scored in the 1998 FA Cup final?
2. Horse racing – Who's the jockey with a record 30 Classic victories in his career?
3. Tennis – Who won the Wimbledon ladies' singles title in 2000?

4 Swimming – Which Briton won an Olympic breast-stroke silver medal at the Seoul Olympics?

5 Rugby Union – Name Scotland's most-capped player.

6 Football – Which England defender was signed for a record £18 million by Leeds in 2000?

7 Horse racing – Amateur jockey Charlie Fenwick rode which horse to victory in the 1980 Grand National?

8 Cricket – Name the England all-rounder who took a hat trick against the West Indies in 1995.

9 Football – Name the former Southend full-back who won the FA Cup with Tottenham in 1991.

10 Football – Who managed Sunderland in the 1992 FA Cup final defeat against Liverpool?

11 Athletics – Which British athlete set a world 10,000 metres record in 1973?

SCOREBOARD		

game **22**

round one — name the year

The following events all happened in the same year, but which one?

1 Desert Orchid wins the Cheltenham Gold Cup.
17-year-old Michael Chang wins the French Open.
Stuart McCall scores twice in an FA Cup final yet still finishes on the losing side.
Curtis Strange becomes the first man to retain the US Open Golf title since Ben Hogan in 1951.
Michael Thomas's last-minute goal at Anfield gives Arsenal the League title.

Now for the second year:

2 Graeme Hick scores 2,004 runs, becoming the youngest to reach this figure.
Greg Norman wins the Open at last – the first Australian to take the title since Peter Thomson in 1965.
American Greg Lemond wins the Tour de France for the first time.
The football World Cup is held in Mexico City.
Liverpool beat Everton in the FA Cup final.

SCOREBOARD

round two — picture board

Take a look at picture C on page 2 of Picture Board 1. Who is it?

Take a look at picture D on page 4 of Picture Board 2. Who is it?

SCOREBOARD

round three — twenty sporting questions

20 questions with a connection to Australia.

1 Rugby Union – Who captained the 1999 World Cup-winning team?
2 Which Australian batsman made a record 153 consecutive Test match appearances between 1979 and 1994?
3 Which country did Australia beat 31–0 in a World Cup qualifier in 2001?
4 Golf – Which Australian won the Open in 1986 and 1993?
5 Where in Australia would you find a Rugby League side called the Knights?
6 Australian goalkeeper Mark Schwarzer played in the 1998 League Cup final for which club?
7 Who was Wimbledon men's singles champion in 1987?
8 Who played in the last of his 101 Rugby Union internationals in 1996 after scoring a record 64 tries?
9 Which goalkeeper joined Chelsea from Manchester United in January 2001?
10 Which spinner during 2000 become Australia's all-time top wicket-taker?
11 Where in Australia would you find the WACA?
12 In which sport might you see a game between Essendon and Geelong?
13 Which woman won the 400m hurdles gold medal at the 1988 Olympics?
14 Which swimmer known as 'Thorpedo' won four medals at Sydney?
15 Which European country beat Australia in a play-off to qualify for the 1986 World Cup?
16 In which year did Melbourne host the summer Olympics?
17 Who won the Wimbledon men's singles title four times during the 1960s?
18 Which former Australian captain known as 'Tubs' ended his 104-Test career with a record 157 catches to his credit?
19 Which Australian woman won the 2000 US Women's Open?
20 For which Premiership club did Jacob Burns and Harry Kewell appear during season 2000–01?

SCOREBOARD		

round four — sporting links

1 What do the following have in common: former Minister of Sport Colin Moynihan, Crown Prince Constantin of Greece and Brazilian footballer Ronaldo?

2 Apart from winning Olympic medals, what else do long-distance runner Ron Clarke, decathlete Rafer Johnson and 400 metre runner Cathy Freeman have in common?

SCOREBOARD		

round five — where am I?

From the following two clues you must work out which place is being described.

1 In this city there are teams called Spartak which play both ice hockey and football, and it also staged the Olympics where Allan Wells won 100m gold.

2 The birthplace of Kenny Dalglish is home to the football teams which play at the Broadwood Stadium and the Firhill Stadium. Where is it?

SCOREBOARD		

round six — what happened next?

All you have to do in this round is decide which of the three options is the correct answer.

Football. Germany against Greece in a World Cup under-21 qualifying match. The Greek keeper is about to take a goal kick. What happened next?

- **a** Strong winds blow large amounts of rubbish on to the field and the game is stopped for 15 minutes while the ground is tidied up.
- **b** A dog runs on the pitch and it takes the ground staff five minutes to catch him.
- **c** The referee pulls a muscle in his leg but there is no fourth official, so a local league manager has to take over as one of the linesmen.

2001 Boat Race. Both crews have been rowing for one mile. What happened next?

- **a** The crews clash and a Cambridge rower loses his oar.
- **b** The Cambridge crew sink.
- **c** A family of swans swim across the river causing the Oxford crew to take evasive action.

SCOREBOARD		

round seven — home or away

football Name the Welsh international striker who has made appearances for his country while at ten different clubs.

athletics	Which sprinter has won medals at both 100m and 200m at the past two Olympics?
rugby league	Which English international forward played in the 2000 Australian Rugby League Grand Final?
tennis	Which player first won the Wimbledon singles title in 1974, but didn't win his second Wimbledon championship until eight years later when he defeated John McEnroe?

SCOREBOARD

round eight — captain's away

True or false. All these names contain parts of the body and you have to decide which are genuine and which have been made up.

1 Shin Sang-Shik competed in the Greco-Roman wrestling for Korea at the 1968 Olympics.

2 Puck van Heel played left-half for Feyenoord.

3 Declan Kidney is the coach of the Munster Rugby Union side.

4 Wendy Elbow rode in the 1986 Melbourne Cup.

5 Arthur Nostril played 20 cricket test matches for Australia.

6 Perris Kneebone won an Olympic hockey gold medal with Australia.

7 Johnny Moustache has played international football for the Seychelles.

8 Roger Eyelid competed in the 1984 World Bowls Championships.

SCOREBOARD

round nine — mystery guest

Can you guess the identity of these sporting stars from the four clues below? The more clues you need, the fewer points you get.

1 I was born in 1957 in Hayes, Middlesex. (4 points)
I scored on my England debut in 1979. (3 points)
I played in three FA Cup finals in the 1980s, scoring in 1982. (2 points)
I have managed Swindon, Chelsea, England, Southampton and Spurs. (1 point)

2 I was born in Melbourne in 1969 and made my debut for Victoria in 1990–1. (4 points)
I made my Test debut after just seven appearances. (3 points)
I took a hat-trick against England in Melbourne and have also played for Hampshire recently. (2 points)
I am particularly well-known for a ball which captured Mike Gatting's wicket. (1 point)

SCOREBOARD

round ten — on the buzzer

These questions are all about rules and regulations.

1 Football – How far from the goal line is the penalty spot?
2 Cricket – How many runs are awarded if the ball hits a fielder's helmet which is lying on the ground?

3 What is the height of a squash net?

4 Athletics – What is the first event in the heptathlon?

5 Golf – What is the maximum number of clubs in a bag?

6 Which sport's playing surface is 72 square feet?

7 Which sport's most famous tournament is held in London SW19?

8 In which sport can you win by a TKO?

9 Football – What were referees and their assistants issued with for the first time in 1999?

10 Cricket – Which English batsman was given out in a Test match in 1993 for handling the ball?

11 Rugby League – How many points for a dropped goal?

12 Which sport has a net six inches (15.25 cm) high?

13 In which sport can you be penalised for travelling?

14 Motor racing – How many points do you get for winning a Grand Prix?

15 Athletics – What is 11 inches long, 5 inches round and covers 400 metres in 38 seconds?

16 Football – Since 1997, what have players been able to do direct from the kick-off?

SCOREBOARD		

game 23

round one — name the year

The following events all happened in the same year, but which one?

1 Ayrton Senna clinches his second World Championship.
Hale Irwin at 45 years is the oldest winner of the US Open.
Stefan Edberg beats Boris Becker to take the Wimbledon men's singles title.
Manchester United win the FA Cup after a replay.
England lose 4–3 on penalties to West Germany in the World Cup semi-final.

Now for the second year:

2 England's cricket tour of South Africa is cancelled eight days before its start.
Jochen Rindt wins the World Drivers' Championship but sadly is killed in practice at Monza before the season ends.
Nijinsky wins the Derby in the fastest time for 34 years.
Everton win the League; Celtic lose in the European Cup final.
Brazil win the World Cup in Mexico with possibly the greatest team performance in history.

SCOREBOARD

round two — picture board

Take a look at picture C on page 1 of Plicture Board 2. Who is it?

Take a look at picture A on page 4 of Picture Board 1. Who is it?

SCOREBOARD

round three — twenty sporting questions

Twenty questions on the history of Rugby Union.

1 Who captained England to the Five Nations Grand Slam in 1991?

2 Name the Scottish winger who retired in 1998 after scoring a record-equalling 24 tries in internationals.

3 Which team won the 2001 Principality Cup in Wales?

4 Which French flanker won 59 caps from 1975–84 including 34 as captain?

5 The victorious 1974 British Lions were captained by which Irish lock forward?

6 In which city was the first World Cup final played in 1987?

7 Which Australian did Neil Jenkins overtake to be top world points-scorer?

8 Who scored four tries against England in the 1995 World Cup semi-final?

9 Which team did Martin Johnson captain to victory in the 2001 Zurich Championship final?

10 Against whom in 1995's World Cup did New Zealand score 21 tries in a game?

11 Which club have won the Middlesex Sevens on most occasions?

12 Who scored the crucial drop-goal for South Africa in the 1995 World Cup final?

13 Which famous Irish club's name is often used to describe a high kick, often a favourite tactic of the club?

14 Which country did Italy defeat in their first ever Six Nations match?

15 Which two countries compete for the Bledisloe Cup?

16 Name the Argentinean outside-half who scored 530 points during a 28-year career which ended in 1990.

17 Which country, whose men's side are known as the Eagles, won the inaugural Women's World Cup in 1991?

18 Which Welsh club side play their home games at the Brewery Field?

19 What is the surname shared by JPR and JJ – two of Welsh rugby's greatest names during the 1970s?

20 What cup do Scotland play England for every season?

SCOREBOARD

round four — sporting links

Which of these Olympians has appeared in the most feature films?

1 Wrestling bronze medallist Ken Richmond; five-times gold medal-winning swimmer Jonny Weissmuller; weight-lifting silver medallist Harold Sakata.

Which of the following sports people has written the most best-selling books: but you'll have to guess their names first?

2 The cricket umpire who stood in 66 Tests; Manchester United's 1994 double-winning captain; Devon Loch's jockey in the 1956 Grand National.

SCOREBOARD

round five — where am I?

From the following two clues you must work out which place is being described.

1 If you had been watching the 1999 Cricket World Cup match between Kenya and South Africa, you would have been in the home country of the winner of the 1996 Wimbledon men's single title. But which country?

2 The nationality of squash legend Jahangir Khan will lead you to the country with international cricket venues at Rawalpindi and Lahore. Which country?

SCOREBOARD

round six — what happened next?

All you have to do in this round is decide which of the three options is the correct answer.

Football from the Bundesliga. Hansa Rostock against Bayern Munich, and a corner for Bayern. What happened next?

- **a** Bayern 'keeper Oliver Kahn comes up for the corner and punches the ball into the Rostock net.
- **b** The ball goes through the side-netting but the goal is allowed to stand.
- **c** Bayern Munich score but the goal is disallowed when the referee realises that they have 12 players on the field.

Tennis, and Marc Philippoussis is about to serve. What happened next?

- **a** Play is interrupted by a young lady who runs on to the court to present Philippoussis with a rose.
- **b** Play is interrupted by a noisy crow, so Philippoussis hits balls at it to make it go away.
- **c** Play is interrupted when the umpire faints and falls out of his chair.

SCOREBOARD		

round seven — home or away

tennis Who held the Wimbledon Men's singles title from 1976 to 1980?

golf	Name the wild-card entry who won the 1991 USPGA, replacing Nick Price on the day before the start of the tournament?
cricket	Who during the 1999 season became the youngest English player to score a first-class triple century, with 303 not out for Northants?
football	Name the Scotsman who lifted the European Cup for Liverpool in 1984.

SCOREBOARD

round eight — captain's away

Here are anagrams of two England stars – can you unscramble them?

1 Whole cinema
Leaky ringer

And now for a couple of famous footballing names from Scotland...

2 Elk having lager.
Local mystic.

SCOREBOARD

round nine — mystery guest

Can you guess the identity of these sporting stars from the four clues below? The more clues you need, the fewer points you get.

1 Born in Glasgow in 1951, I played for the city's hooped side. (4 points)
I scored over 100 league goals in two countries. (3 points)
My goal won the 1978 European Cup final. (2 points)
I won the league title in England as manager of two clubs. (1 point)

2 Born in 1957, I am considered one of the all-time greats. (4 points)
I have won three Open championships, as well as playing for and captaining the European Ryder Cup teams. (3 points)
I won the Masters in 1980; the first player from my country to do so. (2 points)
My most famous shot was played from a car park! (1 point)

SCOREBOARD		

round ten — on the buzzer

These answers are all associated with animals.

1. Golf – Who won three consecutive US amateur titles in the '90s?
2. Football – Name the striker who scored against Scotland on his England debut, whilst playing in the third division.
3. Cricket – Which former Yorkshire and Leicestershire batsman of the 60s is now a best-selling author?

4 Athletics – Who was the first British female to run the 800 metres in less than two minutes: she's now a BBC commentator?

5 Which city do the Rhinos Rugby League team come from?

6 Golf – Which American is nicknamed 'the Walrus'?

7 Football – What is the name of the Rams who play at Pride Park?

8 Athletics – Which Scotsman led the silver medal-winning men's 4 x 100 relay team at the Seoul Olympics?

9 Cricket – Name the South African-born batsman who played for Northants and captained England.

10 Football – Which Premiership club are known as the Black Cats ?

11 Cricket – Which England spinner is nicknamed 'the Cat'?

12 Football – Name the club known as the 'Foxes'.

13 Rugby League – Name the brothers who played for the Bradford Bulls in the 2001 Challenge Cup final against St Helen's.

SCOREBOARD		

game **24**

round one — name the year

The following events all happened in the same year, but which one?

1 The 12–1 shot Shaamit ridden by Mick Hills wins the Derby.
Alan Shearer becomes the world's most expensive player at £15 million.
Britain's Roger Black wins Olympic silver.
A Frenchman scores the winning goal in the FA Cup final.
Steve Redgrave wins his fourth consecutive Olympic Gold medal.

Now for the second year:

2 In the Cricket World Cup final, Australia beat England by seven runs.
Mike Gatting and umpire Shakoor Rana call a truce after their finger-wagging row in Pakistan.
Ian Woosnam leads Wales to Golf's World Cup win.
Europe successfully defends the Ryder Cup at Muirfield Village under the captaincy of Tony Jacklin.
Everton win the League.

SCOREBOARD		

round two — picture board

Take a look at picture E on page 6 of Picture Board 1. Who is it?

Take a look at picture E on page 7 of Picture Board 2. Who is it?

SCOREBOARD		

round three — twenty sporting questions

20 questions on Italian sport and sports stars.

1. Which striker was the leading goal-scorer at the 1990 World Cup?
2. Name the fly-half whose 29 points gave Italy their first-ever Six Nations victory, against Scotland in 2000.
3. In which sport did Alberto Tomba win three gold and two silver medals at the Winter Olympics?
4. Which UK-born long-jumper took World Championship gold for Italy in 1995?
5. Where in Italy would you find the Luigi Ferraris stadium, venue for the Republic of Ireland's World Cup victory over Romania in 1990?
6. Which famous race did Marco Pantani win in 1998?
7. Which legendary goalkeeper captained Italy to the World Cup in 1982?
8. Klaus Dibiasi won three consecutive Olympic titles in which sport?
9. Which Italian driver won nine consecutive Grands Prix in 1952 and 1953?
10. In which sport have Carmine, Guiseppe and Agostino Abbagnale all won Olympic gold medals?
11. Name the Italian golfer who finished runner-up in the Open in 1995?
12. Which Italian football team have won five European Cup finals?
13. Name the father and son who've both ridden winners of the 2000 Guineas?
14. In which sport has Giacomo Agostini won more world titles than anyone else?
15. Which Italian midfielder scored in three Wembley finals between 1997 and 2000?
16. Which boxer won the world heavyweight title in 1933?
17. Livio Berruti and Pietro Mennea have both won Olympic gold in which event?
18. In 1976, Adriano Panatta won a major title in which sport?
19. In which sport did Nedo Nadi win five gold medals at one Summer Olympics?
20. In which city did Paul Gascoigne shed tears after being booked in the World Cup semi final?

SCOREBOARD		

round four — sporting links

Now for some detailed testing of your Olympic records knowledge.

1 Which of the following sportsmen has won gold medals at the greatest number of consecutive Olympic Games: rower Sir Steven Redgrave, fencer Aladar Gerevich or yachtsman Durwood Knowles?

2 Which of these countries won the most medals at the Winter Olympic Games in the 20th century: China, Liechtenstein or Uzbekistan?

SCOREBOARD		

round five — where am I?

From the following two clues you must work out which place is being described.

1 Manchester United played a Cup Winner's Cup tie here in 1977, while the Albion play Rugby Union. Where?

2 This town had a Football League team until 1929: a few years later it was the birthplace of Jack and Bobby Charlton. Where?

SCOREBOARD		

round six — what happened next?

All you have to do in this round is decide which of the three options is the correct answer.

Tennis. John McEnroe is playing against Michael Stich. The game comes to a halt. What happened next?

- **a** McEnroe is forced to leave the court to change his shorts, which have just ripped.
- **b** McEnroe objects to two people in the crowd who are smoking pipes.
- **c** McEnroe's mobile phone in his bag begins ringing.

Football from the 1999 FA Cup, and a game between Yeovil and Cardiff. Yeovil keeper Tony Pennock has the ball in his hands. What happened next?

- **a** Pennock rolls the ball out too far and Cardiff score the winner.
- **b** Pennock scores from his hands to win the game for Yeovil.
- **c** Pennock throws the ball into his own net, sending Cardiff through to the next round.

SCOREBOARD		

round seven — home or away

golf On which championship course would you find the 'Postage Stamp' hole?

rugby league Which former Great Britain scrum-half won nine Challenge Cup winners medals during his career?

athletics At the 2000 Olympics in Sydney, which woman won a track and field gold medal 17 years after winning a World Championship gold medal in the same event?

cricket How many pieces of wood are on the field of play at the start of a match?

SCOREBOARD

round eight — captain's away

What links the following sports stars?

1 What do these three American sports stars have in common: Olympic weight-lifting silver medallist Harold Sakata, five-times Olympic gold medal-winning swimmer Johnny Weissmuller and basketball superstar Michael Jordan?

2 What sporting connection is shared by Julio Iglesias, David Icke and Pope John Paul II?

SCOREBOARD

round nine — mystery guest

Can you guess the identity of these sporting stars from the four clues below? The more clues you need, the fewer points you get.

1 I was born in 1969 and named after my father's favourite footballer. (4 points)
I won the UEFA and the Cup Winners Cups with Ajax. (3 points)
I also played in Italy with Inter Milan. (2 points)
In 1998 I missed the FA Cup final through injury, not through fear of flying. (1 point)

2 I was born in 1935 and had my first race in 1948. (4 points)
I competed for more than 40 years. (3 points)
I won nine Epsom Derbies, my first in 1954, my last in 1983. (2 points)
I have won more English classics than anyone else. (1 point)

SCOREBOARD		

round ten — on the buzzer

The answers in the buzzer round are in alphabetical order. In the case of a person's name it will be the surname that counts. Starting with A...

1. Golf – What do you score if you complete a hole in three under par?
2. Football – Which club lost to Manchester United in the final of the 1999 Champions' League?
3. Which all-rounder hit the winning runs for England against the West Indies in the second Test of 2000?

4 Snooker – Name the player who holds the record for the fastest-ever frame?

5 Football – Who are known as the Toffees?

6 How many points is a brown worth in snooker?

7 American football – In which city do the Packers play?

8 Athletics – Which Olympic event did Dick Fosbury revolutionise at the 1968 Olympics?

9 Football – Which Middlesborough and England midfielder is known as The Guv'nor?

10 Athletics – Which athlete won gold in the 110m hurdles at the 1999 World Championships in Seville?

11 Cricket – Which South African all-rounder was named Man of the Tournament at the 1999 World Cup?

12 Which Midlands Rugby Union club are known as the Tigers?

13 Formula One – Name the 1992 World Champion.

14 Which golfer, known as the Golden Bear, won the US Masters six times?

15 Football – Who's made the record number of appearances for Arsenal?

SCOREBOARD		

game 25

round one — name the year

The following events all happened in the same year, but which one?

1 The San Francisco 49ers win the Super Bowl for the second year running.
Italian sides dominate European club competition with AC Milan winning the Champions Cup and Sampdoria and Juventus winning the other two trophies.
Steve Backley sets a World Javelin record of 90.98m.
Amateur Marcus Armytage wins the Grand National on 16–1 shot Mr Frisk.
Paul Gascoigne sobs in the World Cup game after a booking against Germany.

Now for the second year:

2 The first London Marathon is staged.
Sebastian Coe breaks the World Record for the 800m in Florence.
Alexis Arguello takes the WBC Lightweight title from Scotland's Jim Watt.
John Wark scores 14 goals in the UEFA competition including two in the final.
Alan Kennedy scores the only goal of the European Cup final as Liverpool beat Real Madrid in Paris.

SCOREBOARD		

round two — picture board

Take a look at picture E on page 1 of Picture Board 1. Who is it?

Take a look at picture E on page 2 of Picture Board 1. Who is it?

SCOREBOARD		

round three twenty sporting questions

20 questions where the answers all begin with M.

1 Which football club known as the Stags play at the Field Mill Ground?
2 In which sport did Kate Allenby win a bronze medal at the Sydney Olympics?
3 Which horse ridden by Richard Dunwoody won the 1994 Grand National?
4 Where do Scotland play their home Rugby Union internationals?
5 Which city hosted the 1956 Summer Olympics?
6 Which former Australian wicket-keeper retired in 1984 with a then-world record of 355 dismissals to his name?
7 Which US Davis Cup player lost to André Agassi in the 1999 US Open final?
8 What nationality is Khalid Skah, winner of the 1992 Olympic 10,000 metres?
9 Which club, who play at the Moss Rose Ground, were promoted into the football league in 1997?
10 Snooker – Which Scot was 1994's Benson & Hedges Masters champion?
11 Who was Formula One World Champion in 1992?
12 Which county did Mark Ramprakash leave to join Surrey in 2001?
13 Which Russian woman won the 800m and 1500m at the 1996 Olympics?
14 Which Scottish side play their home games at Fir Park Stadium?
15 From which city do the American Football team known as the Vikings come?
16 Which golfer won the European Order of Merit for seven successive years between 1993-2000?
17 Who scored the winning goal in the 1990 FA Cup final replay?
18 Which British female won the 400 metres bronze at the Sydney Olympics?
19 Which boxer did Frank Bruno defeat to become WBC heavyweight champion in 1995?
20 At which ground do Wolverhampton Wanderers play their home matches?

SCOREBOARD		

round four — sporting links

1 What connects the two-man bobsleigh at the Nagano Olympics, the 1973 Five Nations rugby and the 1981–82 National Hunt champion jockey's title?

2 What connects Spurs winger and Test cricket umpire Fanny Walden, the first Women's Olympic high-jump competition and the Chair at Aintree?

SCOREBOARD		

round five — where am I?

From the following two clues you must work out which place is being described.

1 The nationality of former Derbyshire bowler Ole Mortensen will lead you to the country which has football teams which have won the national championship called Brondby and Aarhus. Which country?

2 In this South American country Barcelona have been League Champions many times and the Lapentti brothers are the rising tennis stars. Which country?

SCOREBOARD		

round six — what happened next?

All you have to do in this round is decide which of the three options is the correct answer.

Football. Liverpool vs Porto from the quarter-finals of the UEFA Cup. Liverpool take a free kick into the Porto area. What happened next?

- **a** Sami Hyypia takes a tumble over the advertising hoardings.
- **b** Jamie Carragher takes the kick but his boot comes off and flies into the crowd.
- **c** Christian Ziege attempts to head the ball but only manages to head the post and knocks himself out.

Golf from the Players' Championship in Florida. American Brad Fabel has hit his shot on to the 17th green. What happened next?

- **a** A seagull picks up Fabel's ball and drops it in the water.
- **b** A disgruntled fan runs on to the green and throws the ball into the water.
- **c** Fabel's playing partner Fred Funk hits his approach which knocks Brad's ball in to the water.

SCOREBOARD		

round seven — home or away

swimming Which British swimmer won the 200m Breaststroke and set a world record at the 1976 Olympic Games?

motor racing	At which track would you drive past Maggotts to get to Hangar Straight?
football	Which club played in three consecutive Champions' League finals between 1996 and 1998?
rugby union	Name the brothers who played for New Zealand in the 1995 Rugby Union World Cup final.

SCOREBOARD

round eight — captain's away

Here are three definitions of a sporting term - two are complete nonsense but one is genuine. Which one?

1 Kushti is a traditional form of wrestling in Iran where the competitors wear tight leather trousers which can be used for holds.
Kushti was a slang term used in the East End of London for an apprentice footballer.
Kushti is the protective guard which is used to protect an Ice Hockey's goal minder's lower regions.

2 Kaboom was the original name for tennis in the 18th Century.
Kaboom is the official noise which is made by a starter's gun in athletics.
Kaboom is a backward somersault in a tuck position used in trampolining.

SCOREBOARD

round nine — mystery guest

Can you guess the identity of these sporting stars from the four clues below? The more clues you need, the fewer points you get.

1 I was born in Ireland in 1952 and by 1974 was a champion in my sport – the youngest for 50 years. (4 points)
I had a younger brother, Paul, who followed me into the sport. (3 points)
I rode Grundy, Golden Fleece and Quest for Fame to victory in the Epsom Derby. (2 points)
I was still riding in the year 2000, having won my first race in 1969. (1 point)

2 I was born in 1952 and played in an FA Cup final in the '80s alongside a fellow-South American. (4 points)
I won the World Cup with Argentina in 1978. (3 points)
Chas and Dave took me and Spurs to the top of the charts. (2 points)
I later managed Spurs as well as Swindon and Newcastle. (1 point)

SCOREBOARD		

round ten — on the buzzer

These questions are all about famous sporting venues.

1 Football – Which Austrian club play their home games at the Arnold Schwarzenegger stadium?

2 What major sporting event was held at the Millennium Stadium in Cardiff on 6 November 1999?

3 In which sport might you compete at Longchamp?

4 Football – Which French club plays their home games at la Stade Velodrome?

5 Tennis – In 1999, where did Serena Williams win her first Grand Slam tournament?

6 Athletics – In which country will you find the Bislett stadium?

7 Which sport's world championship is held at Potter's Holiday Camp in East Anglia?

8 Which world-famous race finishes on the Champs d'Elysee?

9 Which sport holds a World Championships at the Circus Tavern, Purfleet?

10 Football – What is the real name of the Shakers, who play at Gigg Lane?

11 Golf – At which course would you find Amen Corner?

12 Cricket – In which country would you find the WACA, the GABBA and the SCG?

13 Motor racing – At which track is the Italian Grand Prix held?

14 Horse racing – At which course is the Irish Derby run?

SCOREBOARD		

game **26**

round one — name the year

The following events all happened in the same year, but which one?

1 Ally McCoist scores the first goal of the year for Kilmarnock against Motherwell.
Darren Gough takes an Ashes hat-trick, the century's first by an Englishman.
Bobby Jo wins the Grand National, ridden by Paul Carberry.
A last-minute try by Scott Gibbs for Wales against England gives Scotland the Five Nations title.
Giggs's late goal gives Manchester United an FA Cup semi-final win over Arsenal.

Now for the second year:

2 Foinavon wins a sensational Grand National at odds of 100–1.
Spurs win the first all-London FA Cup final defeating Chelsea 2–1.
Foot and mouth disease curtails the horse racing calendar.
The last amateur Wimbledon Singles are won by John Newcombe and Billie-Jean King.
Celtic become the first British club to win the European Cup.

SCOREBOARD		

round two — picture board

Take a look at picture D on page 3 of Picture Board 1. Who is it?

Take a look at picture F on page 4 of Picture Board 1. Who is it?

SCOREBOARD		

round three — twenty sporting questions

20 questions on the World Athletics Championships.

1 Where were the first Championships held in 1983?
2 Which athlete won gold medals at the first six Championships?
3 Calvin Smith took consecutive titles in which event?
4 Who finally added individual gold to six silver and bronze medals when she won the 200 metres in 1993?
5 What linked the winners of the women's 100 metres and the men's shot putt at Seville in 1999?
6 In 1983, Tiina Lillak's last-round javelin throw cost which Briton a gold medal?
7 Who ran the anchor leg in 1991's winning British 4 x 400 metres relay team?
8 In which event were both the men's and women's world records broken at the 1995 Championships in Gothenburg?
9 1991: which hammer-thrower took gold, 15 years after his first Olympic title?
10 At which Championships did Linford Christie, Sally Gunnell and Colin Jackson all win gold medals?
11 Where does 1995 high-jump champion Troy Kemp come from?
12 In 1983, which Briton added a world title to his Olympic, European and Commonwealth gold medals?
13 What was unusual about the athletes who finished second in the women's 400 metres hurdles in 1993 and 1995.
14 In 1991, in which event did Carl Lewis lose for the first time in ten years?
15 Which country does 1997 discus champion Beatrice Faumuina represent?
16 Which former Olympian's daughter won gold in the 200m in Seville in 1999?
17 Which Briton has won silver and bronze over 200 metres?
18 In 1991, which Briton added a world title to her 1988 Olympic silver?
19 Samuel Matete won which country's first world title in 1991's 400m hurdles?
20 Which American took gold in nine world Championship finals?

SCOREBOARD		

round four — sporting links

1 What connects discus-thrower Al Oerter, yachtsman Paul Elvstrom and long-jumper Carl Lewis?

2 What connects the British heavyweight champion who fought Floyd Patterson and Muhammad Ali for the world title, Samoa's record Rugby Union try-scorer and the President of Real Madrid, who built the side's home stadium?

SCOREBOARD		

round five — where am I?

From the following two clues you must work out which place is being described.

1 Greg Blewett scored a century on his debut for Australia here in 1995, but England won the match. Nigel Mansell saw his world title hopes explode along with his tyre in 1986. Where?

2 You could watch two versions of football at Lansdowne Road, then see a third at Croke Park. Where?

SCOREBOARD		

round six — what happened next?

All you have to do in this round is decide which of the three options is the correct answer.

Belgian football, and a match between Charleroi and Geel. The Charleroi 'keeper handles outside the box. What happened next?

- **a** A Charleroi defender, thinking a free kick will be awarded, kicks the ball into his own net, but the referee awards the goal.
- **b** The keeper is sent off, Geel take a quick free kick and score. Unfortunately, the referee orders it to be re-taken as Charleroi did not have a nominated goalkeeper on the field at the time.
- **c** The assistant referee flags for a foul, but is over-ruled. As Geel protest, Charleroi's 'keeper throws the ball upfield and they score.

Rugby Union: the 2000 Heineken Cup quarter-final between Llanelli and Cardiff. Owen Williams and Ian Boobyer are sent to the sin-bin. What happened next?

- **a** The timer in the sin-bin is faulty, and they spend too long off the field.
- **b** The fourth official tells the referee the sin-bin rule is not in operation, so he has to let the players back on.
- **c** Thinking they've been sent off, the players have already showered and changed when they are told they can go back on!

SCOREBOARD		

round seven — home or away

golf Which player finished runner-up in three out of the four major tournaments during 2000 ?

football Who, in 2000, became the first Derby County player to win an England cap for nine years?

athletics Which sprinter won the 100m at the Moscow Olympics in 1980 ?

boxing Which boxer won the Commonwealth Featherweight title in 1978 and regained the World Super-Featherweight title 17 years later in 1995?

SCOREBOARD

round eight — captain's away

Here are two riddles from the often unusual world of sport. Can you tell me...

1 In which sport can you serve a giraffe, drop a shot on the penthouse and suffer from cramped odds?

2 In which sport might you warm up with a doughnut, though you're not allowed to put it on a plate?

SCOREBOARD

round nine — mystery guest

Can you guess the identity of these sporting stars from the four clues below? The more clues you need, the fewer points you get.

1 I was born in London in 1966 and I'm the son of a vicar. (4 points)
I first broke the World Record in my event in Salamanca. (3 points)
In 1995 I won World Championship gold and set a world record. (2 points)
I eventually won Olympic gold at the Sydney Olympics. (1 point)

2 I was born in England in 1960 and had my first major race in 1992. (4 points)
I won my first World Championship race in 1993. (3 points)
My only world title came in a Williams in 1996. (2 points)
My father also won the world title. (1 point)

SCOREBOARD

round ten — on the buzzer

All of these questions are to do with sporting relatives:

1 Golf – Andrew Coltart's sister is married to which other European Ryder Cup player?

2 Tennis – Which British player's grandmother was the first to serve over-arm in the Ladies' singles at Wimbledon?

3 Boxing – Which American brothers won Olympic gold in 1976, and both became world heavyweight champions?

4 Athletics – Name the four-times Olympic long-jump champion whose sister won a World Championship medal in 1983?

5 Golf – Which Spanish father and son have both played for Europe's Ryder Cup team?

6 Rugby Union – Name the brothers who played for the All-Blacks in the 1995 World Cup final?

7 Name this pair of cousins: one played football for West Brom and England; the other was European men's 200 metres champion?

8 Football – How is Ronaldo related to Brazilian international Luiz Nazario de Lima?

9 Cricket – Name the Australians who are the only twins to play in the same Test team?

10 Football – In season 2000–01, at which Premiership club would you have found a manager, his assistant and a young midfielder from the same family?

11 Formula One – Name the son who followed his father by winning the world title for Britain in 1996?

12 Horse racing – Which father and son have both won the 2000 Guineas since 1970?

13 Football – At the 1998 World Cup, which country's team were captained by the son of their coach?

14 Rugby Union – He is the son of a former England cricket captain and has played rugby union for Cardiff, West Hartlepool and Newcastle. Who is he ?

15 Rugby Union – Name the nephew of one of England's 1966 soccer heroes who is a rugby union international with England.

SCOREBOARD		

game **27**

round one — name the year

The following events all happened in the same year, but which one?

1 Pete Sampras wins the first of his many Wimbledon singles titles.
Sally Gunnell runs the race of her life to win the world title in Stuttgart.
A dramatic Wimbledon ladies' final ends in tears as Steffi Graf comes from behind to beat Jana Novotna.
The Grand National is not run.
Arsenal beat Sheffield Wednesday in both the FA Cup and the League Cup finals.

Now for the second year:

2 Muhammad Ali loses for the first time in his career to Joe Frazier.
Pele scores his last international goal against Austria.
Evonne Goolagong wins the Wimbledon ladies' singles.
The British Lions become the first to win a series in New Zealand.
Arsenal do the League and FA Cup double.

SCOREBOARD		

round two — picture board

Take a look at picture C on page 7 of Picture Board 1. Who is it?

Take a look at picture D on page 4 of Picture Board 1. Who is it?

SCOREBOARD		

round three — twenty sporting questions

20 questions on giant-killers.

1. In 1989, which non-League side knocked Coventry City out of the FA Cup?
2. Name the 42–1 outsider who knocked out Mike Tyson to win the world heavyweight title in 1990?
3. Which non-Test-playing country beat the West Indies at the 1996 World Cup?
4. 1999: who was the first qualifier to win the Open under the exemption system?
5. Wimbledon, 1999: which Australian beat Martina Hingis in the first round?
6. Which 150–1 outsider won the 1986 World snooker title?
7. In 1993, whose try for Wales handed England their first Five Nations defeat in almost three years?
8. Name the Ligier driver who won the 1996 Monaco Grand Prix.
9. Which country created the biggest shock in World Cup history when they defeated Italy to reach the quarter-finals in 1966?
10. Name the Greek sprint hurdler who took the 1992 Olympic title.
11. Which country won the Cricket World Cup undefeated in 1996?
12. Which 100–1 shot won the 1967 Grand National?
13. In 1996, which club ended Wigan's run of 43 unbeaten Challenge Cup ties?
14. Which British welterweight beat Don Curry in 1986?
15. In 1972, who ended the USA's 36-year winning streak in Olympic basketball?
16. Which US golfer – a last-minute entrant – won the 1991 USPGA?
17. Which country defeated holders Argentina in the opening match of the 1990 World Cup, eight years after holding eventual winners Italy to a draw?
18. Which country beat Wales 16–13 in Cardiff and qualified for the quarter-finals of the 1991 Rugby Union World Cup?
19. Which 17-year-old beat the reigning Australian and Wimbledon champions on his way to winning the 1989 French Open?
20. In 1981, who became the first wild-card team to win the Superbowl?

SCOREBOARD		

round four

sporting links

1 What links the American who's won the most Solheim Cup matches, the Welsh striker who played for Leicester, Newcastle and Birmingham and the US Ryder Cup golfer who was USPGA runner-up in 1980 and 1989?

2 What links the 1967 USPGA winner, the British swimmer who took bronze in the 400 metres freestyle in the 1984 Olympics and the Italian who took the 1995 world long-jump title?

SCOREBOARD

round five

where am I?

From the following two clues you must work out which place is being described.

1 Ex-footballer Darren Campbell won the European 100 metres title here in 1998; the England football team suffered their heaviest defeat in the same city 34 years earlier. But where?

2 Roberto de Vincenzo won the Open here in 1967, while five British Grands Prix have been staged – at a venue more commonly associated with another sort of racing. Where?

SCOREBOARD

round six — what happened next?

All you have to do in this round is decide which of the three options is the correct answer.

Football, and Brentford are at home to Preston in 1999. Jonathan Macken scores for the visitors and both teams run back to kick off again. What happened next?

a Macken is immediately sent off for lifting his shirt to reveal an insulting message.

b Brentford equalise direct from the re-start.

c A fan parachutes down on to the pitch.

Rugby, and San Isidro against the Penguins at the Middlesex 7s. Carl Izaat intercepts for the Penguins and heads for the try line; what happened next ?

a Izaat has his shorts pulled off, and scores in his underpants!

b Izaat somersaults over the San Isidro full-back and touches down.

c Izaat starts showboating and runs into the goalpost.

SCOREBOARD		

round seven — home or away

football Which country has lost on penalties in the last three World Cups ?

motor racing	Which Scottish driver won the Formula One World Championship three times during the 1960s and '70s ?
rugby union	Name the Irishman who during 2001 scored a hat-trick of tries on Ireland's first visit to Italy in the Six Nations.
horse racing	Who is the only jockey to have won the Grand National in both the '80s and '90s?

SCOREBOARD

round eight — captain's away

Here are two riddles from the often unusual world of sport. Can you tell me...

1 There are two English teams whose names contain the first five letters of the alphabet, A, B, C, D, and E – can you name them?

2 Name the two Scottish League teams whose names contain A, B, C, D and E.

SCOREBOARD

round nine — mystery guest

Can you guess the identity of these sporting stars from the four clues below? The more clues you need, the fewer points you get.

1 I led England Schools on three occasions in 1984. (4 points)
I was appointed England captain by Geoff Cooke in 1988, the youngest captain since 1931. (3 points)
I led England to the Grand Slam in 1991, 1992 and 1995. (2 points)
I played in the centre for Harlequins from 1987. (1 point)

2 I was born in February 1967 in Caldegno, Italy. (4 points)
I once cost a world-record £7.7 million in 1990. (3 points)
In 1993 I was voted FIFA World Footballer of the Year. (2 points)
I missed a penalty in the 1994 World Cup final. (1 point)

SCOREBOARD		

round ten — on the buzzer

These are all about Sues, Allys and Johns...or variations such as Susan, Alison and Jonathan.

1 Golf – Who won the 1991 USPGA?

2 Athletics – Which female Scottish 400 metres runner won silver at the 1998 Commonwealth Games?

3 Football – Name the former Liverpool winger who won 79 caps for England.
4 Rugby Union – Who captained Australia to the '99 World Cup?
5 Boxing – Which world heavyweight champion's daughter turned pro in 1999?
6 Swimming – Name Britain's only female gold medallist at the '99 European championships.
7 Golf – Which British woman won the US Open in 1997?
8 Athletics – Which man holds the British 200 metres record?
9 In which sport was Suzanne Dando a British champion?
10 Rugby Union – In 1998, which fly-half made his England debut aged 18?
11 Football – Who managed Scotland to defeat by Peru at the 1978 World Cup?
12 Golf – Name the Frenchman who was runner-up at the 1999 Open.
13 Motor racing – With which team did Colin McRae win the World Rally Championship?
14 Snooker – Which 20-year-old knocked Stephen Hendry out of the 1999 Grand Prix?
15 Football – Who was the top scorer at France '98?

SCOREBOARD		

game **28**

round one — name the year

The following events all happened in the same year, but which one?

1 Niki Lauda miraculously survives a horrendous crash at the German Grand Prix, and races again just six weeks later.
The West Indies win the Wisden Trophy in Cricket.
John Curry wins the Olympic ice skating gold medal.
Liverpool win the FA Cup and UEFA Cup.
Bjorn Borg wins the first of his five successive Wimbledon Singles titles.

Now for the second year:

2 Two Welshmen reach the World Snooker Final at the Crucible.
Tiger Woods wins three of the four Major titles.
Tranmere reach the Worthington Cup Final.
Audley Harrison wins an Olympic gold medal.
Steve McManaman wins a European Cup winners' medal.

SCOREBOARD		

round two — picture board

Take a look at picture A on page 8 of Picture Board 1. Who is it?

Take a look at picture F on page 2 of Plicture Board 1. Who is it?

SCOREBOARD		

round three — twenty sporting questions

20 questions on cricket.

1. For which country did Sunil Gavaskar score more than 10,000 Test runs?
2. Who has taken most Test wickets for New Zealand?
3. Who was the first Zimbabwean to take more than 100 Test match wickets?
4. Which county play their home games at Sophia Gardens?
5. Who won the 1983 World Cup?
6. Which famous England batsman's middle name is Ivon?
7. Who captained Gloucestershire to three one-day trophies in 2000?
8. For which country did Lance Gibbs take more than 300 Test wickets?
9. In which city would you find the SCG?
10. Against which team did Brian Lara score his world record 501 not out?
11. On which ground did Gary Sobers hit six sixes in an over in 1968?
12. Which prolific Indian batsman made his Test match debut, aged 16, in 1989?
13. For which trophy do England play Australia in Test matches?
14. Which England batsman made 333 and 123 in a 1990 game against India?
15. Where was the first-ever Test match played?
16. Which England bowler took 19 wickets in a match against Australia in 1956?
17. Name the Pakistani fast bowler who took hat-tricks in successive matches during the series against Sri Lanka in 1998/99.
18. For which county have Viv Richards, Greg Chappell and Martin Crowe played?
19. Which Test match country have Paul Strang, Eddo Brandes and Craig Evans all represented?
20. Who hit the winning runs in the 1999 World Cup final and has also played for Yorkshire?

SCOREBOARD		

round four — sporting links

1 What connects these three football managers: Herbert Chapman, Brian Clough and Kenny Dalglish?

2 What connects these three Test cricketers: Alan Davidson of Australia, Ian Botham of England and Imran Khan of Pakistan?

SCOREBOARD		

round five — where am I?

From the following two clues you must work out which place is being described.

1 In this Welsh town John Aldridge began his football league career and the Black and Ambers play Rugby Union at Rodney Parade. Where ?

2 This North American city has an American Football side known as the Seahawks and a basketball side known as the Supersonics. But where in the USA is it?

SCOREBOARD		

round six — what happened next?

All you have to do in this round is decide which of the three options is the correct answer.

Motor racing from Road America in Wisconsin. Bryan Herta brakes hard to avoid his team leader Bobby Rahal and spins off the track. What happened next?

- **a** Another competitor drives straight over the top of Herta's car.
- **b** On the very next lap, Rahal spins off in exactly the same place and comes to rest next to his team-mate's car.
- **c** Herta waits for the rest of the field to go past and is about to re-join the track when the marshals arrive and spray his car with their fire extinguishers. He has to retire.

Tennis from the Albert Hall, and Mansour Bahrami is playing Henri Leconte. Henri smashes the ball at Mansour and it whistles just past his head. What happened next?

- **a** Mansour tries to persuade the umpire to swap places
- **b** Mansour puts on a helmet to protect himself.
- **c** Mansour is appointed assistant manager at Tottenham Hotspur.

SCOREBOARD		

round seven — home or away

athletics Which British-born athlete won her second successive Olympic silver medal in Sydney to go with World Championship gold, silver and bronze?

rugby league Which player won the Man of the Match award in the 2000 Grand Final, seven years after he had also been Man of the Match against Wigan in the Premiership Final?

sailing Which sailor exacted revenge on Brazilian Robert Scheidt to reverse the result from the 1996 Olympics and take the gold medal in the Laser class at Sydney?

boxing Who, by defeating Reggie Johnson in 1999, claimed the IBF Light-Heavyweight title to add to his WBA and WBC belts ?

SCOREBOARD

round eight — captain's away

True or false. Here are the names of sportsmen and all you have to do is decide whether they are genuine or not.

1. Cagney and Lacy have both played international rugby for Ireland.
2. Dempsey and Makepeace have both been heavyweight boxing champions of the world.
3. Julius Caesar has played county cricket.
4. Peter Stringfellow played in midfield for Oldham and Gillingham.
5. Lennon, McCartney, Harrison and Starr have all played League football since the war.
6. Pugh, Pugh, Barney, Mulgrew, Cuthbert, Dibble and Grubb have all played League football.

SCOREBOARD

round nine — mystery guest

Can you guess the identity of these sporting stars from the four clues below? The more clues you need, the fewer points you get.

1 I was born in 1962 and have played most of my career in Scotland. (4 points)
I won the European Golden Boot in 1992. (3 points)
I scored Scotland's only goal during Euro '96. (2 points)
I have starred on small and big screen, most often on a sports quiz show. (1 point)

2 I was born in Brighton in 1966 but never won a national title. (4 points)
I was a respected World Champion and more than a little extrovert. (3 points)
I fought Nigel Benn, Michael Watson and Steve Collins. (2 points)
I was the first celebrity voted out of *Celebrity Big Brother* in 2001. (1 point)

SCOREBOARD		

round ten — on the buzzer

Which of these statements are genuine and which are made-up?

1 Football – Ryan Giggs was born in England, Michael Owen was born in Wales.

2 Golf – Tiger Woods hit his first hole in one at the age of three.

3 As a youngster athlete Iwan Thomas was one of the world's top BMX bikers.

4 Rugby Union – Will Carling's real first name is Wilfred.

5 Snooker – Steve Davis has appeared on Essex Radio as a DJ.

6 Bobsleigh – Jamaica won their first Winter Olympic medal in the four-man bob in Nagano.

7 Football – Emmanuel Petit has appeared on *The Bill.*

8 Motor racing – Murray Walker finished ninth in the 1952 British Grand Prix.

9 At the Melbourne Olympics of 1956, boomerang-throwing was a demonstration sport.

10 Rugby Union – England captain Martin Johnson has appeared naked on billboard adverts.

11 Tennis – Vijay Amritraj starred in *Nine Deaths Of The Ninja.*

12 Football – Under Graham Taylor, Geoff Thomas won more England caps than Paul Gascoigne.

13 Golf – South Africa once issued a stamp with Gary Player's face on it.

14 Athletics – Double Olympic hurdles champion Roger Kingdom now plays basketball for the Atlanta Hawks.

15 Snooker – Ronnie O'Sullivan beat John Parrott in the 2001 World Championship final.

SCOREBOARD		

game 29

round one — name the year

The following events all happened in the same year, but which one?

1 Steffi Graf completes tennis's Grand Slam.
Great Britain win their first Olympic hockey gold medal.
Sugar Ray Leonard collects his record fifth world title at different weights.
Ben Johnson is stripped of his Olympic 100 metres gold medal.
The Olympics are held in Seoul.

Now for the second year:

2 The Americans retain the Ryder Cup at the Belfry.
In July, cyclist Chris Boardman breaks the world hour record.
Evander Holyfield defeats Riddick Bowe to retain the World Heavyweight title.
Alain Prost wins the Formula One World Drivers' Championship.
England, under Graham Taylor, fail to qualify for the World Cup despite beating San Marino 7–1.

SCOREBOARD		

round two — picture board

Take a look at picture F on page 1 of Picture Board 2. Who is it?

Take a look at picture E on page 5 of Picture Board 2. Who is it?

SCOREBOARD		

round three — twenty sporting questions

20 questions on South Americans.

1 Which legendary Argentinian scored in the first five European Cup finals?
2 Which Guyanese cricketer captained his team to the most Test match victories?
3 Who won three Wimbledon ladies' singles titles in the 50s and 60s?
4 In 1999, in which sport did Argentina become the first South American side to reach the World Cup quarter-finals?
5 In which event have athletes Adhemar Ferreira da Silva, Nelson Prudencio and Joao Carlos de Oliveira all won Olympic medals?
6 Which Formula One driver won 24 of his 51 Grands Prix and five world titles?
7 What is Pele's real name?
8 Who won the 1967 Open golf title?
9 Francisco Rodriguez won Venezuela's first Olympic gold in 1968: in what?
10 Guillermo Vilas, Andres Gomez and Gustavo Kuerten have all won the men's singles at which Grand Slam tournament?
11 Who in 1972 became the youngest Formula One world champion?
12 Why did Uruguay's winger Ruben Moran look odd in 1950's World Cup final?
13 Which country is golfer Carlos Franco from?
14 Which prop forward helped win European Cup finals for Bath and Northampton?
15 Brazilians took men's and women's silver medals in which sport at Sydney?
16 Which driver won five consecutive Monaco Grands Prix in 1989–93?
17 Which Guyana and West Indies spinner broke Fred Trueman's record of Test wickets in 1976?
18 In which sport have Brazilians Aurelio Miguel and Rogerio Sampalo both won Olympic gold medals?
19 Which country hosted the 1962 World Cup finals?
20 Which country did the Lapentii brothers lead to victory over Great Britain in the 2000 Davis Cup?

SCOREBOARD		

round four — sporting links

1 What connects these three European Ryder Cup golfers: Nick Faldo, Bernhard Langer and Ian Woosnam?

2 What links these four British athletes: decathlete Daley Thompson, sprinter Linford Christie, hurdler Sally Gunnell and triple-jumper Jonathan Edwards?

SCOREBOARD

round five — where am I?

From the following two clues you must work out which place is being described.

1 After watching the football team with the most European Cups, it's just a short walk to watch the basketball side who can boast the same thing. But where?

2 Dundee United played in a European final here in 1987, while Michael Johnson collected three world championship gold medals in 1995. But where?

SCOREBOARD

round six — what happened next?

All you have to do in this round is decide which of the three options is the correct answer.

Flat racing from Caulfield in Australia. Andrew Payne is on Hong Kong Star which stumbles as the field rounds the home turn. What happened next?

- **a** Andrew falls, but his foot is caught in a stirrup and he is dragged all the way to the finishing line
- **b** Andrew is catapulted over the railings.
- **c** Andrew ends up on board Cogitate, which had thrown his brother-in-law, Jason Patton.

Boxing, and an IBF world flyweight fight between Mark 'Too Sharp' Johnson and Luis Rolon. Johnson is well ahead in the middle of the eighth round. What happened next?

- **a** Rolon wrestles Johnson out of the ring. 'Too Sharp' isn't sharp enough to get back in time and the referee counts him out!
- **b** Johnson stops punching, and for the rest of the fight just dodges blows.
- **c** Rolon's corner throws in the towel, but he disagrees with them and tries to continue fighting.

SCOREBOARD		

round seven — home or away

rugby Who, in 2001, became the first player in history to win an English domestic cup winner's medal in both rugby codes?

athletics	Who in 1995, by winning the 5000m, became the only Irish woman in history to win a World Championship gold medal?
cricket	Who has taken the most Test wickets for England?
cycling	Which Spaniard won the Tour de France for five consecutive years between 1991–95?

SCOREBOARD

round eight — captain's away

Here are two riddles from the often unusual world of sport. Can you tell me...

1 Golf – At the 1999 World Championships, held in the Netherlands, three players went round in just 18 strokes. How?

2 Who is the single-handed champion of the world?

SCOREBOARD

round nine — mystery guest

Can you guess the identity of these sporting stars from the four clues below? The more clues you need, the fewer points you get.

1 I was born in Montreal in 1973 but don't represent Canada. (4 points)
I switched to Great Britain in 1995 to compete at international level. (3 points)
I was a quarter-finalist at Wimbledon in 1997. (2 points)
I play Davis Cup tennis for Britain, partnering Tim Henman. (1 point)

2 I was born in 1966 in Paris. (4 points)
I made my league debut in 1983 and my international bow four years later. (3 points)
I have a reputation as a tempestuous character, which was proved at Selhurst Park in 1995. (2 points)
I left my beloved Old Trafford in 1997, presumably to follow the trawler with some seagulls. (1 point)

SCOREBOARD		

round ten — on the buzzer

These answers are all sporting heroes from the British Isles.

1 Football – Before Ally McCoist, who was the last British player to win the European Golden Boot?

2 Boxing – Name the British heavyweight champion who fought Mike Tyson during 2000.

3 Motor racing – Which former Grand Prix driver was knighted in the 2000 New Year's Honours list?

4 National Hunt racing – Which jockey won a record 1,699 races in Britain?

5 Athletics – Name the first Briton to win two world titles.

6 Snooker – Which Welshman won the World Championships in 2000?

7 National Hunt racing – In 1999, which jockey reached 1,000 career victories in record time?

8 Football – Whose two goals against Scotland took England to Euro 2000?

9 Boxing – In the '90s, which British heavyweight was twice WBO champion?

10 Hockey – Nicknamed Jasper, who is Britain's record goal scorer?

11 Football – Name the England striker who was substituted in his last international by Graham Taylor during Euro '92.

12 In which sport would you find British Paralympian Simon Jackson competing?

13 Name the British Olympic legend who started the 2001 London Marathon.

14 Football – Who replaced Kevin Keegan as manager of Newcastle United in January 1997 ?

15 Golf – Name the Scotsman who won the 1985 Open at Sandwich.

SCOREBOARD		

game **30**

round one — name the year

The following events all happened in the same year, but which one?

1 Charlotte Brew creates history as the first female jockey to ride in a Grand National.
Ian Botham makes his Test debut.
Barry Sheene of Great Britain is the 500cc Motor Cycling World Champion.
Don Revie resigns as England manager.
Liverpool win the European Cup for the first time.

Now for the second year:

2 Istabraq wins a second Champion Hurdles in a row.
Stephen Hendry wins a record seventh World Snooker Championship.
France defeats England at Wembley for the first time, Nicolas Anelka scoring both goals in a 2–0 win.
Allan Nielsen's last-minute goal wins Tottenham the League Cup Final.
Australia cruise to an eight-wicket World Cup final win over Pakistan.

SCOREBOARD

round two — picture board

Take a look at picture A on page 2 of Picture Board 2. Who is it?

Take a look at picture B on page 4 of Picture Board 2. Who is it?

SCOREBOARD

round three — twenty sporting questions

20 questions on sporting events from 1991.

1. Who won the FA Cup by beating Nottingham Forest 2–1?
2. Which Australian won the Open at Royal Birkdale?
3. Alan Munro won the Derby on which horse?
4. What nationality is Moses Tanui, 1991's 10,000 metres world champion?
5. Name the British driver who won his third British Grand Prix in 1991.
6. Which London team were third in the English first division in 1990–91?
7. Who won the all-German Wimbledon men's singles final?
8. Which country won their first Five Nations Grand Slam for 11 years?
9. Which West Indian did Richard Illingworth dismiss with his first ball in a Test?
10. Who won their third consecutive World Championship 100 metres gold?
11. Who did Manchester United defeat in the European Cup Winners' Cup final?
12. Which horse, ridden by Nigel Hawke, won the Grand National?
13. Rugby League – who did Wigan beat 13–8 to win the Challenge Cup?
14. Name the Welshman who won the US Masters.
15. Who won Rugby Union's World Cup?
16. Which legendary West Indian batsman retired after scoring 24 Test centuries?
17. Which team beat Dundee United to win the Scottish FA Cup for only the second time in their history?
18. Who did John Parrott defeat to become snooker's World Champion?
19. Which country beat the USA 3–1 to win tennis' Davis Cup?
20. Who was Arsenal's leading scorer in their successful League championship campaign?

SCOREBOARD		

round four — sporting links

1 What connects the second Test match between the West Indies and England in 1990, the first leg of the 1971 Fairs Cup final between Juventus and Leeds and the 1973 world snooker championship quarter-final between Alex Higgins and Fred Davis?

2 What connects cricketer Kepler Wessels, rugby player Inga Tuigamala and footballer Ladislao Kubala?

SCOREBOARD

round five — where am I?

From the following two clues you must work out which place is being described.

1 In this US city, the 1987 and 1988 Formula One Grands Prixs were won by Ayrton Senna, and there is a Major League Baseball side known as the Tigers. Where?

2 In which American city would you find an ice hockey team called the Penguins and an American football team known as the Steelers?

SCOREBOARD

round six — what happened next?

All you have to do in this round is decide which of the three options is the correct answer.

Football. A 2000 FA Cup tie between Northwich Victoria and Leyton Orient. Scott Houghton chases a back pass into the Northwich box. What happened next?

- **a** As the 'keeper clears the ball it rebounds off Houghton into the net.
- **b** Houghton beats the 'keeper to the ball, rounds him – and shoots wide.
- **c** The 'keeper takes a huge swing at the ball, misses completely and his boot flies off and hits Houghton. The ball goes behind for a corner.

American Football. The New England Patriots are losing 24–27 to the Miami Dolphins. With the last play of the game the Patriots fumble the ball, re-gather it but throw an illegal forward pass. The referee declares the Dolphins the winners. What happened next?

- **a** Half an hour later the referee decides the forward pass was actually a lateral, so the teams have to go back into the empty stadium to repeat the final play.
- **b** Half an hour later the referee decides the Dolphins had 12 men on the field during the Patriots' final drive. They have to replay the game's final minute.
- **c** Half an hour later, the referee decides the fumble was actually an incomplete pass, and there are still three seconds to play. The teams have to go back out into an empty stadium to play them.

SCOREBOARD		

round seven — home or away

snooker Who won the 1998 World Championships?

golf	In what respect did Rodney Pampling of Australia make unwanted history at the 1999 Open at Carnoustie?
cricket	Which Essex and England player in 1999 batted for 71 minutes against New Zealand, yet failed to get off the mark?
tennis	In the first round of Wimbledon 1999, how did Jelena Dokic emulate Charlie Pasarell in 1967 and Lori McNeil in 1994?

SCOREBOARD

round eight — captain's away

Here are two riddles from the often unusual world of sport. Can you tell me...

1 Name the Scottish League teams with the longest and shortest names.

2 Name the English league teams with the longest and shortest names.

SCOREBOARD

round nine — mystery guest

Can you guess the identity of these sporting stars from the four clues below? The more clues you need, the fewer points you get.

1 I was born in England in 1974 and turned professional in 1992. (4 points)
I am regarded by many as the most naturally-talented player in my sport. (3 points)
In 1993 I became the youngest player to win a ranking tournament. (2 points)
I won the world snooker title in 2001. (1 point)

2 I am one of this programme's regular guests and enjoy football and horse racing. (4 points)
I was born in Dublin and joined Arsenal as a professional in 1983. (3 points)
I also played for Manchester City before moving to the North East. (2 points)
I've partnered Kevin Phillips at the Stadium of Light. (1 point)

SCOREBOARD		

round ten — on the buzzer

All of these questions involve sporting near-misses.

1 Football – Which team have played in eight World Cups, but never made it past the first round?

2 Golf – Who hasn't picked up a Major but won the European Order of Merit for seven years in a row during the 1990s?

3 Horse racing – Which jockey never won the Grand National, but did ride a then-record 1,680 winners in his career?

4 Motor racing – Which driver won 16 Grands Prix in the '50s and '60s, and was runner-up in the world championship for four consecutive years?

5 Football – Who was never capped for England, but captained Manchester United to the double in 1994?

6 Tennis – Which man never won the Wimbledon singles title, but collected eight other Grand Slam singles titles in the '80s and '90s?

7 Athletics – Which Briton holds indoor and outdoor world records, but has never won the Olympics?

8 Football – Which team collected two Amateur Cups in the 1890s, but has never won the League, FA Cup or League Cup?

9 Horse racing – Who during the '90s didn't win the Derby, but rode the winners of seven English Classics?

10 Boxing – Which British heavyweight never won the British title, but was European and World champion?

11 Football – Who won 80 caps, scoring 48 goals for England, and was never booked?

SCOREBOARD		

game **31**

round one — name the year

The following events all happened in the same year, but which one?

1 Frankie Dettori wins all seven races on the card at Ascot.
France beat Sweden 3–2 to win the Davis Cup final.
Phil de Glanville succeeds Will Carling as England Rugby Union captain.
Manchester United achieve a second double.
Gareth Southgate's miss costs England a European Championship final place.

Now for the second year:

2 The first B&H Cup is staged in cricket, Leicestershire beating Yorkshire.
The Five Nations Championship is left undecided.
Emerson Fittipaldi wins the World Drivers' Championship finishing the season 16 points clear of Jackie Stewart.
Olga Korbut makes her mark in the Olympics at Munich.
Rangers win the Cup Winners' Cup and West Germany win the European championships

SCOREBOARD		

round two — picture board

Take a look at picture D on page 5 of Picture Board 2. Who is it?

Take a look at picture E on page 5 of Picture Board 1. Who is it?

SCOREBOARD		

round three — twenty sporting questions

20 questions about the Premiership and Football League.

1 How many clubs formed the Football League in 1888?
2 Which team won a hat-trick of titles in the 1920s?
3 Who in 1997 became the first player to appear in 1,000 League matches?
4 Which team has won the most League titles?
5 What decided the Football League title for the only time in 1989?
6 Which striker scored a record 357 first division goals between 1957 and 1971?
7 Which side went from the first division to the fourth between 1984 and 1986?
8 What was introduced to English League football in 1981, and helped Blackburn win the title in 1995?
9 Who scored 250 League goals, then took two teams to the first division title?
10 How did seven Aston Villa players make history in 1981's title-winning season?
11 Newton Heath and Ardwick joined the League in 1892; where were they from?
12 Two members of Arsenal's 1989 title-winning side also won the League with different clubs; name either.
13 In 1962, which team won the title in their first season in the top flight?
14 Who played in his team's first Championship side in 1951, then managed them to their second in 1961?
15 What did the League neglect to purchase until their third season?
16 Which third division team won their first 13 matches in the 1985–86 season?
17 Who scored in seven consecutive Premiership games for Chelsea in 1993–94?
18 Which team have been in the top-flight since 1919?
19 Who collected his eighth Championship medal in 1990?
20 Why wouldn't Newcastle have minded losing 9–1 at home to Sunderland in 1908 for too long?

SCOREBOARD		

round four — sporting links

1 What connects France's World Cup-winning midfielder who's played for Arsenal and Barcelona, the Warwickshire fast bowler who played for England in the 1987 World Cup final and the brothers who managed on opposite sides when Stoke played York in the 1998–99 season?

2 What connects the winger, then with Nottingham Forest and who played for England during Euro '96, with the brothers who have played for Zimbabwe more than 40 times and the golf-loving US President whose grandfather presented the Walker Cup?

SCOREBOARD

round five — where am I?

From the following two clues you must work out which place is being described.

1 You could watch a contest for the single-handed championship of the world, then bet on the Greyhound Derby. Where?

2 More commonly known as a boxing venue, this place also staged two Formula One Grands Prix in 1981 and 1982.

SCOREBOARD

round six — what happened next?

All you have to do in this round is decide which of the three options is the correct answer.

Football. The 2001 UEFA Cup 4th round second leg match between Liverpool and Roma. Vincenzo Montella's cross hits Markus Babbel. What happened next?

- **a** The ball gets stuck between Babbel's legs! The Roma players make several attempts to kick it out before the referee rescues the German by awarding a free-kick.
- **b** The ball bursts! Delvecchio pumps it into an empty net but the referee disallows the goal and orders a drop-ball.
- **c** The ball goes behind, but the referee appears to point for a penalty. Then he realises his mistake and instead awards a corner after all.

NHL ice hockey between Boston and Tampa Bay. Two players are challenging for the puck behind the goal. What happened next?

- **a** Their skates get stuck together and they collide with the goal net.
- **b** One player takes a giant swing and knocks the other's helmet off.
- **c** One of the players smashes the other into the glass surrounding the rink and shatters it.

SCOREBOARD		

round seven — home or away

football Which Scottish international scored both goals for Leicester City in the 2000 Worthington Cup Final victory?

athletics Which man ran in his fifth world 100 metres final in the 1999 games in Seville and equalled his national record?

rugby union Who in 1999 became the last player to score a hat-trick of tries in the Five Nations, yet still ended up on the losing side?

cricket During the Fourth Test against India in January 1985, two England batsmen scored double centuries in the same innings – the only time in England's test history. Mike Gatting was one player, but who was the other?

SCOREBOARD		

round eight — captain's away

Here are two riddles from the often unusual world of sport. Can you tell me...

1 In 1946 Kevin O'Flanagan played on the right wing for Ireland on consecutive weekends – what was unique about this?

2 In which sport might a Clash in San José lead to a Mutiny in Tampa Bay and a Revolution in New England?

SCOREBOARD		

round nine — mystery guest

Can you guess the identity of these sporting stars from the four clues below? The more clues you need, the fewer points you get.

1	I made the first of my Olympic appearances in 1988 and retired from Internationals after the Sydney Olympics.	(4 points)
	I was nicknamed Jasper.	(3 points)
	I won a hockey bronze medal at the 1992 Olympics.	(2 points)
	I am England's leading scorer.	(1 point)
2	I was a nine-pound baby but grew up into a rather bigger man.	(4 points)
	I made my professional debut in 1982 but it lasted only 15 seconds.	(3 points)
	I supported Michael Barrymore at the Dominion Theatre in London, dressed as a genie.	(2 points)
	I fought Mike Tyson and Lennox Lewis for a world title.	(1 point)

SCOREBOARD		

round ten — on the buzzer

There's a real Valentine's theme to these questions.

1 Where would you find Valentine's Brook?

2 What's the lowest score you can get in tennis?

3 Football – Leeds and Ireland's Gary Kelly is related to which of his team-mates?

4 Cricket – Name the brothers who have both scored more than 2000 Test runs for Zimbabwe?

5 Golf – Name the amateur who finished fourth at the 1998 Open.

6 In which sport could an unintended kiss cost you seven points?

7 Football – Against which team did Ally McCoist play his last competitive game for Rangers?

8 Cricket – Which two counties play in the Roses match?

9 Athletics – Marion Jones married which other world champion?

10 Football – Which team play at Love Street?

11 Golf – Which American won the '92 US Masters?

12 In which sport can you compete on the rings?

SCOREBOARD		

game **32**

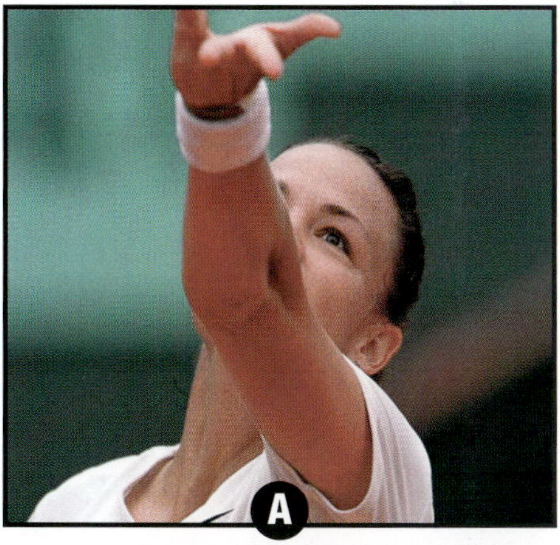

A

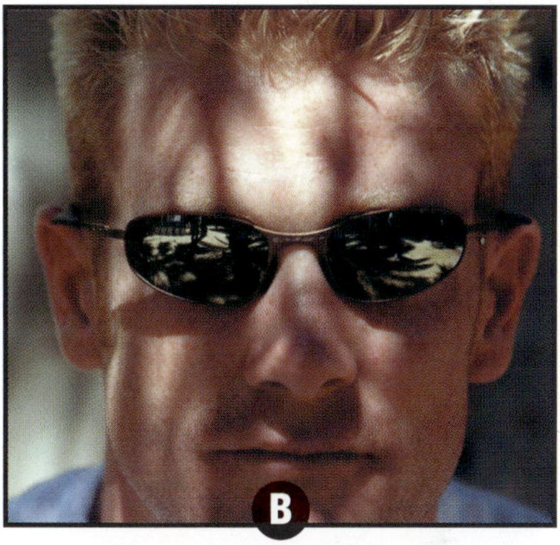

B

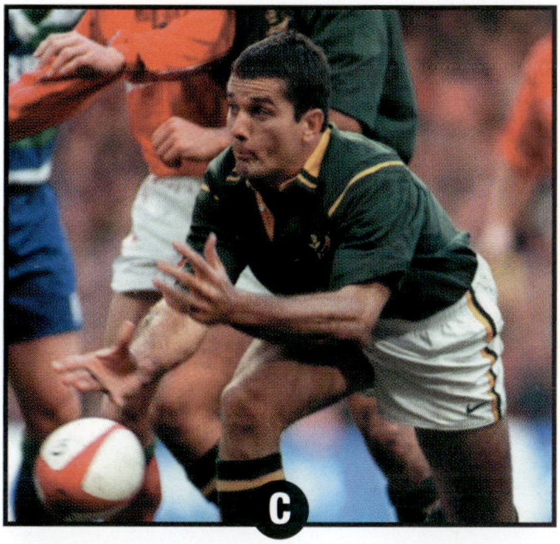

C

D

E

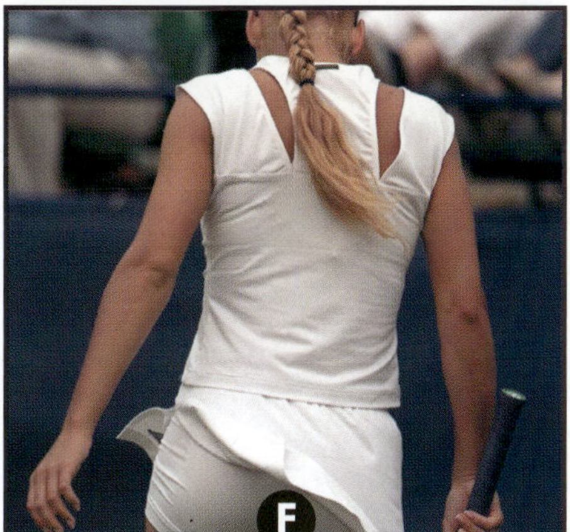

F

A

B

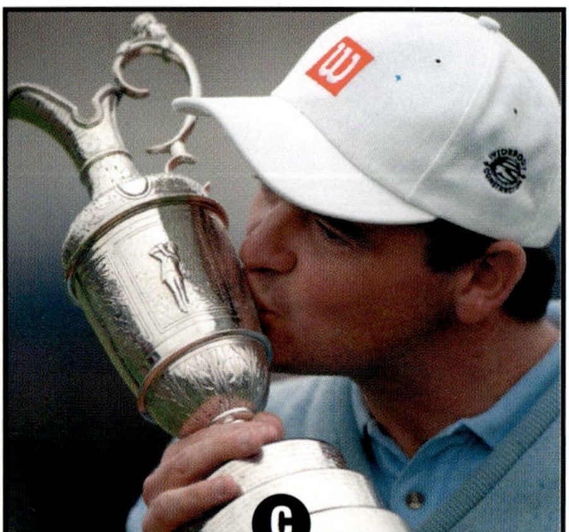
C

D

E

F

A

B

C

D

E

F

A

B

C

D

E

F

A

B

C

D

E

F

Picture Board 2

A

B

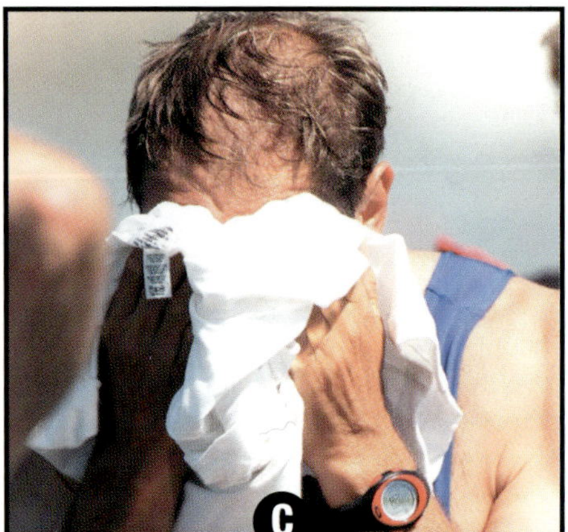

C

D

E

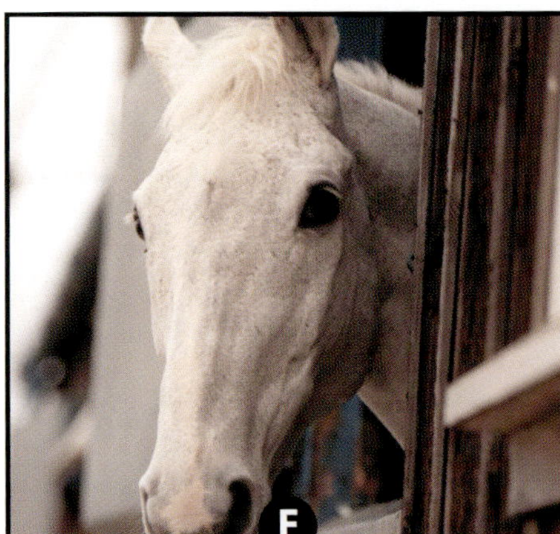

F

A

B

C

D

A

B

C

D

round one — name the year

The following events all happened in the same year, but which one?

1 Hank Aaron of the Atlanta Braves hits his 715th home run, breaking the record set by Babe Ruth in 1935.
Brendan Foster breaks the 3000 metres world record in Gateshead.
Muhammad Ali defeats George Foreman in Zaire.
Bayern Munich win the first of three successive European Cups.
Beckenbauer caps a memorable year by lifting the World Cup.

Now for the second year:

2 Devon Malcolm takes 9–57 against South Africa at the Oval.
Laura Davies wins on five different tours in the course of a year.
Michael Schumacher takes the title by one point from Damon Hill.
Colombian Andreas Escobar scores an own goal in the World Cup and on his return home is shot dead.
Alan Smith scores Arsenal's winner to beat Parma in the Cup Winners' Cup Final.

SCOREBOARD		

round two — picture board

Take a look at picture F on page 3 of Picture Board 1. Who is it?

Take a look at picture F on page 6 of Picture Board 1. Who is it?

SCOREBOARD		

round three — twenty sporting questions

20 questions with a connection to **A Question of Sport.**

1 In which year was *A Question of Sport* first broadcast?
2 He was captain of England's Grand Slam-winning side in 1980 and on *A Question of Sport* from 1982–96. Who is he?
3 Who did HRH the Princess Royal threaten to hit with her handbag in 1987?
4 Who was the very first presenter?
5 He joined the programme in 1979 and was one of the greatest rugby players of all time, appearing in 53 consecutive matches for Wales. Who is he?
6 Which former captain rode nearly 4,000 winners, including 17 Classics?
7 A captain on the show, he floored Cassius Clay at Wembley in 1963. Who is he?
8 Which cricketer helped Worcestershire win the County Championship twice, scored more than 5,000 Test runs and collected 383 wickets for England.
9 Ally McCoist started his career at which Scottish club?
10 David Coleman won the Manchester Mile in the 1940s. True or false?
11 Which Welsh fly-half won 29 caps in the 1950s and was a *QS* captain?
12 Sue Barker reached the Wimbledon semi-finals in 1977. Who beat her?
13 I stood in for Ian Botham as a captain while he was away at the 1992 Cricket World Cup and won silver in the men's 400m at the 1996 Olympics. Who am I?
14 Who beat John Parrott in snooker's 1989 World Championship final?
15 Who appeared as a *QS* captain for eight programmes in the 1970s and was the first cricketer to take 300 Test match wickets?
16 Who has appeared most times as a guest on *A Question of Sport*?
17 George Best appeared as a guest on the very first programme. True or false?
18 He won 108 caps for England, collected a World Cup winner's medal in 1966 and was a guest captain on a number of occasions in the 1970s. Name him.
19 Where did Ally McCoist score Scotland's only goal of Euro '96?
20 Who won the men's 10,000 metres at the 1974 European Championships?

SCOREBOARD		

round four — sporting links

1 What connects the former Spurs and Manchester United striker who won the UEFA Cup with Ipswich, the American boxer who twice beat Thomas Hearns in world title fights and the horse on which Piero d'Inzeo won the 1959 European Show Jumping Championships?

2 What connects the 1992 Derby-winning jockey, Charlton's South African international defender and the first Australian bowler to take 300 Test wickets?

SCOREBOARD

round five — where am I?

From the following two clues you must work out which place is being described.

1 An England cricket captain was born here in 1968, and this country has reached Davis Cup finals in 1974 and 1987. Where is it?

2 Seve Ballesteros won two Open Championships here, while it's also the headquarters of the Football League. Where?

SCOREBOARD

round six — what happened next?

All you have to do in this round is decide which of the three options is the correct answer.

Ice hockey from the NHL, and the New Jersey Devils face the Philadelphia Flyers in 2000. The Devils are on the attack and let fly with a shot. What happened next?

- **a** The puck shatters the plastic screen around the rink.
- **b** The puck gets stuck in the goal-tender's face mask.
- **c** The puck demolishes the automatic goal sensor above the net.

Tennis from the 2001 Australian Open. Sebastien Grosjean aces Magnus Norman on match point and goes to shake hands. What happened next?

- **a** The umpire calls a let, so Norman concedes the point and the match!
- **b** The line judge foot-faults Grosjean and the Frenchman is so incensed he walks off court, forfeiting the match.
- **c** An extremely large streaker runs on court to 'congratulate' Grosjean! It takes four stewards to escort him away.

SCOREBOARD

round seven — home or away

rugby union Name the Scottish flanker who captained the British Lions to a series victory over Australia in 1989.

swimming Which Australian female swimmer won six gold medals at the 1998 Commonwealth Games?

tennis Which former professional tennis player appeared in the James Bond film *Octopussy*?

football Which on-loan striker equalled a post-war record of scoring in 10 consecutive league matches in 2000–01?

SCOREBOARD		

round eight — captain's away

Here are two riddles from the often unusual world of sport. Can you tell me...

1 How was the Battle of Hastings won by a Scot in 1996 after starting ten years earlier with victory over France?

2 Why were the England Football Team pleased to see another Norman Conquest in 1951. Unusually, it was still followed by Norman Rule later that decade?

SCOREBOARD		

round nine — mystery guest

Can you guess the identity of these sporting stars from the four clues below? The more clues you need, the fewer points you get.

1 I was born in Italy in 1970 and followed my father into the sport. (4 points)
I came to the fore in Britain in 1990 when I won more than 100 races as a teenager. (3 points)
In 1994 I was Champion Jockey for the first time. (2 points)
My first name is Lanfranco but I'm known by a shorter version of that. (1 point)

2 I won consecutive junior Amateur Titles in 1991, 1992 and 1993. (4 points)
In 1994 I became the youngest winner of the US Amateur Championship. (3 points)
I was the youngest US Masters Champion. (2 points)
I won four successive Major golf titles in 2000–2001? (1 point)

SCOREBOARD		

round ten — on the buzzer

These answers are all in alphabetical order... but backwards!

1 We start with Z. Football – Who was the 1998 European Footballer of the Year?

2 Cricket – For which county does Darren Gough play?

3 Football – Which Everton defender played for Benfica and PSV Eindhoven?

4 Golf – At which course is the World Matchplay held?

5 What is the correct name for a cycling track?

6 Rugby Union – Name the tight head prop in England's 1995 Grand Slam-winning team.

7 Football – In what colour do Dundee United play?

8 Tennis – How old was Boris Becker when he won his first Wimbledon title?

9 American football – Which NFL team is based in Washington?

10 Football – At which club did Sir Alex Ferguson begin his playing career?

11 Which sport is played on the biggest field?

12 Football – What have Tommy Hutchison, Gary Mabbutt and Des Walker all scored in FA Cup finals?

13 Horse racing – Which horse did Lester Piggott ride to victory in the Derby, 2000 Guineas and St Leger in 1970?

14 Which city will stage the 2002 Commonwealth Games?

15 Where was athlete Steve Smith born?

SCOREBOARD		

game 33

round one — name the year

The following events all happened in the same year, but which one?

1 Seb Coe and Daley Thompson retain their Olympic titles.
Seve Ballesteros wins his second Open Championship.
Liverpool win the European Cup.
Torvill and Dean win Olympic Gold with their dazzling *Bolero* routine.
Carl Lewis takes four gold medals in the Olympics.

Now for the second year:

2 Britain's first gold medal of the Olympics comes in cycling.
Steve Redgrave wins his fifth Olympic gold medal.
Australia beat New Zealand in the Rugby League World Cup final.
Semi-final goals from Chelsea's Gustavo Poyet ruin Newcastle's hopes of a third consecutive FA Cup final.
Roberto de Matteo scores the last FA Cup final goal at Wembley.

SCOREBOARD		

round two — picture board

Take a look at picture B on page 8 of Picture Board 1. Who is it?

Take a look at picture C on page 4 of Picture Board 1. Who is it?

SCOREBOARD		

round three — twenty sporting questions

20 questions on golf.

1. Who in 1988 became the first Briton to win the US Masters?
2. What is presented to the winner of the Open?
3. From which year were players from the continent of Europe allowed to compete in the Ryder Cup?
4. What nationality is the 1992 and '94 USPGA champion Nick Price?
5. Which Italian did John Daly beat in a play-off to win the 1995 Open?
6. Name the winner of the 1987 US Women's Open.
7. Who in 1961 became the first non-American to top the USA tour money list?
8. For which trophy do the male Amateur players of Great Britain and Ireland play their American counterparts?
9. What is a hole completed three under par known as?
10. Which player is known as 'the Great White Shark'?
11. On which course is the US Masters played annually?
12. Which American golfing legend won successive Open titles in 1961 and 1962?
13. What nationality was the winner of the 1999 Open?
14. Which Swede won the 1990 Women's British Open?
15. Which Spaniard was Amateur Champion in 1998 and a Ryder Cup player the following season?
16. Who was the only South American to win the Open during the 20th century?
17. Which South African won the US Open in 1994 and '97?
18. With what colour jacket is the winner of the US Masters presented?
19. Which highly successful American golfer finished runner-up at the Open seven times between 1964–1979?
20. On which course has the Open been played most frequently?

SCOREBOARD		

round four — sporting links

1 What connects the Welsh centre who made his debut against England in 1983 and went on to win 32 caps, the world welterweight champion who took the middleweight crown from Sugar Ray Robinson in 1957 and the venue of the 1994 and 1995 Pacific Grands Prix?

2 What connects the granite-chinned boxer who lost the world middleweight title to Sugar Ray Robinson in 1951, the winning jockey in the 1981 Grand National and two British gold medallists at the 1924 Olympics?

SCOREBOARD

round five — where am I?

From the following two clues you must work out which place is being described.

1 If you were in the country which hosted the Winter Olympics in 1988 and the home of the 1980 snooker world champion, where would you be?

2 If you were in the home country of ice skating legend Sonja Henie and footballer Steffan Iversen, where would you be?

SCOREBOARD

round six — what happened next?

All you have to do in this round is decide which of the three options is the correct answer.

Ski-ing. The 2001 world championships in St Anton. Samir Azzimani of Morocco is about to start his first run in the men's giant slalom. What happened next?

- **a** Samir does the whole run on one ski, having lost the other at the start!
- **b** Samir does the whole run with one arm in a sling, having suffered an injury in training!
- **c** Samir does the whole run trailing part of the starting-gate behind him!

Still in St Anton, and Win-Jack Pai of Taiwan is about to start his first run in the men's giant slalom. What happened next?

- **a** He trips over coming out of the starting-gate, his skis come off and slide down the course on their own!
- **b** He makes it to the finish in the slowest time on record... and is then disqualified!
- **c** He catches the last control gate and crashes a yard from the finish.

SCOREBOARD		

round seven — home or away

athletics Which female sprinter won individual gold and silver medals at the 1999 World Championships, to add to the Olympic silver and bronze medals won by her father?

boxing	Between Terry Downes in 1961 and Nigel Benn in 1990 only one British boxer held the World Middleweight title: who?
horse racing	Which jockey retired in 1996 after riding 3,828 winners?
football	Which player appeared in four League Cup finals between 1997 and 2001, finishing as a winner on three occasions?

SCOREBOARD

round eight — captain's away

Here are two riddles from the often unusual world of sport. Can you tell me...

1 American Alan Shepard hit a unique and memorable golf shot in 1971: but where was he playing?

2 In 1918, Piggott landed first at Gatwick: but what did he win?

SCOREBOARD

round nine — mystery guest

Can you guess the identity of these sporting stars from the four clues below? The more clues you need, the fewer points you get.

1 I made my name in Staffordshire and was the greatest in my sport in the 1980s. (4 points)
I won the first of my five world titles in 1980. (3 points)
Phil Taylor has since broken my records for most world titles. (2 points)
I am known as the Crafty Cockney. (1 point)

2 I was born in Tunbridge Wells and played for Leicestershire and Hampshire. (4 points)
I won my first cap in 1977. (3 points)
I played in 117 Tests and only Graham Gooch has scored more runs for England than me. (2 points)
I now play opposite Gary Lineker on the BBC. (1 point)

SCOREBOARD		

round ten — on the buzzer

The Christian and surnames in these answers both start with the same letter!

1 Tennis – Which man won the '99 French and US Open singles titles?
2 Athletics – Which man held the world long-jump record for 23 years from 1968?

3 Who captained England in the fourth Test against the West Indies in 1988?

4 Football – Name the Aston Villa and England striker who was the Premier League's joint leading scorer in 1998?

5 Which Briton came last in both ski-jumping events at the 1988 Winter Olympics?

6 Golf – Which American has had five victories on the PGA Tour since 1992?

7 Cricket – Name the opening batsman who scored 19 centuries in 108 Tests for the West Indies?

8 Athletics – Name the female German high-jumper who won the world title in 1991 and the Olympics in 1992?

9 Motor racing – Which British driver won the 1961 US Grand Prix for Lotus?

10 Who was the world snooker champion in 1986?

11 Football – Name the Republic of Ireland midfielder who's played for Preston, West Brom and Sunderland.

12 Cricket – Which county won the Sunday League in 1999?

13 Athletics – Which former Commonwealth 200 metres champion coaches Dwain Chambers?

SCOREBOARD		

game **34**

round one — name the year

The following events all happened in the same year, but which one?

1 Britons Hugh Jones and Joyce Smith win the London Marathon.
Tom Watson becomes the fifth player to win the Open and US Open in the same year.
Daley Thompson wins the European Championship decathlon with a world record total of 8,774 points.
Paolo Rossi is the World Cup's leading scorer as his country wins the tournament.
Aston Villa win the European Cup, the fourth English team to collect the trophy.

Now for the second year:

2 Duke McKenzie wins a world title in a third division, the first Briton to do this.
On his way to the Championship, Nigel Mansell wins nine out of 16 Grands Prix.
Pakistan win the Cricket World Cup in Melbourne.
Linford Christie wins the Olympic 100 metres in 9.96 seconds.
Gary Lineker's international career is ended during the European Championship match against Sweden.

SCOREBOARD		

round two — picture board

Take a look at picture B on page 6 of Picture Board 1. Who is it?

Take a look at picture C on page 5 of Picture Board 1. Who is it?

SCOREBOARD		

round three — twenty sporting questions

20 questions on tennis.

1. Who was the first man to achieve the tennis Grand Slam in a single year?
2. Which competition was first held in 1900?
3. Who won the ladies' singles in Wimbledon's centenary year?
4. In which year did Wimbledon become open to professionals?
5. Which pair took a silver medal in the men's doubles at the 1996 Olympics?
6. Which man reached eight consecutive US Open singles finals in the 1980s?
7. On what surface was the US Open played between 1975 and 1977?
8. Who is the only woman to hold all four Grand Slams at the same time, in singles and doubles?
9. With which player did John McEnroe win his last Wimbledon men's doubles title in 1992?
10. Which women's team competition was discontinued in 1989?
11. Who won 1973's 'Battle of the Sexes' before the biggest audience in the history of the sport?
12. Which man won six French Open titles between 1974 and 1981?
13. What distinguishes Dorothea Lambert Chambers and Evonne Cawley (though not Evonne Gollagong) from all other Wimbledon ladies' singles champions?
14. Which woman achieved a 'Golden Grand Slam' in 1988?
15. Which Australians won five consecutive men's doubles titles in the 1990s?
16. What was unusual about the 1977 Australian Championships?
17. Which Cameroon-born player won the 1983 French Open men's singles title?
18. Which woman won a Grand Slam singles title every year from 1974 to 1986?
19. Who achieved the junior Grand Slam in 1983, before winning Wimbledon, the US and Australian Opens as a senior?
20. In 1946, Yvon Petra was the last Wimbledon champion to wear what?

SCOREBOARD		

round four — sporting links

1 What connects England's Footballer of the Year in 1997, Argentina's record points-scorer in rugby union and a midfielder who made his debut for Walsall before appearing for Sheffield Wednesday, West Bromwich Albion, Grimsby and Scunthorpe?

2 What is unusual about the German World Cup-winning teams in 1954 and 1974 and the victorious Argentines in 1978?

SCOREBOARD		

round five — where am I?

From the following two clues you must work out which place is being described.

1 After watching the Rhinos, there's only a short distance to travel if you want to see United play at Elland Road. Where?

2 Steve Backley set his first world javelin record here in 1990, while Gary Lineker won his last international cap two years later; but where?

SCOREBOARD		

round six — what happened next?

All you have to do in this round is decide which of the three options is the correct answer.

Boxing from the Ebbw Vale Leisure Centre, between Jason Williams and Mark Ramsay. The two boxers are squaring up in the middle of the ring. What happened next?

- **a** a) A light-bulb shatters, and the fight is halted while the ring is cleared of glass.
- **b** Williams' cornerman Nobby Nobbs throws in the towel, just as he knocks Ramsay out. Ramsay is the winner, despite being flat out on the canvas.
- **c** Ramsay launches a haymaker and flattens the referee. The fight is abandoned.

A 2001 FA Cup tie between Leeds and Liverpool. Rio Ferdinand challenges Jamie Carragher for the ball near the touchline. What happened next?

- **a** The ball goes out for a throw-in, both players try to take it and a scuffle ensues. Leeds' boss David O'Leary defuses the situation by picking up the ball and taking the throw himself.
- **b** Carragher concedes a free-kick. He tries to stop Ferdinand taking it quickly by hiding the ball up his shirt.
- **c** Ferdinand knocks the assistant referee over the perimeter wall.

SCOREBOARD		

round seven — home or away

ski-ing What nationality is double Olympic champion Hermann Maier?

athletics Tanni Grey-Thompson has won the women's London Wheelchair Marathon a record five times, but can you name the British man who has four wins to his name – also a record?

football Name the two Scotsmen who scored both goals for Everton in their 1984 FA Cup final victory?

golf In golf, who is nicknamed 'The Wild Thing'?

SCOREBOARD

round eight — captain's away

Here are two riddles from the often unusual world of sport. Can you tell me...

1 Golf – Between 1980 and 2000 only five men with Zs in their surnames have won major titles – who?

2 Horse racing – Between 1977 when Red Rum won his third Grand National and 2001, five other horses beginning with 'R' have won the race. Name them.

SCOREBOARD

round nine — mystery guest

Can you guess the identity of these sporting stars from the four clues below? The more clues you need, the fewer points you get.

1 I started my career as a Rugby Union player with Rosslyn Park. (4 points)
However, I am better known as a Rugby League player. (3 points)
I set a world record when I moved from Widnes to Wigan for £440,000. (2 points)
I am one of the greatest try-scorers in the game and now play for Salford. (1 point)

2 I was born in Huyton in Liverpool, and made my league debut with Bolton. (4 points)
I collected many major trophies at Goodison Park. (3 points)
I later moved into management with Manchester City. (2 points)
I am now manager at the Stadium of Light. (1 point)

SCOREBOARD		

round ten — on the buzzer

All the surnames in these answers have four letters!

1 Football – Who captained Chelsea to four major trophies from 1997 to 2000?

2 Rugby Union – Name the Irish hooker who played for the British Lions on their victorious tour of South Africa in 1997.

3 Cricket – Which batsman holds the world record for the highest Test and first class innings?

4 Formula One – Which British driver took his 22nd and last Grand Prix victory for Jordan at Spa in 1998?

5 Golf – Who was the first Briton to win the US Masters?

5 Football – Which Liverpool striker scored the very first goal on *Match of the Day* in 1964, and also helped England win the World Cup?

7 Rugby Union – Which All-Black has scored more World Cup tries than any other player?

8 Athletics – Which Briton set three middle-distance world records in 1985?

9 Cricket – Which Tasmanian batsman scored 7,422 Test runs for Australia?

10 Football – Which Welsh striker has scored five goals for Liverpool in FA Cup finals?

11 Rugby Union – Which England forward scored a drop goal in the 1999 Six Nations?

12 Tennis – Which woman won the Wimbledon singles title seven times in the '80s and '90s?

13 Cricket – Which Northants batsman scored more than 4,000 runs for England in the '80s and '90s?

SCOREBOARD		

game **35**

round one — name the year

The following events all happened in the same year, but which one?

1 Ian Woosnam wins the US Masters.
Grand National winner Seagram shares his name with the sponsors of the race.
Kenny Dalglish sensationally resigns as manager of Liverpool.
Paul Gascoigne scores with a terrific free-kick in the FA Cup semi-final against Arsenal at Wembley.
Boris Becker loses to fellow-German Michael Stich in the Wimbledon men's singles final.

Now for the second year:

2 Australia beat England 4–1 to win the Ashes in Australia.
Tom Watson wins the first of his five Opens.
Lescargot beats Red Rum to win the Grand National.
West Ham beat Fulham in the all-London FA Cup Final.
Bayern Munich beat Leeds to win their second successive European Cup Final

SCOREBOARD		

round two — picture board

Take a look at picture B on page 1 of Picture Board 2. Who is it?

Take a look at picture C on page 2 of Picture Board 2. Who is it?

SCOREBOARD		

round three — twenty sporting questions

20 questions on Scottish football.

1. Which club play their home games at Pittodrie?
2. Which team won the European Cup Winners' Cup in 1972?
3. Which Liverpool defender missed a penalty in 1984's European Cup final penalty shoot-out?
4. Who did Scotland beat 3–2 at the 1978 World Cup thanks to Archie Gemmill?
5. Which club were sponsored by pop group Wet Wet Wet during the 1990s?
6. Who scored for Manchester United in the 1994 FA Cup final after coming on as a substitute?
7. Who are the only Scottish club to play in the English FA Cup final?
8. Kenny Dalglish and Denis Law share the record for Scottish international goals, but how many?
9. Which Wolves striker scored the only goal of 1980 English League Cup final?
10. Which club are nicknamed the Buddies?
11. Who did Celtic defeat to win the 2001 League Cup final?
12. ...and who scored a hat-trick in the 3–0 win?
13. Who did Aberdeen beat in the final of the 1983 European Cup Winners' Cup?
14. To which Caribbean country did Scotland lose in the 1990 World Cup final?
15. Which team beat Bon Accord by a record 36–0 in 1885?
16. Who managed Scotland at the 1986 World Cup?
17. Kenny Dalglish and which other Scot scored for Liverpool in the 1981 League Cup final replay?
18. Which club are known as 'the Pars' and play at East End Park?
19. Who scored the goal from Scotland to defeat England 1–0 at Wembley in the Euro 2000 play-off?
20. Who was the only Scotsman to appear in the 2001 FA Cup final?

SCOREBOARD		

round four — sporting links

1 What links the 1988 Women's Olympic 200 metres backstroke champion Kristina Egerszegi, 1976 Women's All-Around Gymnastics gold medallist Nadia Comaneci and Eammon Collins, when he played for Blackpool in an Anglo-Scottish Cup tie in 1980?

2 What connects the Johannesburg-born opening batsman who made his debut for Middlesex in 1998, the Sunderland full-back whose only England cap came in a 13–2 victory over Ireland and the 1999 world decathlon champion?

SCOREBOARD

round five — where am I?

From the following two clues you must work out which place is being described.

1 The 1936 Summer Olympics will lead you to the city which is the birthplace of golf's Peter Alliss – but where is it?

2 The venue of the 1928 Summer Olympics is also home to famous football club Ajax: where is it?

SCOREBOARD

round six — what happened next?

All you have to do in this round is decide which of the three options is the correct answer.

Rugby A 2000–01 Heineken Cup tie between Gloucester and Llanelli. Gloucester are behind in injury time, when scrum-half Elton Moncrieff goes for a drop goal. What happened next?

- **a** The ball is deflected over the bar by a Llanelli player to win the game for Gloucester.
- **b** The ball is deflected over the bar by a Gloucester player, but the score is disallowed for accidental offside, costing them the game.
- **c** The ball is deflected over the bar by the referee, who is knocked to the ground. He can't give a decision so has to award a scrum to Gloucester.

Cricket, and the England team are celebrating at the end of their historic victory in Pakistan in December 2000. What happened next?

- **a** Darren Gough pulls down Ashley Giles' trousers to reveal that he is wearing his girlfriend's underwear!
- **b** Alec Stewart opens a bottle of champagne and the cork shatters a lightbulb.
- **c** Craig White accidentally wallops Mike Atherton on the nose with his bat!

SCOREBOARD		

round seven — home or away

cricket Name the Australians who are the only twins to play Test cricket in the same team.

football How did Wendy Toms, Janie Frampton and Amy Rayner make history in Kidderminster's game against Nuneaton Borough during 1999?

rugby union Who scored two tries for Leicester in their 2001 Heineken Cup victory over Stade Français?

boxing In May 2001, which heavyweight won his first professional fight against Mike Middleton?

SCOREBOARD

round eight — captain's away

Here are some sporting arenas from around the world. For your points you must state which sport you would be watching there.

1 Pumpkin Ridge.
The Arnold Schwarznegger Stadium.
Happy Valley.
Coonabarabran.
The Brickyard.
Sun Devil Stadium.
The Jungle.
Rugby Park.

SCOREBOARD

round nine — mystery guest

Can you guess the identity of these sporting stars from the four clues below? The more clues you need, the fewer points you get.

1 I was born in 1961, the son of a former top jockey. (4 points)
I have won the Epsom Derby on three occasions. (3 points)
I've also won the 1000 Guineas, 2000 Guineas and the Oaks. (2 points)
My Derby winners were Shahrastani, Lammtarra and Shergar. (1 point)

2 I was born in September 1976 and wear a number 7 shirt. (4 points)
I represented England in the 2000 World Cup. (3 points)
I was 'the Man of Steel' in 2000 and helped my club to success in three major finals soon afterwards. (2 points)
I play alongside Tommy Martyn at St Helen's. (1 point)

SCOREBOARD		

round ten — on the buzzer

The answers to all these are record-breakers!

1 Boxing – In 1994, who won back the world heavyweight title at the age of 46?

2 Cricket – who is India's youngest-ever Test player?

3 Football – In 1998–99, who played for England in Hungary after only 12 Premiership starts in his career?

4 Motor racing – Which driver won nine Grands Prix in 1992?

5 Rugby Union – England's most capped forward is?

6 Golf – In 1993, who shot a record 267 to win the Open?

7 Football – In 1997, who broke Cliff Bastin's Arsenal goal scoring record?

8 Snooker – Who scored 167 points in one frame at the 1999 World Championships?

9 Boxing – Which fighter has won world titles at six different weights?

10 Ice skating – In 1984, which pair achieved the highest scores in Olympic history?

11 Football – In 1999, against which Premiership team did Manchester United score eight away from home?

12 Rugby Union – England's record try scorer is?

13 Cricket – In 1993, whose record for Test match runs did Allan Border break?

14 Athletics – Which pole vaulter set 17 outdoor world records between 1984 and 1994?

15 Horse racing – Which jockey won nine Derbies in his career?

16 In 1999, in which sport did Leroy Rivett score four times in a final?

SCOREBOARD		

game 36

round one — name the year

The following events all happened in the same year, but which one?

1 To celebrate 100 years of the Ashes a Centenary Test is held in Melbourne.
Willie Duggan (Ireland) and Geoff Wheel (Wales) are the first players to be sent off in a Five Nations Rugby Tournament.
Virginia Wade wins the ladies singles at Wimbledon.
Manchester United defeat Liverpool in the FA Cup Final.
Red Rum wins his third Grand National.

Now for the second year:

2 Marat Safin defeats Pete Sampras to win the US Open Singles.
Rugby Union's Five Nations becomes the Six Nations Championship.
England win a Test Series in Pakistan.
Manchester United play in the World Club Championship rather than the FA Cup.
France beat Italy 2–1 in the Final of the European Championships.

SCOREBOARD		

round two — picture board

Take a look at picture C on page 5 of Picture Board 2. Who is it?

Take a look at picture B on page 8 of Picture Board 2. Who is it?

SCOREBOARD		

round three — twenty sporting questions

20 questions with a colourful connection.

1 Which horse won the 2001 Grand National?
2 Who managed Scotland to Euro '96 and World Cup '98?
3 In snooker, which ball is worth five points?
4 Which Welsh rugby Union side nicknamed the Scarlets?
5 By what name were Bristol Rovers originally known?
6 Where did Maurice Greene win his first world title, and two years later break the world 100 metres record?
7 Where is the Embassy World Darts Championship held?
8 What is the name of Toronto's Major League baseball team?
9 Which country do Wayne and Byron Black represent in the Davis Cup?
10 Who is the Yorkshire and England all-rounder who made his Test Debut in 1994?
11 What colour jersey is worn by the leader of the Tour de France?
12 Who won the men's 400 metres gold medal at the 1990 European Championships?
13 Football – Who are the Blues who play at St Andrews?
14 From which city do the American Football team the Packers come from?
15 What is the name of the Rugby League side from Salford?
16 Which football side are known as the Sky Blues?
17 Who won the 2001 ladies wheelchair London Marathon?
18 Which golfer is known as 'the Golden Bear'?
19 In what colour shirts do Dundee United play?
20 Name the Surrey batsman who made a century in his third one-day international for England in 1996.

SCOREBOARD		

round four — sporting links

1 What connects the 1988 Olympic welterweight freestyle wrestling champion, the Nigerian athlete who made the world 400 metres finals in 1993 and 1995, and the 1991 League Cup winners?

2 What connects the USSR's victory over Spain in the 1960 Nations' Cup quarter-finals, the 1972 Olympic heavyweight boxing final won by Teofilio Stevenson, and Wyndham Halswelle's victory in the 1908 Olympic 400 metres final?

SCOREBOARD

round five — where am I?

From the following two clues you must work out which place is being described.

1 The home country of footballers Boniek and Lato will lead you to the same nation where teams such as Lech Poznan and Widzew Lodz have been League Champions. Which country ?

2 Olympic swimming champion Le Jingyi will lead you to the country where Phil Neville made his England debut. Where?

SCOREBOARD

round six — what happened next ?

All you have to do in this round is decide which of the three options is the correct answer.

Football. A 2000–01 FA Cup tie between Cardiff City and Crewe Alexandra. The Crewe keeper does a long throw out and Jason Bowen of Cardiff chases the ball down the near touchline. What happened next?

- **a** An over-enthusiastic ball boy picks up the ball before Bowen can reach it.
- **b** Bowen isn't looking where he's going and runs into the corner flag.
- **c** Bowen tries to play a back-pass to his keeper... and puts the ball into his own net.

The 2001 Paris-Dakar rally. Maimon Pascal tries to overtake Jose Maria Servia, but hits a tree in the process and is forced to stop a mile later with a puncture. What happened next?

- **a** Servia pulls over to help Pascal change his wheel, but is then unable to re-start his car which is stuck in the sand!
- **b** Pascal stands in the middle of the track to try and force Servia to stop... and is almost run over!
- **c** Servia cruises past, making crude hand signals... and promptly crashes into another tree!

SCOREBOARD		

round seven — home or away

football Who is the only England player since Geoff Hurst to score a hat-trick in the final stages of a World Cup ?

athletics	Which female sprinter won a record eighth Olympic medal at the Sydney games ?
rugby union	Who scored 30 points in the 2001 Heineken Cup final but still finished on the losing side?
bowls	What nationality is Ian Schuback, who was World Indoor Champion in 1992 ?

SCOREBOARD

round eight — captain's away

Here are two riddles from the world of golf. Can you tell me...

1 Name the three golfers to have won a Major between 1980 and 2000 whose surnames end in a Y.

2 Name the three major winners between 1980 and 2000 whose surnames begin with B.

SCOREBOARD

round nine — mystery guest

Can you guess the identity of these sporting stars from the four clues below? The more clues you need, the fewer points you get.

1 I am one of the great South Africans to have played my sport. (4 points)
I was only the second South African to win the US Open. (3 points)
I won the World Matchplay title in three successive years. (2 points)
I was runner-up in three major tournaments in 2000. (1 point)

2 I was born in 1956 and was in the Leicester side which won threesuccessive cup finals. (4 points)
I made my England debut in 1980 and toured with the Lions that year. (3 points)
I was a centre and won the Grand Slam in my first season. (2 points)
In September 1997 I was appointed England coach. (1 point)

SCOREBOARD		

round ten — on the buzzer

The answers to these questions are in alphabetical order. The first answer will have the initials AB, the second CD and so on...

1 Cricket – Which batsman has scored the most runs in Test history?

2 Which British Olympic gold medallist formerly work as a policeman alongside footballer Steve Ogrizovic?

3 Football – Which Scottish team play at Bayview?

4 Football – Which former school-teacher is manager of Liverpool?

5 Rugby Union – Which second-row won 79 caps for the All-Blacks before joining Gloucester ?

6 Where were the 1998 Commonwealth Games held?

7 Tennis – Which woman won 56 Grand Slam titles between 1974 and 1995?

8 Horse racing – Which jockey won the Derby in 1998 on High Rise?

9 What name is given to the original laws of boxing?

10 Cricket – Which Indian batsman has scored the most centuries in one-day internationals?

SCOREBOARD		

game **37**

round one — name the year

The following events all happened in the same year, but which one?

1 In the World Matchplay Golf Championship, Lee Westwood beats defending champion Colin Montgomerie in the Final.
Pete Sampras wins his seventh Wimbledon Singles Title.
Celtic lose to Inverness Caledonian Thistle in the Scottish Cup.
Denise Lewis wins Olympic Gold
Emily Heskey becomes the third most expensive player to be traded between Premiership clubs

Now for the second year:

2 The New York Giants win their first Super Bowl.
Dennis Conner's Stars and Stripes wins the America's Cup for the USA.
Nick Faldo wins the Open for the first time.
A Midlands side win the FA Cup.
Pat Cash wins his only Wimbledon men's singles title.

SCOREBOARD		

round two — picture board

Take a look at picture B on page 3 of Picture Board 1. Who is it?

Take a look at picture B on page 4 of Picture Board 1. Who is it?

SCOREBOARD		

round three — twenty sporting questions

20 questions on British involvement in European football.

1 Who were the first British team to win a European trophy?
2 Which British player scored in two European Cup finals, seven years apart?
3 Who picked up European Cup winner's medals with two different English clubs, despite only playing for eight minutes in the two games?
4 Where did Real Madrid beat Eintracht Frankfurt 7–3 in the 1960 European Cup final?
5 Who captained Celtic to the European Cup in 1967?
6 What is unique about the 1972 UEFA Cup final?
7 Whose goal won 1970's Cup Winners' Cup final – he later became chairman?
8 Which Chelsea striker scored eight against Jeunesse Hautcharage in 1971?
9 Which team qualified for Europe for the only time in 1970 by finishing sixth in the Football League?
10 How did Liverpool defeat Cologne in the 1965 European Cup quarter finals?
11 Who played for different British clubs in the European Cups of 1992–93 and 1993–94?
12 Apart from Glasgow, which other British city has two teams which have both reached European Cup semi-finals?
13 Which British player made his Champions League debut in the 2000–01 competition, before he'd played in the Premiership?
14 Who was the first British player to win the European Cup with a foreign club?
15 Which British team knocked Porto out of the Cup Winners' Cup in 1984?
16 Before Solskjaer, who last scored a winner for a British team at the Nou Camp?
17 Which British team have lost two European finals in penalty shoot-outs?
18 Which British team won the 1969 Fairs Cup?
19 Who scored 14 goals in the 1981 UEFA Cup?
20 Which British team twice knocked Internazionale out of the Fairs Cup?

SCOREBOARD		

round four — sporting links

All of these sports stars have long or unusual names.

1. What's the real name of the US golfer who won the Open in 2000?
2. Name the Bath winger who made his England debut against Italy in 1996, and also played against Australia and New Zealand the following year.
3. Which Zairean striker joined Newcastle from Colchester in 2000?
4. What's the full name of the former Manchester United and Chelsea striker who later became manager of Wales?
5. Which Yugoslav made the men's singles semi-finals at Wimbledon in '86?
6. Who was the Tour de France cyclist nicknamed 'the Terror of Tashkent'?

SCOREBOARD		

round five — where am I?

From the following two clues you must work out which place is being described.

1. David Gower made his debut for this place in 1975, and you'll find a replica of the Statue of Liberty next to its Premiership football ground.
2. Birthplace of the 1982 Formula One world champion, and home country of the 1952 Summer Olympics, where is this?

SCOREBOARD		

round six — what happened next?

All you have to do in this round is decide which of the three options is the correct answer.

Tennis. The Australian Open, and a match between André Agassi and Paul Goldstein. Agassi to serve. What happened next?

- **a** A member of the crowd shouts out 'How's Steffi?' Agassi playfully hit the ball at him.
- **b** A bird overhead interrupts play by dropping its lunch on the court.
- **c** As he strikes the ball, Andre's racket falls to pieces.

Ski-ing from Garmisch Partenkirchen in the 2000–01 season. Simon Bastelica of France is about to begin his run in the men's downhill. What happened next?

- **a** He's forgotten his poles!
- **b** He's only wearing one ski!
- **c** He isn't wearing a number!

SCOREBOARD		

round seven — home or away

cricket What feat did Andy Caddick perform in 2000 which only Maurice Allom in 1929, Chris Old in 1978 and Wasim Akram in 1991 had previously achieved in Test cricket?

football Who was the first English player to score for a foreign club in a European Cup final?

rowing Which British rower who had won medals at the previous two Olympics narrowly missed out on making it three in a row at Sydney by finishing fourth in the coxless pairs with Ed Coode?

cycling Which British cyclist won the World Championship twice during the 1990s?

SCOREBOARD

round eight — captain's away

Here is a riddle from the often unusual world of sport. Can you tell me...

1 Name the 13 Football League clubs which have a unique second name. (eg. Athletic doesn't count because there are Charlton, Oldham and Wigan).

SCOREBOARD

round nine — mystery guest

Can you guess the identity of these sporting stars from the 4 clues below? The more clues you need the fewer points you get.

1 I took up my sport as a 13-year-old and turned professional in 1976. (4 points)
I was fourth in the Open in 1982 and made my breakthrough by winning the title in 1987. (3 points)
I then won the Masters in 1989 and 1990 and my second Open in 1990. (2 points)
Since then I've become one of the greatest British golfers by winning a third Open and a third Masters title. (1 point)

2 I was born in Germany in 1959 and was one of my sport's greatest players. (4 points)
I won three Wimbledon and four US Open titles. (3 points)
I represented and captained the USA in the Davis Cup. (2 points)
I was renowned for my tantrums on court. (1 point)

SCOREBOARD		

round ten — on the buzzer

The first letter of these surnames will spell out a famous player from Euro '96... backwards! See how quickly you can guess who it is:

1 Who scored Scotland's goal against Brazil at the '82 World Cup?

2 Which Arsenal defender played for England in both the 1988 and 1996 European Championships?

3 Name the Italian defender who played under his father's managership during the 1998 World Cup.

4 Who scored England's opening goal against Colombia at the '98 World Cup?

5 Which English Euro '96 referee also took charge of the '94 FA Cup final?

6 Who was top scorer at the '98 World Cup?

7 Who captained his side to victory in the 1998 World Cup final?

8 Who represented England in Euro '96 while playing for Inter Milan?

9 Which football pundit came on as sub for Liverpool in the '89 FA Cup final?

10 Name the French goalkeeper who was a substitute for Liverpool in the 2001 UEFA cup final.

11 Which Chelsea defender scored for AC Milan in the '94 European Cup final?

SCOREBOARD		

game **38**

round one — name the year

The following events all happened in the same year, but which one?

1 At 17, Boris Becker is Wimbledon's youngest winner of the Men's Singles.
The Open played at Sandwich is won by Sandy Lyle.
Everton win their only European trophy.
England beat Australia 3–1 in cricket's Ashes series.
Everton also win the League, while Norwich win the League Cup.

Now for the second year:

2 20–1 outsider High Rise storms to an Epsom Derby win.
Jana Novotna finally overcomes nerves to win Wimbledon.
Charlton defeat Sunderland 7–6 on penalties after a 4–4 draw in the First Division play-off final.
Britain's athletics team wins nine golds at the European Championships.
France defeats Brazil in the World Cup Final.

SCOREBOARD		

round two — picture board

Take a look at picture F on page 2 of Picture Board 2. Who is it?

Take a look at picture F on page 6 of Picture Board 2. Who is it?

SCOREBOARD		

round three — twenty sporting questions

20 questions on the history of the Commonwealth Games.

1. Name the venue of the 1998 Commonwealth Games.
2. Who won her second Commonwealth gold medal in the women's heptathlon in 1998?
3. Which country staged the Games for the only time in 1958?
4. In which sport was Sarah Hardcastle a Commonwealth champion in 1986?
5. Who at the age of 40 won the women's shot competition at the '98 Games?
6. Who delighted the home crowd by winning gold in the women's 10,000 metres in '86?
7. After nine major silver and bronze medals, which athlete finally ended his wait for a gold medal in the 100 metres hurdles at the '98 Games?
8. Which city staged the 1950 and 1990 Commonwealth Games?
9. In which event did Julian Golding win gold at the '98 Games?
10. In which sport did Fiona Smith win gold in '90?
11. He completed a clean sweep of titles in 1998, winning the European, World Cup and Commonwealth titles in the men's 400 metres. Name him.
12. Which boxer won gold in the super-heavyweight division at the '98 Commonwealth Games and the 2000 Olympics?
13. In which event did Joanne Wise win a Commonwealth title in '98?
14. Australia last staged the Games in which year?
15. Who won gold in the men's discus in '98, 16 years after he won the hammer?
16. Ato Boldon won the 100 metres title in '98. Which country did he represent?
17. At the '86 Games, England won the most gold medals. True or false?
18. Which boxer won the bantamweight title for Northern Ireland in 1978?
19. Name the high-jumper from England who won his first major outdoor title at the '98 Games.
20. Name the venue for the 2002 Games.

SCOREBOARD		

round four — sporting links

Who are the stars who all recorded the best performance by a Briton in their particular event?

1 In which sport was Konrad Bartelski second in a World Cup event in 1980?
2 Which British woman has won the US Tennis Open?
3 Who is the only Briton to win a medal at the world gymnastics championships?
4 In which sport has Britain won nine Olympic silver medals but only one gold, by Gillian Sheen in 1956?
5 Name the only British man to win a world judo title.
6 In 1964, in which sport did Anthony Nash and Robin Dixon collect a Winter Olympics gold medal?

SCOREBOARD		

round five — where am I?

From the following two clues you must work out which place is being described.

1 In the city where the 1988 Winter Olympics were held, you'd find an ice hockey team known as the Flames. Where might that be?

2 In which American city would you find an American Football team known as the Chiefs and a baseball side named the Royals?

SCOREBOARD		

round six — what happened next?

All you have to do in this round is decide which of the three options is the correct answer.

Premiership football between Manchester City and Charlton Athletic in December 2000. Charlton's Claus Jensen challenges Richard Dunne for the ball near the centre circle. What happened next?

- **a** Both make contact with the ball simultaneously and it bursts.
- **b** Jensen's challenge sends the ball flying off the pitch and it shatters the roof of the home dugout.
- **c** Dunne's clearance hits Jensen and flies past Nicky Weaver into the net.

Football between Newcastle and Everton in 2000. Newcastle have a free kick and three players line up to take it. What happened next?

- **a** All three run over the ball, expecting the others to take it!
- **b** Two of the players start arguing, the Everton defenders try to separate them and Robert Lee chips the ball into an unguarded net!
- **c** Norberto Solano slices the ball so badly he hits the corner flag!

SCOREBOARD		

round seven — home or away

tennis In the boycott year of 1973, which European player added Wimbledon to his two French Open titles?

rugby union In the game between Australia and the USA at the 1999 World Cup, what did American full back Juan Grobler do, that no other player in the tournament managed ?

football In 1999 against Belgium, which midfielder became only the third player to follow his father into the England team?

golf What was unusual about Aaron Baddeley's victory at the 1999 Australian Open?

SCOREBOARD

round eight — captain's away

Here are two riddles from the often unusual world of sport. Can you tell me...

1 In which sport does a single digit straight down a buttock indicate a blockage down the line, whilst an inverted V would lead you to cross the court ?

2 In which sporting event in 2000 did Watford complete 220 yards ahead of both Swansea and Birmingham, while pre-event favourite Scunthorpe trailed well behind ?

SCOREBOARD

round nine — mystery guest

Can you guess the identity of these sporting stars from the four clues below? The more clues you need, the fewer points you get.

1 I started go-karting in 1982 at the age of 11 and won Scottish titles. (4 points)
I made my Formula One debut in 1994. (3 points)
My first Grand Prix win came in 1995, and in 1998 I came third in the World Championship. (2 points)
I drove for McLaren in 2001 with Mika Hakkinen. (1 point)

2 I had my first winner in 1983 at the age of 19. (4 points)
In 1993–94 I rode 198 winners to become Champion Jockey for the second successive time. (3 points)
I rode over 1,000 winners in National Hunt but also enjoy Motor Racing. (2 points)
I won the Grand National on West Tip and Minnehoma and also rode winners in the Cheltenham Gold Cup and the Champion Hurdles. (1 point)

SCOREBOARD

round ten — on the buzzer

These questions are all about unusual sporting terms and words

1 In which sport might a bad flipper cost you sundries?
2 Where would you find a niblick?

3 In which sport have teams used the W, catenaccio and Christmas tree formations?

4 In which sport might you use a grubber after a play-the-ball?

5 Where would you find Cyclops?

6 Athletics – In which event could you use a scissors, a straddle or a flop?

7 In 10-pin bowling, what are known as Scooby-Doos?

8 In which sport could a night-watchman score a Nelson?

9 In which sport can you play a 'cock hat double?'

10 In which sport does the Old Lady of Turin play the Viola in Florence?

11 In which sport aren't you allowed to feed the tight five?

12 Athletics – In which events can competitors be penalised for 'timber topping?'

SCOREBOARD		

game **39**

round one — name the year

The following events all happened in the same year, but which one?

1 Tim Henman is in the Wimbledon semi-finals, the first British male since 1973.
John Higgins beats Ken Doherty to win the World Snooker Title.
Gérard Houllier is announced as joint manager of Liverpool.
Justin Rose, the 17-year-old amateur, finishes equal fourth at Royal Birkdale in the Open.
Substitute Gianfranco Zola wins the Cup Winners' Cup for Chelsea.

Now for the second year:

2 Neath beat holders Llanelli to win the Welsh Rugby Cup.
Rangers win the Scottish League: Richard Gough is named Footballer of the Year.
The first all-weather horse racing track in Britain is introduced at Lingfield Park.
Peter Scudamore reaches a historic 201 winners in a National Hunt season.
The Lions, captained by Gavin Hastings, win the series against Australia

SCOREBOARD

round two — picture board

Take a look at picture C on page 7 of Picture Board 2. Who is it?

Take a look at picture D on page 1 of Picture Board 2. Who is it?

SCOREBOARD

round three — twenty sporting questions

20 questions where all the answers begin with T.

1 In which sport is Desmond Douglas a former British Champion?
2 What was the name of Dennis Lillee's fearsome bowling partner for Australia during the 1970s?
3 Which club play their home games at Prenton Park?
4 Which American golfer won the 1971 US Open and was known as Tex-Mex?
5 In which sport during the 1990s were Britons Spencer Smith and Simon Lessing world champions?
6 Who rode Royal Athlete to success in the 1995 Grand National?
7 The Wightman and Federation Cups are competed for in which sport?
8 Who did the League and Cup double in 1961?
9 Where were the 1964 Summer Olympics held?
10 In which country do Galatasaray and Besiktas compete?
11 Name the Indian batsman who became the first player ever to score 10,000 runs in one-day internationals.
12 How many times did Liverpool play in the FA Cup final during the 1980s?
13 Who was world snooker champion in 1985?
14 Ski-ing – Which Italian won Olympic slalom and giant slalom gold in 1988?
15 Rugby Union – Which Welsh full-back kicked a last-minute conversion to win the third-place play-off in the 1987 World Cup?
16 In the North American Ice Hockey League, from which city do the Maple Leafs come?
17 On which course did Nick Price win the 1994 Open?
18 Which club play their home games at Plainmoor?
19 Who in 1987 became undisputed Heavyweight champion of the world?
20 Where do Dundee United play their home games?

SCOREBOARD		

round four — sporting links

1 What connects 1992 European Football champions Denmark, the 1980 Olympic men's downhill gold medallist Leonhard Stock and Carl Llewellyn, who won Grand Nationals on Party Politics and Earth Summit?

2 What connects the following Olympic gold medallists: Hasely Crawford, who won the 100 metres in 1976; Anthony Nesty, who took the 100 metres butterfly in 1988; and John Akii Bua, who won the 400 metres hurdles in world record time in 1976?

SCOREBOARD

round five — where am I?

From the following two clues you must work out which place is being described.

1 Which country is home to cyclist Eddie Merckx and hosted the match between Italy and Romania during Euro 2000?

2 Tennis player Hicham Arazi comes from the North African country who played in the 1970 World Cup finals. Which one?

SCOREBOARD

round six — what happened next?

All you have to do in this round is decide which of the three options is the correct answer.

Tennis, and the 2000 Masters final between Pat Cash and John McEnroe. Cash is about to serve. What happened next?

- **a** His headband falls over his eyes! He attempts to play on anyway!
- **b** The ball explodes! Pat flexes his arm in a 'he-man' gesture!
- **c** A car the tournament sponsors have suspended on wires behind the court crashes down! McEnroe jokes about women drivers!

Cricket between Australia and the West Indies. Australia's Colin Miller is about to bowl the first over of the day. What happened next?

- **a** Miller takes off his sweater to reveal that he has forgotten to put on a shirt!
- **b** Miller takes off his sunglasses to reveal that he is wearing eye shadow!
- **c** Miller takes off his hat to reveal that he has dyed his hair blue overnight!

SCOREBOARD		

round seven — home or away

rugby league Which team lost to St Helen's in the 1996 and 1997 Challenge Cup finals?

athletics Which British track athlete competed in her fourth consecutive Olympics at Sydney, having reached the final in her first in 1988?

football Name the former Aston Villa striker who was joint top-scorer at Euro 2000 with five goals.

baseball Name the Baltimore Orioles player who holds the record for most consecutive games – 2,632.

SCOREBOARD

round eight — captain's away

Here are two riddles from the often unusual world of sport. Can you tell me...

1 What is three inches in diameter, one inch high, made of vulcanised rubber, black and cold?

2 What is unique about Bob Charles' victory in the 1963 Open?

SCOREBOARD

round nine — mystery guest

Can you guess the identity of these sporting stars from the four clues below? The more clues you need, the fewer points you get.

1 Born in Cheshire, I played for England with three counties. (4 points)
I also played in the Football League. (3 points)
I am considered England's greatest all-round cricketer. (2 points)
I teamed up with Bill Beaumont on *A Question of Sport*. (1 point)

2 I was born in Jamaica in 1960 and competed for Great Britain in three Olympic Games. (4 points)
I was an Olympic Gold medal winner in 1992. (3 points)
I am accepted as Britain's greatest-ever sprinter. (2 points)
You might also have seen me presenting on television. (1 point)

SCOREBOARD		

round ten — on the buzzer

All the answers are countries.

1. Snooker – In 1999, in which country did John Parrott win his first tournament for three years?
2. Football – Paulo Wanchope was the first Premiership player from which country?
3. Rugby League – In 1996, where was the very first Super League match played?

4 Golf – Where did the 1998 USPGA champion come from?
5 Cricket – In 1998, in which country did Australian captain Mark Taylor declare after scoring 334 not out?
6 Athletics – Deon Hemmings was which country's first female Olympic champion?
7 Rugby Union – Who joined the Five Nations in the year 2000, when it became the Six Nations?
8 Golf – Where was the Ryder Cup held for the first time in 1997?
9 Football – In 1998, who came third at their debut World Cup?
10 Rugby League – For which country has Apollo Perelini played for?
11 Athletics – Which nation's athletes won five consecutive women's European Championship marathons?
12 Cricket – Who do England play for the Wisden trophy?
13 Rugby League – Which country did Australia beat 86–6 at the 1995 World Cup?
14 Football – Which country scored the first goal of France '98?
15 Golf – Which country won the World Cup for the first time in 1998?

SCOREBOARD		

game **40**

round one — name the year

The following events all happened in the same year, but which one?

1 Greg Rusedski loses in the US Open final to Patrick Rafter.
Martina Hingis wins three of the four major singles titles.
Jacques Villeneuve wins his first World Drivers' Championship.
The British Athletic Federation goes bankrupt.
Seve Ballesteros skippers Europe to victory over the Americans in the Ryder Cup at Valderrama.

Now for the second year:

2 Martina Navratilova wins her first Wimbledon singles title.
Bjorn Borg beats Jimmy Connors to win his third successive Wimbledon singles title.
Scotland fail in the World Cup despite Archie Gemmill's superb goal to beat Holland.
Ian Botham's 8–34 vs Pakistan are the best figures by an England bowler since Jim Laker in 1956.
Nottingham Forest under Brian Clough win the League title for the first time.

SCOREBOARD		

round two — picture board

Take a look at picture B on page 3 of Picture Board 2. Who is it?

Take a look at picture E on page 4 of Picture Board 2. Who is it?

SCOREBOARD		

round three — twenty sporting questions

20 questions on sporting veterans.

1. Name the 36-year-old who was Man of the Match in Liverpool's dramatic victory over Alaves in the 2001 UEFA Cup final.
2. Who won his fifth successive gold medal at the Sydney Olympics?
3. In what did Judy Oakes win gold at the '98 Commonwealth Games?
4. Who marked his 50th cap for Scotland with the only goal of the game against Australia in 1996?
5. Mark O'Meara won the Open in '98. How old was he?
6. Which British rider won the first of his four Superbike world titles in 1994?
7. Which ex-Everton 'keeper made a comeback for Bradford aged 41 in 2000?
8. Who in 1996 became the first British woman to earn over £1m in a year?
9. Harold 'Dickie' Bird umpired his final Test match in June '96. England were playing India, but where?
10. Tim Henman and Neil Broad lost in the final of the men's doubles at the Atlanta Olympics. Who beat them?
11. Which tennis legend marked his debut as a professional golfer with an 11-over-par round of 82 in the Czech Open in '96?
12. Who replaced Ruud Gullit as manager of Newcastle United?
13. Which two golfers both won the US Masters three times in the 1960s?
14. John Parrott lost his place in the world's top 16 after losing to which player in the 2001 World Snooker Championship?
15. Coventry legend Steve Orgrizovic also played for Liverpool. True or false?
16. Three-day eventing – Which country does Mark Todd represent?
17. Who won his sixth world athletics title in Athens?
18. Who broke Cliff Bastin's 58-year-old scoring record for Arsenal?
19. Whose drop goal sealed victory for the Lions 18–15 in the 1997 Test?
20. In which famous race did veteran Rosemary Henderson finish fifth in 1994?

SCOREBOARD		

round four — sporting links

1 What connects the 1998 Danish World Cup player who scored with his first touch after coming on against Nigeria, the Welsh prop forward who made his debut against Tonga in 1994, and the right-back who won the League Cup with Luton in 1988 and went on to play for West Ham?

2 What connects the Lancashire and Nottinghamshire batsman who played three Tests against the West Indies and South Africa in 1995, the Australian fly-half who won the World Cup in 1991 and the Nigerian striker who joined Arsenal from Internazionale?

SCOREBOARD		

round five — where am I?

From the following two clues you must work out which place is being described.

1 You could watch the Cardinals baseball team in the city which hosted the Olympic Games in 1904. Where?

2 Home of legendary athlete Alberto Juantorena, this country has also won two Olympic gold medals in baseball. Where?

SCOREBOARD		

round six — what happened next?

All you have to do in this round is decide which of the three options is the correct answer.

Football, and a 2000 UEFA Cup tie between Boavista and Barry Town. Barry 'keeper Lee Kendall is about to take a goal kick. What happened next?

- **a** The advertising logo on the front of Kendall's shirt falls off!
- **b** The number on Kendall's back falls off!
- **c** Kendall's hairpiece falls off!

The 2000 Superleague, and Halifax are playing the Huddersfield/Sheffield Giants. The Giants' Dale Cardoso has the try line at his mercy. What happened next?

- **a** Cardoso runs right through the in-goal area and touches down over the dead ball line!
- **b** The hooter goes as Cardoso crosses the line; he mistakenly thinks time is up and kicks the ball away in frustration!
- **c** Cardoso tries to run round behind the posts, trips on a divot and knocks on!

SCOREBOARD		

round seven — home or away

athletics Name the British track and field athlete who set an Olympic record at Sydney but only managed to win a silver medal.

football Which Irish international scored an FA Cup-winning goal against Everton, and later went on to play for them ?

rowing Bruce Philip and Richard Young are the only two rowers in Boat Race history to do what?

tennis Who partnered John Newcombe to five Wimbledon men's doubles titles?

SCOREBOARD

round eight — captain's away

Here are two riddles from the often unusual world of sport. Can you tell me...

1 In which sport did a Wolf win a world championship race at its first attempt in 1977?

2 In which sporting event did Ronaldo set a world record in 1998?

SCOREBOARD

round nine — mystery guest

Can you guess the identity of these sporting stars from the four clues below? The more clues you need, the fewer points you get.

1 I am an Olympic Champion from Merseyside. (4 points)
In Barcelona, I won Britain's first gold medal in my sport since 1920. (3 points)
I used a Lotus-built Dreammaker, and also competed in the Tour de France. (2 points)
In 2000 I set another cycling world record (1 point)

2 I was born in Finland and in 2001 celebrated my 10th year in the sport at the top level. (4 points)
My first major win came in 1997. (3 points)
In 1998 I won eight races and became World Champion. (2 points)
My biggest rival is Michael Schumacher. (1 point)

SCOREBOARD		

round ten — on the buzzer

These questions are all about sports stars with interesting nicknames.

1 Football – Name the England midfielder who likes to call himself 'the Guv'nor'.
2 Cricket – Which wicketkeeper is known as 'Chuckie'?
3 Snooker – Which former world champion is nicknamed 'the Grinder'?

4 Golf – Who's the former American Ryder Cup player known as 'the Walrus?'

5 Rugby Union – Name the former England flanker they call 'the Munch'.

6 Cricket – Which England batsman is known as 'Creepy?'

7 Darts – Who is the former world champion known as 'the Crafty Cockney'?

8 Rugby League – Which Great Britain winger is known as 'Chariots'?

9 Football – Name Manchester United's 'Baby Faced Assassin'.

10 Golf – Who's the 'Wild Thing'?

11 Football – Which England winger was labelled 'Sicknote' by his team-mates?

12 Cricket – The former England coach they call 'Bumble' is?

13 Snooker – Who's the former world champion nicknamed 'Dracula'?

14 Golf – Who is 'the Golden Bear'?

15 Boxing – Which multi-world champion is normally known as 'the Hitman'?

16 Football – Name the former England goalkeeper known as 'the Cat'.

SCOREBOARD		

game **41**

round one — name the year

The following events all happened in the same year, but which one?

1 American Justin Leonard wins the Open at Troon, finishing 12 under par.
Jansher Khan wins his sixth successive British Open squash title, beating 24-year-old Peter Nicol.
Australia beat England 3–2 to retain the Ashes.
The British Lions beat their hosts in South Africa.
England make it to the World Cup finals by holding Italy to a draw in Rome.

Now for the second year:

2 The first World Athletics Championships are held in Helsinki, with Steve Cram winning the 1500 metres.
The British Lions under Ciaran Fitzgerald lose all four tests in New Zealand.
Europe taste defeat in the Ryder Cup by a single point in Palm Beach.
Tom Watson wins the Open for a second time in succession and fifth time in total.
Hamburg win the European Cup beating Juventus 1–0.

SCOREBOARD		

round two — picture board

Take a look at picture E on page 3 of Picture Board 2. Who is it?

Take a look at picture C on page 4 of Picture Board 2. Who is it?

SCOREBOARD		

round three — twenty sporting questions

20 sporting questions to do with 1994.

1 Name the referee who awarded two penalties in the 1994 FA Cup final.
2 Who defeated the Buffalo Bills to retain the Superbowl?
3 Name the former England manager who took charge of Wolves in March 1994.
4 Which Spaniard won the US Masters?
5 Which British tennis player won the Korean Open?
6 Which team won the women's Rugby World Cup?
7 Which Italian team did Arsenal defeat in the European Cup Winners' Cup final?
8 Which jockey won his fourth Derby on Erhaab?
9 Name the Spaniard who won the men's French Open singles title.
10 Who defeated Ray Close to defend his WBO super-middleweight world title?
11 Which fast bowler took 9–57 against South Africa at the Oval?
12 Du'aine Ladejo won which event at the 1994 European Championships?
13 From which club did Liverpool sign Phil Babb for £3.75 million?
14 Which German won his first Formula One Drivers' Championship?
15 Which country won Rugby Union's Five Nations?
16 Which sprinter won his third successive European Championship 100 metres crown?
17 Name the Welsh international who scored twice for Aston Villa in the League Cup final.
18 In which country were the World Cup finals staged?
19 Which Italian club defeated Barcelona 4–0 in the final of the European Cup?
20 For which county did Brian Lara score over 2,000 runs in the County Championship?

SCOREBOARD		

round four — sporting links

1 What connects the 1987 Wimbledon men's singles champion, the Somerset off-spinner who took an England-record 5 for 39 against Sri Lanka in the 1983 World Cup and the Romanian who scored four goals at the 1994 World Cup and joined West Ham in 1996?

2 What connects the former Liverpool apprentice who managed Bradford into the Premiership in 1999, the winning jockey at the 2000 Grand National and the team promoted to the Football League in 2001?

SCOREBOARD		

round five — where am I?

From the following two clues you must work out which place is being described.

1 In which country, the birthplace of pole-vaulting legend Sergey Bubka, do Dynamo Kiev play their home games?

2 Which country was a runner-up at Euro '96 and also home to the Wimbledon women's singles winner in 1998?

SCOREBOARD		

round six — what happened next?

All you have to do in this round is decide which of the 3 options is the correct answer.

World League American football between Rhein Fire and the Amsterdam Admirals. Eric Turner charges into the endzone. What happened next?

- **a** Eric crashes into the goalpost!
- **b** Eric collides with a television cameraman!
- **c** Eric falls down the players' tunnel!

Football from the 2000–01 FA Cup between Forest Green Rovers and Morecambe. A hopeful ball loops into the Forest Green box. What happened next?

- **a** A Forest Green defender tries to blast the ball clear, but mis-cues it into his own net.
- **b** A Morecambe striker gets in a header and one of his team-mates on the goal-line tries to tap the ball in, but slices it wide of the open goal.
- **c** The referee collides with the Forest Green goalkeeper and leaves Morecambe with an open goal.

SCOREBOARD		

round seven — home or away

football In 2000, which 39-year-old Englishman became the oldest player ever to appear in a Champions League match?

hockey	Stephan Veen scored the winning penalty and captained which country to the gold medal at the 2000 Olympics?
athletics	Which French 400 metres hurdler finished fourth, third, first and second in four consecutive World Championships?
golf	Having won 20 titles, which man holds the record for the most Major wins?

SCOREBOARD

round eight — captain's away

Here are two riddles from the often unusual world of sport. Can you tell me...

1 Name the four English League teams whose names appear on a Monopoly board.

2 Horse racing – there are six racecourses in Britain which contain all of the letters of the word RACE in their name. Name four.

SCOREBOARD

round nine — mystery guest

Can you guess the identity of these sporting stars from the four clues below? The more clues you need, the fewer points you get.

1 I was born in Leytonstone and made my first-class debut in 1973. (4 points)
I made my England debut in 1975 and made a pair against Australia. (3 points)
I once scored 333 against India at Lords in 1990. (2 points)
I played for Essex and have scored a record number of runs for England in Test matches. (1 point)

2 I was born in Essex in 1964 and made my Formula 1 debut with Benetton in 1989. (4 points)
In 1991 I was victorious in the Le Mans 24 hour race. (3 points)
I won my first Grand Prix on my home track in 1995, and then followed up with victory in Italy. (2 points)
I was one of three Britons to win a Grand Prix in 1999, along with David Coulthard and Eddie Irvine. (1 point)

SCOREBOARD

round ten — on the buzzer

These answers are all managers, coaches and captains.

1 Football – Which manager was known as Stroller in his playing days?
2 Snooker – Who captained Wales to victory in the 1999 Nations Cup?

3 Football – In 1998, which team sacked their coach after he'd led them to victory in the Champions' League?

4 Football – In 1998, who led his team to the Scottish League title and then resigned?

5 Rugby Union – Who is the England coach?

6 Football – Which Premiership manager won 12 major trophies in the 1990s?

7 Tennis – Who is Britain's Davis Cup captain?

8 Football – In the 1990s, which manager won seven successive Scottish titles?

9 Athletics – Who was the high-jumper who captained the British men at the 1998 European Championships?

10 Football – Who resigned as manager of West Ham in May 2001?

11 American Football – Which team did Mike Shanahan coach to win the 1999 Superbowl?

12 Football – Name the former Crystal Palace chairman who became manager of Brentford in 1998.

13 Rugby League – Which team did Ellery Hanley coach to the Superleague title in 1999?

14 Golf – In 1985, who captained the first European team to win the Ryder Cup?

15 Cricket – Which Middlesex batsman captained England in 1997 when they won the ashes against Australia?

SCOREBOARD		

game 42

round one — name the year

The following events all happened in the same year, but which one?

1 Troy wins the 200th Epsom Derby.
Sebastian Coe sets his first world record, in the 800 metres in Oslo.
Seve Ballesteros is the first European to win the Open since 1907.
Trevor Francis becomes the first £1 million British footballer.
Arsenal beat Manchester United in a dramatic FA Cup Final.

Now for the second year:

2 A hat-trick is scored in the Scottish League Cup Final.
Steve Waugh becomes only the fifth player to be out 'handled ball' in a Test.
Steve Davis and Jimmy White fail to qualify for the World Snooker Championships.
Jason Robinson makes the Lions Rugby Union Tour in his first season since moving from Rugby League.
Chris Powell is the first Charlton Athletic player to be capped for England since Mike Bailey.

SCOREBOARD		

round two — picture board

Take a look at picture D on page 6 of Picture Board 2. Who is it?

Take a look at picture B on page 7 of Picture Board 2. Who is it?

SCOREBOARD		

round three — twenty sporting questions

20 questions on young sports stars.

1. Brian Close is England's youngest-ever international in which sport?
2. Who won the 1997 Wimbledon ladies' singles title aged 16?
3. Which footballer scored in the 1968 European Cup final on his 19th birthday?
4. In what did 15-year-old Shane Gould win five medals at the 1972 Olympics?
5. In 1992, which future world champion won 38 consecutive matches in world-ranking qualifiers aged 16?
6. Name the 22-year-old New Zealander who won the 1959 US Grand Prix and later founded his own team.
7. In which sport is American Wilfred Benitez the youngest-ever world champion?
8. Which British high-jumper equalled the world junior record in Seoul in 1992?
9. In 1998, who made his debut for the England rugby union team aged 18?
10. Who in 1999 became the first teenager to play in Ryder Cup?
11. In which sport could the Young Boys of Berne play the young men of Turin?
12. Which centre, then with Featherstone Rovers, became the youngest Great Britain Rugby League international in 1989?
13. In 1990, who became the youngest-ever world snooker champion?
14. At the 1988 Olympics, in which athletics event did Steve Lewis become the youngest individual male gold medallist for 80 years?
15. Which 17-year-old scored a century against England at Old Trafford in 1990?
16. Tennis – In 1982, which teenager won the French Open men's singles?
17. Blendi Nallbani was only 17 years and 19 days old when he conceded five goals against England at Wembley in 1989; for which country?
18. Who in 1994 became the youngest New Zealand All-Black ever?
19. Which jockey won the 1954 Derby aged 18?
20. In which major sporting event is Young Tom Morris the youngest-ever winner?

SCOREBOARD		

round four — sporting links

1 What connects former England manager Kevin Keegan, 1982 and 1989 world darts champion Jocky Wilson and three-times world motor racing champion Jackie Stewart – and it's nothing to do with sport?

2 What connects the West Indies' victory in the 1979 Cricket World Cup final, Liverpool's win in the 1984 European Cup final and the success of Tony Jacklin's European Ryder Cup side over Jack Nicklaus's Americans in 1987?

SCOREBOARD		

round five — where am I?

From the following two clues you must work out which place is being described.

1 This country has had its own Grand Prix since 1981, and its football team made a dream start to a game against England in 1993... but to call it a 'home' game requires clarification. Where is this?

2

The birthplace of England goalkeeper Dave Beasant also hosted the 1986 world hockey championships. Where is this?

SCOREBOARD		

round six — what happened next?

All you have to do in this round is decide which of the three options is the correct answer.

American football between the Green Bay Packers and the Carolina Panthers in 2000. Brett Favre throws a pass, but a Panthers player intercepts. What happened next?

- **a** A Packers fan runs on to the field and tries to tackle him!
- **b** A photographer on the sideline trips him up!
- **c** He drops the ball as he's about to cross the goal-line!

Tennis, and Goran Ivanisevic is playing at an event in Brighton in the year 2000. Goran smashes his racket in frustration after losing a point. What happened next?

- **a** Goran has sprained his wrist and has to default the match!
- **b** Goran has already incurred two penalties; he gets a third which automatically means he is disqualified!
- **c** Goran has run out of rackets and has to default the match!

SCOREBOARD		

round seven — home or away

darts Which Dutchman defeated Richie Burnett in 1998 to claim the BDO World Professional Darts Championship ?

football	George Graham was only the second person to manage both Spurs and Arsenal. Who was the first?
athletics	Name the British athlete who won Commonwealth gold in 1982 in a field event, and another in 1998 in a different field event?
horse racing	Which jockey, the son of a famous trainer, rode Garrison Savannah to victory in the 1991 Cheltenham Gold Cup ?

SCOREBOARD

round eight — captain's away

It's odd one out. We will show you four names and you will have to decide who is the misfit.

1 Which of these would feel out of place on a baseball field?

Rollie Fingers.
Yogi Berra.
Picabo Street.
Randy Wolf.

2 Which of these famous names hasn't played top-level basketball?

Patrick Ewing.
Don Maclean.
Joan Crawford.
Kenny Rogers.

SCOREBOARD

round nine — mystery guest

Can you guess the identity of these sporting stars from the four clues below? The more clues you need, the fewer points you get.

1 I was born in 1972, and won an Olympic bronze medal in 1996. (4 points)
I won European and Commonwealth gold medals in 1998 in a multi-event competition. (3 points)
I followed that with Olympic gold in Sydney. (2 points)
I sometimes compete in long jump, but mainly in the heptathlon. (1 point)

2 I was born in Scotland in 1969 and have often been called the greatest player in my sport. (4 points)
In 1999 I won my seventh world title. (3 points)
In 1995 I scored a maximum at the Crucible. (2 points)
I was the youngest World Snooker Champion in 1990. (1 point)

SCOREBOARD		

round ten — on the buzzer

These questions are all about famous sporting venues.

1. Football – At which ground do the Toffeeman play?
2. Rugby Union – Which famous Exiles play at Old Deer Park?
3. What sport is played at Winged Foot and Crooked Stick?

4 Snooker – Where was the 1998 Grand Prix staged?
5 Hockey – Which country won its first Olympic title in Barcelona?
6 Tennis – Where is the French Open held?
7 Football – Who plays at Gay Meadow?
8 In which sport could you play at the Gabba and the Waca?
9 Golf – At which course did Europe regain the Ryder Cup in 1985?
10 Rugby Union – Which ground is known as the Cabbage Patch?
11 Athletics – Where did Linford Christie and Sally Gunnell win their Olympic gold medals?
12 Football – Name one of the two teams which play at the Stadium of Light.
13 Motor racing – Where did Mika Hakkinen clinch the 1998 World Drivers' Championship?
14 Horse racing – Where is thc St Leger held?
15 Cricket – At which ground did England clinch the series with South Africa in 1998?
16 Football – At which ground did Ally McCoist score in Euro '96?

SCOREBOARD		

game **43**

round one — name the year

The following events all happened in the same year, but which one?

1 Baltimore Ravens win the Super Bowl, beating the New York Giants 34–7.
St Helen's beat the Brisbane Broncos to win the Rugby League World Club Challenge.
Red Marauder wins the Grand National at 33–1, as only four horses finish.
St Helens defeat Bradford 13–6 in the Challenge Cup Final at Twickenham.
Foot and mouth disease prevents the Cheltenham Festival from going ahead.

Now for the second year:

2 South Africa return to International Rugby Union.
Goalkeepers are banned from handling deliberate back passes.
England lose in the final of cricket's World Cup.
The Premier League is introduced in England.
The Olympic Games are held in Barcelona.

SCOREBOARD		

round two — picture board

Take a look at picture D on page 3 of Picture Board 2. Who is it?

Take a look at picture D on page 5 of Plate Section 1. Who is it?

SCOREBOARD		

round three — twenty sporting questions

20 questions on sporting connections with Africa.

1. Which Zimbabwean goalkeeper played in the 1984 European Cup final?
2. Who was the first batsman to score over 4,000 Test runs for South Africa?
3. Who was named FIFA World Footballer of the year in 1995?
4. Tennis – Which player won his first title at Queen's Club in 1992?
5. Apart from hosts South Africa, which other African nation qualified for the 1995 Rugby Union World Cup?
6. Which Ethiopian won the Olympic 10,000 metres gold medal at Sydney?
7. Name the South African who was WBA heavyweight world champion in 1983.
8. Alain Prost won the 1993 South African Grand Prix at which circuit?
9. What nationality was Jaroslav Drobny when he won the 1954 Wimbledon men's singles title?
10. Who were 1996 Olympic football champions?
11. Rugby Union – Which player captained South Africa to victory in the 1995 World Cup?
12. Which South African batsman played his 200th one-day international in May 2001?
13. Penny Heyns of South Africa won Olympic gold in which sport in 1996?
14. Which country did Zimbabwe beat in 1995 to record their first ever Test win?
15. Who was Formula One World Drivers' Champion in 1979?
16. Name the South African golfer who won nine Majors.
17. Which South African-born player scored for Liverpool in the 1986 FA Cup final?
18. Which Moroccan broke the world 1500 metres record in 1998?
19. Rugby Union – South African Joel Stransky won the 1999 League Championship with which club?
20. Cricket – Who was named Man of the Tournament at the 1999 World Cup?

SCOREBOARD		

round four — sporting links

1 What connects Grand Slam-winning tennis player Rod Laver, world snooker champion Ken Doherty and world lightweight boxing champion Pernell Whitaker?

2 What connects 1966 Formula One world champion Jack Brabham, 1986 League and FA Cup winner Kenny Dalglish and Arnold Palmer when he played in the 1963 Ryder Cup winning team?

SCOREBOARD

round five — where am I?

From the following two clues you must work out which place is being described.

1 In which American state would you find American Football teams known as the Dolphins and the Buccaneers? The same state was host to the 1992 US Open at Pebble Beach.

2 In this country you would find football teams called Apollon Limassol and Omonia, and it is also the birthplace of Welsh international Jeremy Goss. Where is it?

SCOREBOARD

round six — what happened next?

All you have to do in this round is decide which of the 3 options is the correct answer.

Football between Reading and Oxford in 2000, and a Reading defender hits a back pass to keeper Phil Whitehead. What happened next?

- **a** Whitehead goes to kick the ball clear but it hits a divot and loops into the net.
- **b** Whitehead is behind the goal line receiving treatment! He runs on the field trailing a length of bandage and just manages to clear the ball in time.
- **c** Whitehead tries to prevent the ball going for a corner, but ends up stopping it on the goal-line to give Oxford an easy goal.

Rugby Union between Ireland and South Africa at Lansdowne Road in 2000. Ronan O'Gara takes a penalty. What happened next?

- **a** The kick hits a goal post and lands by the dead ball line. Brian O'Driscoll touches it down, but the referee thinks the ball has gone dead and disallows the try.
- **b** The kick goes wide but both line judges raise their flags and the referee awards the three points.
- **c** The kick hits the crossbar, rebounds back into O'Gara's hands and he drops a goal! The Springboks protest but the score counts.

SCOREBOARD		

round seven — home or away

american football	Former Chicago Bears defensive lineman William Perry was better-known by which nickname?

judo	Which Briton claimed the 1981 World Championship in the under-78kg class?
football	Which current Premiership manager also appeared as a player for the same club in their only FA Cup final appearance?
rugby union	Name the Frenchman who appeared in the first three European finals.

SCOREBOARD

round eight — captain's away

True or False? Here are the names of some boxers from over the years, and all you have to do is decide which of them are impostors.

1 Ray 'Boom Boom' Mancini.
Peter 'Young Rump Steak' Crawley.
Arthur 'Rock Hands' Robson.
Verno 'The Inferno' Phillips.
'Piano Mover' Jones.
Sheila 'La Rockette' Stallone.
Lyndon 'The Man of' Steele.
Harry 'The Human Windmill' Greb.

SCOREBOARD

round nine — mystery guest

Can you guess the identity of these sporting stars from the four clues below? The more clues you need, the fewer points you get.

1 I compete in the same sport as my brother. (4 points)
We both won major races in 2001, but I was the reigning champion. (3 points)
We're from Germany. (2 points)
Mika Hakkinen is my great rival. (1 point)

2 I was born in England in 1957 and turned professional in 1978. (4 points)
I won my first world title in 1981. (3 points)
I went on to win six world titles, the last one in 1989 with an 18–3 defeat of John Parrott. (2 points)
I was involved in a famous final in 1985, when I lost 18–17 to Dennis Taylor on the black ball. (1 point)

SCOREBOARD		

round ten — on the buzzer

In all of these answers, both the Christian and surnames begin with the same letter.

1 Cricket – Who was the Sri Lankan spinner who took 16 wickets against England in 1998?

2 Football – Who scored twice in the 1998 World Cup final?

3 Rowing – Name the Italian Olympic champion whose two brothers have also won gold medals.

4 Golf – Which South African won two US Opens in the '90s?

5 Rugby Union – Who captained England to the Grand Slam in 1980?

6 Snooker – Which player won his only world title in 1986?

7 Football – Name the England striker who moved from Coventry to Aston Villa in 1998.

8 Tennis – Who is the youngest winner of the Wimbledon men's singles title?

9 Cricket – Which England batsman scored 333 in 1990?

10 Snooker – Who won the last of his six world titles in 1978?

11 Athletics – Who currently holds the British high-jump record?

12 Football – Who was the eleventh England manager?

13 Tennis – Name the 1992 Wimbledon men's singles champion.

14 Swimming – Who was Britain's only individual medallist at the 1998 world championships?

SCOREBOARD		

game **44**

round one — name the year

The following events all happened in the same year, but which one?

1 Wigan beat St Helen's 13–8 to win the Challenge Cup for the fourth successive time.
England complete the Grand Slam in Rugby Union.
The Davis Cup Final is won by underdogs France who defeat the USA.
Ian Baker-Finch wins the Open at Royal Birkdale.
Paul Gascoigne injures himself in the FA Cup Final.

Now for the second year:

2 David Bedford set a world record of 27 minutes 30.8 seconds in the 10,000 metres.
This is the year of the Wimbledon boycott: Jan Kodes beat Alex Metreveli in a somewhat devalued championship.
England fail to qualify for the World Cup in October after a 1–1 draw with Poland.
Liverpool win the League and UEFA Cup.
Muhammad Ali has his jaw broken in his defeat by Ken Norton.

SCOREBOARD

round two — picture board

Take a look at picture F on page 3 of Picture Board 2. Who is it?

Take a look at picture F on page 4 of Picture Board 2. Who is it?

SCOREBOARD

round three — twenty sporting questions

20 questions where all the answers begin win the letter D.

1 Which England scrum-half scored for the British Lions against South Africa in the first Test in 1997?

2 Which team play at Pride Park?

3 In which sport were Isabelle Werth and Gigolo Olympic champions in 1996?

4 In which city did Liverpool clinch the 2001 UEFA Cup?

5 Which Spaniard won the 1988 Tour de France?

6 Who rode Lord Gyllene to victory in the 1997 Grand National?

7 What nationality is Wilson Kipketer, who won the 1997 800m World Championship?

8 Name the Dutch goalkeeper who played in the 1998 League Cup final for Chelsea.

9 In which South African city did England play all their group matches in the 1995 Rugby Union World Cup?

10 Who was champion jockey on the flat in 1994 and 1995?

11 Who won the 1991 US PGA Championship?

12 In which sport was John Part a world champion in 1994?

13 Ice hockey – From which American city do the Red Wings come?

14 Which striker was top scorer in the third, second and first divisions in consecutive seasons in the 1980s?

15 Which Scottish club play their home matches at Dens Park?

16 In which event was Dan O'Brien of the USA Olympic champion in 1996?

17 Which county won the 1993 Benson & Hedges Cup?

18 Who beat Mike Tyson in 1990 to claim the WBC Heavyweight belt?

19 Who was world snooker champion six times during the 1980s?

20 Who scored the only goal of the 1978 European Cup final?

SCOREBOARD		

round four — sporting links

1 What connects these Olympic champions: Emil Zatopek, who won a unique treble of long distance golds in 1952; hammer-thrower Harold Connolly, who triumphed in 1956; and Valery Borzov, who won the 100 and 200 metres in 1972?

2 What connects the fifth Test between Australia and South Africa at Melbourne in 1932, Greg Norman's victory at the 1993 Open and Eddie Charlton's defeat by John Parrott at the 1992 World Championships?

SCOREBOARD

round five — where am I?

From the following two clues you must work out which place is being described.

1 Where in England is the traditional pre-Wimbledon ladies' singles tournament held, and where do the Eagles compete in speedway's Elite League?

2 George Best was born in the city which is home to Windsor Park, but where is it?

SCOREBOARD

round six — what happened next?

All you have to do in this round is decide which of the three options is the correct answer.

Baseball, and the New York Mets against the San Francisco Giants. Benny Agbayani of the Mets catches the ball in the outfield. What happened next?

- **a** The marching band think the innings is over and come on to the field! While Agbayani is trying to wade through them, the Giants score a run!
- **b** Agbayani thinks the innings is over and gives the ball to a fan in the crowd. While he is retrieving it, the Giants score two runs!
- **c** The runner on third base thinks the innings is over and starts to walk slowly off the field! On his way Agbayani tags him out, costing the Giants a run!

Swimming from the Sydney Olympics, and the start of the first heat in the Men's 100 metres freestyle. What happened next?

- **a** Four competitors had failed to turn up, guaranteeing the others a place in the next round…but officials still insisted that the race should be swum anyway!
- **b** Two competitors are disqualified for false starts, leaving one swimmer to complete the course in the slowest time on record!
- **c** The officials have inadvertently entered nine competitors but the pool only has eight lanes! So one hapless swimmer has to compete by himself.

SCOREBOARD		

round seven — home or away

american football In which city would you find a baseball team called the Reds and an American Football team called the Bengals?

athletics Which high-jumper broke his national record in the final of the 1999 World Championships in Seville, but did not set a personal best?

football Which defender joined Aston Villa for £3 million in 1998 but left without playing a game?

cricket Who made his Test debut for England in 1999, despite having played for a different country in the World Cup earlier in the year?

SCOREBOARD

round eight — captain's away

Here are two riddles from the often unusual world of sport. Can you tell me...

1 Can you name the first Yorkshire captain to tour Australia?

2 How many legs would you find on a snooker table?

SCOREBOARD

round nine — mystery guest

Can you guess the identity of these sporting stars from the four clues below? The more clues you need, the fewer points you get.

1 I was born in 1967 and won five Olympic gold medals. (4 points)
From May 1990 to June 1992 I was unbeaten over 200 metres in 32 successive races. (3 points)
In 1995 and 1996 I won gold medals over 200 and 400 metres. (2 points)
I hold world records in both events and the 4 x 400 metres relay. (1 point)

2 I was born in Czechoslovakia in 1956, but I also represented the USA. (4 points)
I used to partner Pam Shriver in doubles. (3 points)
I won nine Wimbledon singles titles. (2 points)
My last title came in 1990. (1 point)

SCOREBOARD

round ten — on the buzzer

All of these answers are sporting pundits

1 Football – Who managed Coventry City to the Second Division title in 1967?

2 Golf – Who followed his father Percy into Britain's Ryder Cup team?

3 Cricket – Which former England captain made a notorious flight in a Tiger Moth?

4 Football – Which England World Cup star made a hit record with Chris Waddle?

5 Motor racing – Which British former Grand Prix driver won the Le Mans 24 Hours in 1990?

6 Athletics – Which Olympic gold medallist presented Record Breakers?

7 Football – Who said on Match of the Day, 'For the benefit of those of you watching in black and white, Spurs are in the yellow shirts.'?

8 National Hunt racing – Who shared the 1982 Champion Jockey's title with Peter Scudamore?

9 Tennis – Who won the ladies' singles at the 1976 French Open?

10 Football – In 1999, who had to cut short his holiday in the West Indies to manage Nottingham Forest?

11 Snooker – Who won the 1979 UK title, and can now be seen on *Big Break*?

12 Cricket – Which Australian spinner took 248 Test wickets in the '50s and '60s?

13 Football – Which model Premiership player played 50 games for Brest?

14 Athletics – Which famous commentator won the Manchester Mile in 1949?

SCOREBOARD		

game 1

round one
name the year

1 *1979*
2 *1996*

round two
picture board

1 *Ally McCoist wearing Rangers' tartan after Scotland's 1–1 draw with Norway, France 98*
2 *England's Andrew Caddick relaxes during the 1998 West Indies tour*

round three
twenty sporting questions

1 *Uruguay*
2 *Argentina*
3 *Davor Suker*
4 *Mexico*
5 *1958*
6 *Italy*
7 *Peter Beardsley*
8 *Morocco*
9 *Andreas Brehme*
10 *13*
11 *Norman Whiteside*
12 *Brazil*
13 *Algeria*
14 *Roger Milla*
15 *Lothar Matthaus*
16 *First match held indoors*
17 *Score in every match of the tournament*
18 *He was the Russian linesman*
19 *They were the names of the official mascots*
20 *62*

round four
sporting links

1 *They're all qualified doctors*
2 *They each have a parent who is an ordained minister of religion*

round five
where am I?

1 *Sheffield*
2 *Cardiff*

round six
what happened next?

1 *a)*
2 *c)*

round seven
home or away

1 *Teddy Sheringham*
2 *Neil Jenkins*
3 *Allan Border*
4 *Wentworth*

round eight
captain's away

1 *True*
2 *False*
3 *False*
4 *True*
5 *False*
6 *True*
7 *True*
8 *False*

round nine
mystery guest

1 *Terry Butcher*
2 *Martina Hingis*

round ten
quick-fire

1 *Loftus Road*
2 *Cricket*
3 *Real Madrid*
4 *Doncaster*
5 *Leicester Tigers*
6 *Millennium Stadium, Cardiff*
7 *Chicago Bears*
8 *Bristol*
9 *Stamford Bridge*
10 *Sarajevo*
11 *Roland Garros*
12 *St Andrews*
13 *Turin*
14 *Switzerland (St Moritz)*
15 *Castleford Tigers*
16 *Oslo*
17 *Chicago*
18 *Lords*
19 *Neath*
20 *Darts*

game 2

round one
name the year

1 *1996*
2 *1994*

round two
picture board

1 *South Africa's Allan Donald using a rather larger ball than usual in practice for the 1999 Cricket World Cup Super Six game against Pakistan*
2 *Greg Rusedski on his way to defeat by Slava Dosedel in the first round of the 2000 French Open*

round three
twenty sporting questions

1 *John Higgins*
2 *Hibernian*
3 *Andy Goram*
4 *Jocky Wilson*
5 *Yorkshire*
6 *Fife*
7 *Allan Wells*
8 *Finlay Calder*
9 *Partick Thistle*
10 *Liz McColgan*
11 *Scottish Claymores*
12 *Curling*
13 *St Johnstone*
14 *Eric Liddell*
15 *Stuart McCall*
16 *Sandy Lyle*
17 *Graeme Souness*
18 *Alan Tait*
19 *Sailing*
20 *St Andrews*

round four
sporting links

1 *They've all been in the army*
2 *They've all represented their countries at more than one sport*

round five
where am I?

1 *Paris*
2 *Brisbane*

round six
what happened next?

1 *a)*
2 *c)*

round seven
home or away

1 *Dennis Wise*
2 *Riddick Bowe*
3 *Steve Backley*
4 *Pat Rafter, who won the 1997 and 1998 US Open titles*

round eight
captain's away

1 *Randy Duck is a basketball player and guard is his position. He returned to the London Towers after a loan spell with the Dallas Mavericks*
2 *Augusta National golf course. They're the names of holes*

round nine
mystery guest

1 *Joe Calzaghe*
2 *Graeme Hick*

round ten
on the buzzer

1 *Sonia O'Sullivan*
2 *Long jump*
3 *Yugoslavia*
4 *Modern pentathlon*
5 *Marie-Jose Perec*
6 *Indonesia*
7 *Canoeing*
8 *Maurice Greene*
9 *Athens*
10 *Mozambique*
11 *Equestrianism*
12 *Spain*
13 *Liverpool*
14 *The Derby*
15 *Bill Beaumont*
16 *Boris Becker*
17 *West Indies*
18 *Wimbledon*
19 *Judo*
20 *Michael Thomas*

game 3

round one
name the year

1 *1993*
2 *1995*

round two
picture board

1 *England's Michael Owen reacts after a narrow miss in 2000's friendly against Brazil*
2 *Lindsay Davenport, shortly before crashing out of the 2000 French Open in the first round*

round three
twenty sporting questions

1 *Everton*
2 *Los Angeles*
3 *Ski jumping*
4 *Barry McGuigan*
5 *Bob Champion*
6 *Marco van Basten*
7 *Severiano Ballesteros*
8 *London Marathon*
9 *Headingley*
10 *Jayne Torvill and Christopher Dean*
11 *New Zealand*
12 *Squash*
13 *Liverpool*
14 *The Derby*
15 *Bill Beaumont*
16 *Boris Becker*
17 *West Indies*
18 *Wimbledon*
19 *Judo*
20 *Michael Thomas*

round four
sporting links

1 *They've all competed with or against their fathers. Paul rode Bobbyjo, trained by dad Tommy, to win the '99 Grand National; Eidur came on as a substitute for his dad Arnor in a full international; Neil played his father Geoff in two ranking events in 1986*
2 *They all have degrees*

round five
where am I?

1 *Wales*
2 *Sweden*

round six
what happened next?

1 *b)*
2 *a)*

round seven
home or away

1 *Jose-Maria Olazabal*
2 *Nick Barmby*
3 *Glenn McGrath*
4 *Liz McColgan*

round eight
captain's away

1 *Santa Claus. It won the Derby, ridden by Scobie Breasley*
2 *He was the referee. He stuck out a leg and deflected the ball past Plymouth 'keeper Pat Dunne to win the game 1–0 for Barrow*

round nine
mystery guest

1 *Diego Maradona*
2 *Steve Backley*

round ten
on the buzzer

1 *Tim Curtis*
2 *Curtis Robb*
3 *Rob Andrew*
4 *Drew Henry*
5 *Henry Paul*
6 *Paul Allen*
7 *Alan Sugar*
8 *Sugar Ray Leonard*
9 *Leonard (Len) Ganley*
10 *Gareth Barry*
11 *Barry John*
12 *John Charles*
13 *Charlie (Charles) George*
14 *George Graham*
15 *Graham Henry*
16 *Henry Paul*
17 *Paul Lawrie*
18 *Lawrie Sanchez*
19 *(Arantxa) Sanchez Vicario*

game 4

round one
name the year

1 *1996*
2 *1991*

round two
picture board

1 *Fabien Barthez celebrates France's entry into the Euro 2000 final after victory over Portugal in the semi-final*
2 *Jo Durie in action at Wimbledon in 1984*

round three
twenty sporting questions

1 *Alan Smith*
2 *Robert Jones*
3 *Ann Jones*
4 *Robin Smith*
5 *Alan Jones*
6 *Tommy Smith*
7 *Roy Jones*
8 *Dean Jones*
9 *Steve Jones*
10 *Michelle Smith*
11 *Calvin Smith*
12 *Leeds*
13 *Tom Smith*
14 *Marion Jones*
15 *Boxing*
16 *Ian Jones*
17 *Coventry City*
18 *Steve Smith*
19 *Rob Jones*
20 *Brighton & Hove Albion*

round four
sporting links

1 *They're all former policemen*
2 *They were all born in Devon*

round five
where am I?

1 *Chester*
2 *Northampton*

round six
what happened next?

1 *(b)*
2 *a)*

round seven
home or away

1 *John Lowe, who won titles in 1979, 1987 and 1993*
2 *Leroy Burrell*
3 *Peter Scudamore*
4 *Roy Keane*

round eight
captain's away

1. *The moon! His agent has two tickets for a passenger space shuttle flight in 2002, but Sunderland insist they aren't liable for any mishap he may suffer on the way!*
2. *The Hawaii Ironman, the world's oldest triathlon, which was first held in 1978*

round nine
mystery guest

1. *Nasser Hussain*
2. *Ruud Gullit*

round ten
on the buzzer

1. *Chris Boardman*
2. *Nigel Benn*
3. *Nicky Weaver*
4. *Roy Jones*
5. *Sally Gunnell*
6. *Lance Armstrong*
7. *Gianfranco Zola*
8. *Allan Wells*
9. *Steve Collins*
10. *Steve Davis*
11. *Shane Warne*
12. *Emile Heskey*
13. *Yvonne Murray*
14. *Yannick Noah*
15. *Harold 'Dickie' Bird*
16. *Daley Thompson*
17. *Nelson Piquet*
18. *Teddy Sheringham*
19. *'Marvelous' Marvin Hagler*
20. *Ronnie O'Sullivan*

game 5

round one
name the year

1. *1987*
2. *1994*

round two
picture board

1. *Anke Huber in her first-round match against Meilen Tu in the 2000 US Open tournament*
2. *Arsenal's Lee Dixon tries his hand at basketball during a training session*

round three
twenty sporting questions

1. *Manchester United*
2. *Roberto di Matteo*
3. *Hereford United*
4. *Liverpool*
5. *Trevor Brooking*
6. *Ian Rush*
7. *Be sent off*
8. *Tottenham*
9. *John Aldridge*
10. *Des Walker*
11. *Villa Park*
12. *Paul Rideout*
13. *Tranmere Rovers*
14. *Watford*
15. *John Barnes*
16. *Cardiff City*
17. *Eric Cantona*
18. *Yeovil Town*
19. *Six*
20. *Coventry City*

round four
sporting links

1. *Their brothers all played League football. Glenn's brother Carl played for Barnet, Mike's brother Steve reached the FA Cup final with Brighton, while Peter's brother Shaun played for five different League clubs*
2. *They were all against Romanians. David's penalty for the Republic of Ireland knocked them out of the 1990 World Cup, Jeremy Guscott scored on his international debut in Bucharest in 1989, while Bjorn Borg beat Ilie Nastase in 1976*

round five
where am I?

1. *Derby*
2. *Oxford*

round six
what happened next?

1. *b)*
2. *c)*

round seven
home or away

1. *Kevin Darley*
2. *Mark Hughes – the Welshman has won four (three with Manchester United and one with Chelsea)*
3. *Muttiah Muralitharan*
4. *Triple jump – Jonathan Edwards who claimed gold, Larry Achike who finished fifth and Phillips Idowu, sixth*

round eight
captain's away

1. *American football. Splitting the pile is when a player runs through the line of scrimmage; grinding it out is when a player keeps the ball in play in order to run the clock dead; and a muff is when a player juggles the ball as he catches it rather than taking it cleanly*
2. *Baseball. A fast pitch is known as 'throwing heat', going round the horn is to score a home run, and a blooper is a ball that's hit but doesn't go out of the infield.*

round nine
mystery guest

1. *Ronaldo*
2. *Alec Stewart*

round ten
on the buzzer

1. *'You've got my permission to shoot me.'*
2. *'Liverpool reserves.'*
3. *'The rest I just squandered.'*
4. *'I sting like a bee.'*
5. *'I'd love it if we beat them – love it.'*
6. *'They're expecting sardines to be thrown into the sea.'*
7. *'I can't speak English.'*
8. *'Spurs are the team in yellow.'*
9. *'Another clip round the ear'ole.'*

game 6

round one
name the year

1. *1992*
2. *1985*

round two
picture board

1. *England's Steve McManaman phones home: a 2000 friendly against France*
2. *Leicester Tigers' Martin Johnson wins the ball in a line-out in their clash with Northampton Saints in Zurich Premiership One, 2 September 2000*

round three
twenty sporting questions

1 *Stephen Roche*
2 *Roy Keane*
3 *Lansdowne Road, Dublin*
4 *Ken Doherty*
5 *Eamonn Loughran*
6 *Christy O'Connor Jnr*
7 *Eamonn Coghlan*
8 *Boxing*
9 *Ronnie Whelan*
10 *Jack Charlton*
11 *Keith Wood*
12 *Kerry*
13 *Sonia O'Sullivan*
14 *Shamrock Rovers*
15 *David O'Leary*
16 *Ruby Walsh*
17 *Ray Houghton*
18 *Paul McGrath*
19 *Leopardstown*
20 *Steve Heighway*

round four
sporting links
1 *They were all born in Barnsley*
2 *They all ended 9–0. It was Spurs' record League victory, Yugoslavia equalled the World Cup record score, and Manchester United set a new Premiership record*

round five
where am I?
1 *Greece*
2 *South Africa*

round six
what happened next?
1 *a)*
2 *b)*

round seven
home or away
1 *Cedric Pioline*
2 *Sergio Garcia – aged 19*
3 *Jody Sheckter in 1979*
4 *Wentworth*

round eight
captain's away
1 *Basketball – A Garbage Man cleans up from around the basket, a Cherry Picker is a player who claims free balls from around the hoop, a double pump is when a player fakes to pass twice while in the air and an alley-oop is when the wingman catches the ball in mid-air and slams it in*
2 *Table tennis – a chop is a type of shot, and a sandwich a design of bat.*

round nine
mystery guest
1 *George Graham*
2 *Jonny Wilkinson*

round ten
on the buzzer
1 *FORE!*
2 *9*
3 *1*
4 *21*
5 *Didier Six*
6 *8*
7 *10*
8 *21 (3 and 18)*
9 *5 (Paul Scholes, Steve McManaman, Alan Shearer (2) and Michael Owen)*
10 *George Foreman*
11 *2*
12 *17*
13 *0*
14 *2*
15 *7*
16 *4*

game 7

round one
name the year
1 *1989*
2 *1986*

round two
picture board
1 *Great Britain's silver medalist Steve Backley can't look after missing out on gold in the javelin final at the Sydney Olympics*
2 *The USA's Maurice Greene holds his golden boots aloft after winning the 100m final at Sydney*

round three
twenty sporting questions
1 *Mexico City*
2 *Jason Queally*
3 *USA*
4 *Donovan Bailey*
5 *Cameroon*
6 *Paris, 1924*
7 *Canoeing*
8 *Greg Louganis*
9 *Felix Savon*
10 *Long jump*
11 *Munich, 1972*
12 *Allan Wells*
13 *Muhammad Ali*
14 *Algerian*
15 *One*
16 *Andy Holmes*
17 *High-jump*
18 *Kathy Freeman*
19 *Carl Lewis*
20 *1948*

round four
sporting links
1 *35*
2 *16*

round five
where am I?
1 *Birmingham*
2 *Edinburgh*

round six
what happened next?
1 *a)*
2 *c)*

round seven
home or away
1 *Graeme Hick*
2 *Guin and Miriam Batten*
3 *Robin Reid*
4 *Tony Adams*

round eight
captain's away
1 *Boxing – Douglas was better known as the Marquis of Queensbury*
2 *Underwater hockey – or Octopush! The squid is the puck; the gully is the goal*

round nine
mystery guest
1 *Dennis Wise*
2 *Jeremy Guscott*

round ten
on the buzzer
1 *Kriss Akabusi*
2 *David Beckham*
3 *David Campese*
4 *Dundee United*
5 *Peter Ebdon*
6 *Cathy Freeman*
7 *Gaelic football*
8 *Graham Henry*
9 *Imola*
10 *Marion Jones*
11 *Kilmarnock*
12 *Lord's*
13 *Modern Pentathlon*
14 *Ilie Nastase*
15 *Oakwell*
16 *Matt Pinsent*
17 *Queens Park Rangers*
18 *Rallying*
19 *Graeme Souness*

game 8

round one
name the year
1 *1984*
2 *1990*

round two
picture board
1 *West Indies' Curtly Ambrose leaves the pitch for the last time in a Test, on the fifth day of the Fifth Test in 2000*
2 *Great Britain's Jason Queally wins gold in the Men's 1km Time Trial at the Sydney Olympics*

round three
twenty sporting questions
1 *Manchester United*
2 *Atlanta*
3 *Martina Hingis*
4 *Carl Llewellyn*
5 *Brian Lara*
6 *Australia*
7 *John Parrott*
8 *Damon Hill*
9 *Nick Faldo*
10 *Rangers*
11 *100 metres*
12 *George Foreman*
13 *Italy*
14 *Bayern Munich*
15 *Squash*
16 *Wigan*
17 *Buffalo*
18 *Alan Shearer*
19 *Carnoustie*
20 *Anil Kumble*

round four
sporting links
1 *41*
2 *23*

round five
where am I?
1 *New York*
2 *Rotterdam*

round six
what happened next?
1 *b)*
2 *a)*

round seven
home or away
1 *John McEnroe*
2 *Katerina Witt*
3 *John Barnes: Watford in 1984, Liverpool in 1988 and 1996, Newcastle in 1998*
4 *Javed Miandad of Pakistan: he was a winner in 1992*

round eight
captain's away
1 *Aston Villa, Charlton Athletic, Liverpool, Northampton Town, York City*
2 *Crewe Alexandra, Exeter City, Halifax Town, Oxford United, Wrexham*

round nine
mystery guest
1 *Gianluca Vialli*
2 *Phil Taylor*

round ten
on the buzzer
1 *January – Andre Agassi*
2 *February – Italy*
3 *March – Oxford*
4 *April – Joe Swail*
5 *May – Roberto Di Matteo*
6 *June – 15, a record*
7 *July – Lance Armstrong*
8 *August – Mark Venus*
9 *September – Kathy Freeman*
10 *October – Ally McCoist*
11 *November – Australia*
12 *December – John Higgins*

game 9

round one
name the year
1 *1991*
2 *1992*

round two
picture board
1 *Great Britain's hockey heroine Jane Sixsmith takes a tumble in a preliminary game at the Sydney Olympics*
2 *Great Britain's Steve Redgrave gets cleaned up after the qualifying round of the men's coxless fours at the Sydney Olympics*

round three
twenty sporting questions
1 *Chelsea*
2 *Liverpool*
3 *Five*
4 *London Towers*
5 *Lords*
6 *Saracens*
7 *University Boat Race*
8 *The All-England Tennis Championships, Wimbledon*
9 *Charlton Athletic*
10 *Scott Gibbs*
11 *Fredrik Ljungberg*
12 *London Welsh*
13 *Tottenham Hotspur*
14 *Sheffield Eagles*
15 *Richard Krajicek*
16 *Jimmy White*
17 *Muttiah Muralitharan*
18 *London Marathon*
19 *Twickenham*
20 *West Ham United*

round four
sporting links
1 *b) Ernie Hunt – his famous goal was in 1970*
d) Gareth Edwards – his try was in 1973
c) Seb Coe broke the 800m, 1500m and mile records in 1979
a) Ian Botham helped England win the Ashes in 1981
2 *c) Boris and Steffi were victorious in 1989*
b) Graham made his 'triple Nelson' in 1990
d) Britain's relay team won in 1991
a) Alan scored on his debut in 1992

round five
where am I?
1 *Chester-le-Street*
2 *Doncaster*

round six
what happened next?
1 *b)*
2 *a)*

round seven
home or away
1 *Villa Park*
2 *Dean Macey: his silver medal-winning 8,556 points in the decathlon included six individual personal bests*
3 *Nick Faldo: he appeared in every Ryder Cup from 1977 to 1997*
4 *Martina Navratilova: she was a Czech in 1978 and 1979, but an American when she won from 1982–87 and in 1990*

round eight
captain's away
1 *Those were the two occasions a bowler has taken all 10 wickets in a Test innings: Jim Laker for England against Australia in 1956, and Anil Kumble for India against Pakistan – both spinners. Mr Stokes is believed to be the only person present at both*
2 *Beach volleyball – The International Volleyball Federation thinks it will get the sport more coverage*

round nine
mystery guest
1 *Alan Shearer*
2 *Roger Black*

round ten
on the buzzer
1 *D*
2 *Marco FU*
2 *Robert LEE*
4 *Brian LARA*
5 *Tiger WOODS*
6 *Emile HESKEY*
7 *AINTREE*
8 *Michael ATHERTON*
9 *WIMBLEDON*
10 *DERBYSHIRE*
11 *Martina NAVRATILOVA*
12 *MARK CALCAVECCHIA*
13 *INVERNESS CALEDONIAN THISTLE*

game 10

round one
name the year
1 *1995*
2 *1986*

round two
picture board
1 *Australia's Cathy Freeman focusses on the race ahead in the finals of the women's 400m at Sydney 2000*
2 *Surrey's Ben Hollioake works out on the cycling machine during a visit to the Oval by former PM John Major*

round three
twenty sporting questions
1 *Jose-Maria Olazabal*
2 *Real Madrid*
3 *Tour de France*
4 *Barcelona*
5 *Conchita Martinez*
6 *Uruguay*
7 *Liverpool*
8 *Rallying*
9 *1500 metres*
10 *John Toshack*
11 *Valderrama*
12 *Carlos Moya*
13 *Steve McManaman*
14 *False: only a demonstration sport on three occasions*
15 *Severiano Ballesteros*
16 *Seville*
17 *Albert Ferrer*
18 *Sergio Garcia*
19 *Pedro Delgado*
20 *Athletico Madrid*

round four
sporting links
1 *Steve Waugh: 'Tugga' (as in Tug-of-Waugh!)*
Nigel Benn: 'The Dark Destroyer'
Ted Hankey: 'The Count'
Sue Barker: 'The Paignton Peach'
2 *Craig Stadler: 'The Walrus'*
Joe Swail: 'The Outlaw' (think Clint Eastwood films!)
Maurice Greene: 'The Kansas Cannonball' or 'Fly-mo'
Ally McCoist: 'Alison' ('Super Ally' came later!)

round five
where am I?
1 *Switzerland*
2 *Finland*

round six
what happened next?
1 *a)*
2 *b)*

round seven
home or away
1 *Jennifer Capriati*
2 *Lance Armstrong*
3 *Steve Renouf*
4 *Thomas 'The Hitman' Hearns*

round eight
captain's away
1 *Dundee, Dundee United, Queen's Park, Queen of the South, Aberdeen, Greenock Morton*
2 *Glamorgan, Kent, Somerset, Surrey, Durham*

round nine
mystery guest
1 *Bryan Robson*
2 *Robert Howley*

round ten
on the buzzer
1 *Terry BUTCHER*
2 *Ian BAKER-Finch*
3 *Gilles de BILDE*
4 *Stephanie COOK*
5 *Phil TAYLOR*
6 *Jonny REP*
7 *Paul HUNTER*
8 *Wendell SAILOR*
9 *Darren CLARKE*
10 *Alan JUDGE*
11 *Duncan FLETCHER*
12 *David SEAMAN*

game 11

round one
name the year
1 *1988*
2 *1993*

round two
picture board
1 *Jean Alesi jogging on the track at Melbourne before the opening Grand Prix of 2001*
2 *England's Graeme Hick can't bear to look at an incident during training for the 2000 Third Test vs. Pakistan*

round three
twenty sporting questions
1 *Virginia Wade*
2 *West Germany*
3 *Gareth Edwards*
4 *One*
5 *Sevriano Ballesteros*
6 *James Hunt*
7 *Ian Botham*
8 *Red Rum*
9 *Montreal*
10 *Arsenal*
11 *Figure skating*
12 *Alex Higgins*
13 *Nijinsky*
14 *George Foreman*
15 *Argentina*
16 *West Indies*
17 *Bjorn Borg*
18 *Finnish*
19 *David Wilkie*
20 *Emlyn Hughes*

round four
sporting links
1 *Emile IVANHOE Heskey*
Laurence BRUNO NERO Dallaglio
Peter BOLESLAW Schmeichel
Bob DYLAN Willis (he added the Dylan in honour of the musician)
2 *Mark EVERTON Walters*
Ronnie ANTONIO O'Sullivan
Kriss KEZIE UCHE CHUKWU DURU Akabusi
Alistair MURDOCH McCoist

round five
where am I?
1 *Oslo*
2 *Chicago*

round six
what happened next?
1 *b)*
2 *a)*

round seven
home or away
1 *Neil Jenkins*
2 *Terry Venables – with Spurs in 1991*

3 *Carl Llewelyn – on Party Politics in 1992 and Earth Summit in 1998*
4 *Australia*

round eight
captain's away
1 *Pontefract, Ascot, Newton Abbot, Newmarket*
2 *Crystal Palace, Plymouth Argyle, Rochdale, Port Vale*

round nine
mystery guest
1 *David Seaman*
2 *Peter Scudamore*

round ten
on the buzzer
1 *Zaire*
2 *Yellow*
3 *X-tra time!*
4 *John 'Boy' Walton*
5 *Terry Venables*
6 *Ukraine*
7 *Table tennis*
8 *Sailing*
9 *Rallying*
10 *Queens Park*
11 *Pakistan*
12 *Oxford United*

game 12

round one
name the year
1 *1973*
2 *1981*

round two
picture board
1 *Martin O'Neill, in his playing days for Norwich City, in a Division One clash with Luton Town in April 1982*
2 *Substitute Dwight Yorke wraps up warm at Manchester United's second-stage Champions League game vs. Valencia*

round three
twenty sporting questions
1 *Mark Venus*
2 *Villa Park*
3 *Wycombe Wanderers*
4 *Mark Viduka*
5 *Teddy Sheringham*
6 *Henrik Larsson*
7 *Bayern Munich*
8 *Barnet*
9 *Gary McAllister*
10 *Birmingham*
11 *Inter Milan*
12 *Jean Tigana*
13 *Harry Redknapp*
14 *Terry Venables*
15 *David Beckham*
16 *Steven Gerrard*
17 *Valencia*
18 *Chris Powell*
19 *Celtic*
20 *90*

round four
sporting links
1 *Ray Reardon, 'Dracula' or 'Plod' (he used to be a policeman): Didier Deschamps, 'The Water Carrier': Lester Piggott, 'The Long Fellow': Konishiki, 'The Dump Truck'*
2 *Anthony Hamilton, 'The Sheriff of Pottingham': Darren Anderton, 'Shaggy' or 'Sicknote': Martina Hingis, 'The Swiss Miss': Joel Garner, 'Big Bird'*

round five
where am I?
1 *Bristol*
2 *Ipswich*

round six
what happened next?
1 *a)*
2 *b)*

round seven
home or away
1 *Gail Devers*
2 *Marat Safin*
3 *Peter Ebdon*
4 *Kevin Ratcliffe*

round eight
captain's away
1 *Sir Geoff Hurst. He played one first-class game for Essex in 1962*
2 *Steve Renouf. He joined Wigan in December '99 from the Brisbane Broncos, after their prop forward Shane Webcke agreed to look after his animals*

round nine
mystery guest
1 *Sam Torrance*
2 *Prince Naseem Hamed*

round ten
on the buzzer
1 *Nasser Hussain*
2 *Seve Ballesteros*
3 *Kilmarnock*
4 *Tony Jarrett*
5 *Nigel Benn*
6 *Argentina*
7 *Robbie Fowler*
8 *Desert Orchid*
9 *Gliding*
10 *Robert Weir*
11 *Dickie Bird*
12 *Serena Williams*
13 *Imran Sherwani*
14 *San Francisco 49ers*
15 *Liverpool*

game 13

round one
name the year
1 *1982*
2 *1966*

round two
picture board
1 *Liverpool's keeper Sander Westerveld misses Darren Purse's penalty during the 2000–01 Worthington Cup final vs. Birmingham City*
2 *Jennifer Capriati battles Lindsay Davenport in the 2001 Australian Open*

round three
twenty sporting questions
1 *Andre Agassi*
2 *Jonathan Edwards*
3 *Paul Ince*
4 *Mark O'Meara*
5 *Nicolas Anelka*
6 *Rob Andrew*
7 *Richard Illingworth*
8 *Ronnie O'Sullivan*
9 *John Aldridge*
10 *Martin Offiah*
11 *Derek Underwood*
12 *Michael Owen*
13 *Peter Ebdon*
14 *Ron Atkinson*
15 *Shaun Edwards*
16 *Kriss Akabusi*
17 *Curtley Ambrose*
18 *Stefan Edberg*
19 *Ben Ainslie*
20 *Jean Alesi*

round four
sporting links
1 *They've all released records (Andy's was 'Outstanding,' Naseem did 'Walk Like A Champion' and Jo released 'Wimbledon Lawns')*
2 *Their fathers all played for England as well. Alan Butcher won one cap in 1979, Richard Greenwood captained England in the '60s, while Brian Clough won two caps in 1960*

round five
where am I?
1 *Reading*
2 *Hull*

round six
what happened next?
1 *a)*
2 *c)*

round seven
home or away
1 *Jan Zelezny*
2 *Austin Healey*
3 *Didier Auriol*
4 *They were all ridden by amateurs: Capt Bobby Petre in '46, Tommy Smith in '65, Charlie Fenwick in '80, Dick Saunders in '83 and Marcus Armytage on Mr Frisk in 1990*

round eight
captain's away
1 *Baseball, basketball, beach volleyball, football, gymnastics (rhythmic), handball, hockey, softball, table tennis, tennis, volleyball, water polo*

round nine
mystery guest
1 *Allan Donald*
2 *Martin O'Neill*

round ten
on the buzzer
1 *Andre Agassi*
2 *Ally McCoist*
3 *Brisbane Broncos*
4 *Ellen MacArthur*
5 *Mark Venus*
6 *Katharine Merry*
7 *Darts*
8 *Dagenham & Redbridge*
9 *John Parrott*
10 *Baltimore Ravens*
11 *Mark Foster*
12 *Paul Hunter*
13 *Fulham*
14 *St Helen's*
15 *Martin O'Neill*
16 *Tiger Woods*

game 14

round one
name the year
1 *1995*
2 *1970*

round two
picture board
1 *Dan Luger of England pulls out all the stops in a 2000 Rugby Union friendly against Australia*
2 *Liverpool's Robbie Fowler, on the bench in the 2000–01 UEFA Cup third round game against Olympiakos, watches the fans with a borrowed lens*

round three
twenty sporting questions
1 *Mark Williams*
2 *Last Suspect*
3 *Ian Woosnam*
4 *Swansea City*
5 *Colin Jackson*
6 *Mark Hughes*
7 *Australia*
8 *Chepstow*
9 *Richie Burnett*
10 *Barry John*
11 *Mathew Maynard*
12 *Iwan Thomas*
13 *Arsenal*
14 *Long-jump*
15 *Joe Calzaghe*
16 *JPR Williams*
17 *Ian Rush*
18 *Terry Griffiths*
19 *Ice hockey*
20 *Llanelli*

round four
sporting links
1 *Nigel Mansell. The others were all world champions in 1991: Nigel took the Formula One title in 1992*
2 *Steve Backley. The other three are left-handed*

round five
where am I?
1 *Mexico*
2 *Japan*

round six
what happened next?
1 *a)*
2 *b)*

round seven
home or away
1 *Kapil Dev*
2 *Peter Nicol*
3 *Jonny Wilkinson*
4 *David O'Leary – the Leeds manager appeared for Arsenal in 1978, 1979, 1980 and 1993*

round eight
captain's away
1 *Ally Sloper – 1915*
Tipperary Tim – 1928
Wild Man from Borneo – 1895
Doorknocker won the Champion Hurdles in 1956
2 *Gorilla Jones – 1931*
George Chip – 1913
Max Baer became world heavyweight champion in 1934
Dick Tiger – 1962

round nine
mystery guest
1 *Tim Henman*
2 *Peter Schmeichel*

round ten
on the buzzer
1 *David Platt*
2 *Sally Gunnell*
3 *Richie Woodhall*
4 *Mike Catt*
5 *Motherwell*
6 *John Parrott*
7 *Peter Alliss*
8 *Lester Piggott*
9 *Handball*
10 *Phil Tufnell*
11 *Darren Campbell*
12 *Jamie Redknapp*
13 *James Cracknell*
14 *Kim Barnett*

game 15

round one
name the year
1 *1996*
2 *1997*

round two
picture board
1 *Pete Sampras in action against Juan Ignacio Chela, Australian Open, third round, 19 January 2001*
2 *Carlos Moya celebrates defeating Rainer Schuettler to get into the men's quarter-finals of the 2001 Australian Open*

round three
twenty sporting questions
1 *Martin Peters*
2 *Tommy Hutchison*
3 *Jimmy Glass*
4 *Tottenham Hotspur*
5 *Gary Lineker*
6 *Gerd Muller*
7 *Paul Scholes*
8 *Nayim*

9 *Clive Allen*
10 *Ally McCoist*
11 *Albania*
12 *Trevor Brooking (scored the winning goal in the FA Cup Final)*
13 *Zinedine Zidane*
14 *Andy Gray*
15 *AC Milan*
16 *Eric Cantona*
17 *Kevin Phillips*
18 *Denis Law*
19 *Peter Schmeichel*
20 *Everton*

round four
sporting links
1 *Dean Headley – he's been capped for England. His father and grandfather played for the West Indies*
2 *Harry Redknapp*

round five
where am I?
1 *Hampshire*
2 *Yorkshire*

round six
what happened next?
1 *b)*
2 *a)*

round seven
home or away
1 *Joe Bugner*
2 *Andrei Kanchelskis*
3 *Four*
4 *There was a players' strike.*

round eight
captain's away
1 *Rugby Union – the fourth World Cup*
2 *They are the same person. Richard became Renee in 1976*

round nine
mystery guest
1 *Lennox Lewis*
2 *Jimmy White*

round ten
on the buzzer
1 *Old Trafford*
2 *Cricket*
3 *Milan*
4 *Roker Park*
5 *Leicester Tigers*
6 *Millennium Stadium, Cardiff*
7 *Doncaster*
8 *Chicago Bears*
9 *Turin*
10 *King's Lynn*
11 *Gillingham*
12 *Edinburgh*
13 *Saracens*
14 *Cardiff*
15 *Royal Lytham*
16 *Trent Bridge*

game 16

round one
name the year
1 *1991*
2 *1997*

round two
picture board
1 *John 'Boy' Walton celebrates victory over Ted Hankey in the Embassy World Darts Championship final in January 2001*
2 *Saracens' chief executive François Pienaar with his arm in a sling after an injury in his last game for the club in 2000*

round three
twenty sporting questions
1 *Scunthorpe United*
2 *Speedway*
3 *Swedish*
4 *Swansea*
5 *South Africa*
6 *Scudamore (Peter)*
7 *61*
8 *Sixsmith (Jane)*
9 *Seoul*
10 *Spencer (John)*
11 *Shilton (Peter)*
12 *Sheffield*
13 *Squash*
14 *Surrey*
15 *Spinks (Michael and Leon)*
16 *Stockholm*
17 *Scotland*
18 *St Mirren*
19 *San Marino*
20 *Sunderland*

round four
sporting links
1 *Marc Overmars' goal for Arsenal – all the others didn't count. Gwen Torrence was disqualified for running out of her lane, the 1993 National was declared void after a false start and Phil Edmonds' catch came off a no-ball. Overmars' FA Cup goal against Sheffield United was given and the score stood, though Arsenal agreed to replay the game to decide which team went through.*
2 *Michael Owen – all the others were born outside the country they represent. Andrew Caddick was born in New Zealand, Ashia Hansen in the USA and Nasser Hussain in India. Michael was born in Chester*

round five
where am I?
1 *Wrexham*
2 *Stoke*

round six
what happened next?
1 *b)*
2 *a)*

round seven
home or away
1 *The pools panel*
2 *Iva Majoli*
3 *Prince Naseem Hamed*
4 *Eddie Irvine*

round eight
captain's away
1 *True – James Cannon (1956) and Donald Ball (1979–81), Stephen Ball (1992).*
False – Nicky Banger did but no one called Mash!
True – Vic Marks and Thomas Spencer (1891–1893).
True – John Tate and Ron Lyle (John won it in 1979).
True – Emerson for Middlesborough, Paul Lake for Manchester City and Carlton Palmer with five different clubs.
False – Jim Aitken captained Scotland but not the other two!
False
True – Alan Mills of the LA Dodgers and Bret Boone of the San Diego Padres

round nine
mystery guest
1 *Steffi Graf*
2 *Darren Gough*

round ten
on the buzzer
1 *Chris Boardman*
2 *Rapid Vienna*
3 *Party Politics*
4 *Austin Healey*
5 *Wales*
6 *Minnehoma, in 1994*
7 *Hoylake, Royal Liverpool*
8 *Ron Atkinson*
9 *John Conteh*
10 *Waterloo*

11 *Steve Smith*
12 *'The Toffees'*
13 *John Parrott*
14 *Monday (delayed because of a bomb scare on the Saturday)*
15 *Roy Evans*
16 *Boxing*
17 *Everton*

game 17

round one
name the year

1 *1976*
2 *1980*

round two
picture board

1 *Gary Lineker tries for a £1,000,000 hole in one for charity at the Tiger Woods exhibition match in Hyde Park, November 2000 (He failed to reach the green!)*
2 *England's Marcus Trescothick is out for 13 in the Third Test vs. Pakistan, 8 December 2000*

round three
twenty sporting questions

1 *San Francisco*
2 *Tiger Woods*
3 *John Harkes*
4 *Four – all gold*
5 *Evander Holyfield*
6 *Lance Armstrong*
7 *Baseball*
8 *Mavericks*
9 *Justin Leonard*
10 *Steve Cauthen*
11 *Mario Andretti*
12 *Ski-ing*
13 *Matt Biondi*
14 *Venus Williams*
15 *Roy Wegerle*
16 *Michael Johnson*
17 *Miami*
18 *Jack Nicklaus*
19 *Basketball*
20 *Jimmy Connors*

round four
sporting links

1 *They've all won BBC Sports Personality of the Year. David in 1975, Anita in 1962, Princess Anne in 1971 and Gazza in 1990.*
2 *They've all played first-class cricket. Bader for the RAF, Beckett for Dublin University, Sir Alex for Middlesex and Oxford University, while a Julius Caesar played for Surrey in the 19th century!*

round five
where am I?

1 *Milan*
2 *Halifax*

round six
what happened next?

1 *c)*
2 *a)*

round seven
home or away

1 *India*
2 *Brian London, who fought Patterson in 1959 and Ali in 1966.*
3 *Des Smyth*
4 *Philippe Bernat-Salles*

round eight
captain's away

1 *The piece of Evander Holyfield's ear bitten off by Mike Tyson. Tyson was fined 10% of his $30m purse, as well as losing his boxing license*
2 *The baseball hit by Mark McGuire for his 70th home run of 1998*

round nine
mystery guest

1 *Gary Lineker*
2 *Andre Agassi*

round ten
on the buzzer

1 *Ahmed Barada*
2 *Cool Dawn*
3 *Emerson Fittipaldi*
4 *Graeme Hick*
5 *Ingemar Johannson*
6 *Kenny Logan*
7 *Magnus Norman*
8 *Olivier Panis*

game 18

round one
name the year

1 *1972*
2 *1980*

round two
picture board

1 *England's Andy Farrell during the 2000 Rugby World Cup game against Australia*
2 *Robert Carlos, Real Madrid, in a 2000 Champions League Group A clash with Sporting Lisbon*

round three
twenty sporting questions

1 *Sally Gunnell*
2 *Laura Davies*
3 *Cycling*
4 *Conchita Martinez*
5 *Arsenal Ladies*
6 *Kristin Otto*
7 *The Grand National*
8 *Merlene Ottey*
9 *Three-day eventing*
10 *New Zealand*
11 *Squash*
12 *Jenny Pitman*
13 *Martina Navratilova*
14 *Darts*
15 *Figure skating*
16 *Nadia Comaneci*
17 *Denise Lewis*
18 *Australia*
19 *Golf*
20 *Stephanie Cook*

round four
sporting links

1 *They never missed a game in their entire international careers. Gareth won 53 caps for Wales in the '60s and '70s, John played in 58 consecutive Tests from 1949 to 1965 and Neil played in England's first 27 games after World War II*
2 *All born in Germany: David in Wegberg, John in Wiesbaden and Paul in Hanover*

round five
where am I?

1 *Manchester*
2 *Georgia*

round six
what happened next?

1 *b)*
2 *a)*

round seven
home or away

1 *Gary Havelock – World Champion in 1992*
2 *Shaun Pollock*
3 *Jim Leighton*
4 *Red Rum*

round eight
captain's away

1 *A beret*
2 *Glasses*

round nine
mystery guest

1 *Jurgen Klinsmann*
2 *John Parrott*

round ten
on the buzzer

1. *Robbie Keane*
2. *Greg Norman*
3. *Once – England in 1991*
4. *Ashley Cole*
5. *Kenyan*
6. *Martin O'Neill*
7. *Utah*
8. *Ten-pin bowling*

game 19

round one
name the year

1. *1982*
2. *1995*

round two
picture board

1. *Eric Cantona pops up again in a beach football game, August 2000*
2. *USA's Lance Armstrong signs in for the final stage of the 2000 Tour de France in Paris*

round three
twenty sporting questions

1. *Nick Faldo*
2. *Sri Lanka*
3. *Mick McCarthy*
4. *Cambridge*
5. *Andy Farrell*
6. *Juventus*
7. *Yevgeny Kafelnikov*
8. *Gavin Hastings*
9. *Harold 'Dickie' Bird*
10. *Martina Hingis*
11. *Leicestershire*
12. *St Helens*
13. *Manchester United*
14. *Kenya*
15. *Mick Fitzgerald*
16. *Nevilles (Gary and Phil)*
17. *Royal Lytham*
18. *Dallas*
19. *Les Ferdinand*
20. *Michael Johnson*

round four
sporting links

1. *Jamaica. Gabriel scored the only hat-trick of the 1998 World Cup against them, Linford was born there and Sir Garfield scored a then-world record 365 not out against Pakistan in Kingston in the 1957–58 season.*
2. *They played only one international game: Arnie was in the third Ashes Test in 1985, Andrew helped England beat Australia in 1988 and Brian played nine minutes for England in Saudi Arabia that year.*

round five
where am I?

1. *Newcastle*
2. *Coventry*

round six
what happened next?

1. *c)*
2. *a)*

round seven
home or away

1. *Jason Robinson*
2. *Dottie Pepper*
3. *It was the first golden goal in World Cup history*
4. *Andy Hicks*

round eight
captain's away

1. *The kits they now wear*
2. *Horses named after them have all won races*

round nine
mystery guest

1. *Michael Atherton*
2. *Keiron Cunningham*

round ten
on the buzzer

1. *5*
2. *1*
3. *4*
4. *60*
5. *140*
6. *7*
7. *3*
8. *20*
9. *11*
10. *12*
11. *17th*
12. *30*
13. *6*
14. *26 miles*
15. *49*
16. *5*
17. *5*
18. *18*
19. *13*

game 20

round one
name the year

1. *1974*
2. *1983*

round two
picture board

1. *Manchester United's David Beckham holds his head in his hands as Chelsea beat Manchester United in the 2000 FA Charity Shield*
2. *Mark Philippoussis in action in his third-round match at Wimbledon, 1 July 2000*

round three
twenty sporting questions

1. *Jean van de Velde*
2. *Italy*
3. *Marie-Jose Perec*
4. *Arsène Wenger*
5. *Henri Leconte*
6. *Serge Blanco*
7. *Stade de France, Paris*
8. *Tour de France*
9. *Olivier Peslier*
10. *Rugby Union*
11. *Marseille*
12. *Ellen MacArthur*
13. *Albertville*
14. *Alain Prost*
15. *Michel Platini*
16. *400 metres hurdles*
17. *Longchamp*
18. *David Trezeguet*
19. *New Zealand*
20. *Gérard Houllier*

round four
sporting links

1. *They had all been born with different names. Ali was born Cassius Clay, Pele's real name is Edson Arantes do Nascimento, while Renee was born Richard Raskind – he changed a lot more than just his name!*
2. *They all appeared in the film Escape to Victory alongside noted footballers Michael Caine and Sylvester Stallone.*

round five
where am I?

1. *Nottingham*
2. *Ayr*

round six
what happened next?

1. *b)*
2. *a)*

round seven
home or away

1. *Theatreworld*
2. *Karen Pickering*
3. *Arnie Sidebottom*
4. *Doug Polen*

round eight
captain's away

1 *Trampolining. An Adolph is a forward somersault with three-and-a-half twists; a randy is a forward somersault with two-and-a-half twists*
2 *Water polo. Outfield players are forbidden to stand on the bottom of the pool during the game.*

round nine
mystery guest
1 *Paul Gascoigne*
2 *Sir Steven Redgrave*

round ten
on the buzzer
1 *Dennis Taylor*
2 *David Seaman*
3 *Jason Gardener*
4 *Peter Baker*
5 *David Shepherd*
6 *Henry Cooper*
7 *Michael Schumacher*
8 *Kathy Cook*
9 *George Foreman*
10 *Jim Courier*
11 *Faroukh Engineer*
12 *Alan Shearer*
13 *Wendell Sailor*

game 21

round one
name the year
1 *1968*
2 *1978*

round two
picture board
1 *Motorcycling legend Barry Sheene at the International Classic event at Donington Park in July 2000*
2 *Nottingham Forest's Roy Keane emulates local hero Robin Hood at the 1991 FA Cup final against Spurs*

round three
twenty sporting questions
1 *Ronaldo*
2 *Rangers*
3 *Rowing*
4 *Rosberg (Keke)*
5 *Romanian*
6 *Redskins*
7 *Red Maurader*
8 *Rallying*
9 *Rome*
10 *Red Star Belgrade*
11 *Rafter (Pat)*
12 *Rotherham United*
13 *Rocca (Constantino)*
14 *Rideout (Paul)*
15 *Rahman (Hasim)*
16 *Redknapp (Jamie)*
17 *Russian*
18 *Real Madrid*
19 *Reardon (Ray)*
20 *Robinson (Jason)*

round four
sporting links
1 *They all managed hat-tricks on their debuts. Jeremy scored three tries against Romania in 1989, Damien took a hat-trick of wickets against Pakistan in 1994–95 and Henderson scored three tries against France in 1981*
2 *All signs of the zodiac! Derby are nicknamed the Rams; the Waughs are Twins (Gemini); the snooker was won by John Virgo*

round five
where am I?
1 *Montreal*
2 *Los Angeles*

round six
what happened next?
1 *a)*
2 *a)*

round seven
home or away
1 *Nick Faldo*
2 *Matt Biondi*
3 *Due to the solar eclipse*
4 *Epsom*

round eight
captain's away
1 *Weightlifting. There are two standard lifts: the squat, and the clean-and-jerk!*
2 *Table tennis. The pimpled rubber on the bats was reduced from 1.8mm in height to 1.5mm*

round nine
mystery guest
1 *Ryan Giggs*
2 *Colin Jackson*

round ten
on the buzzer
1 *Marc OverMARS*
2 *LESTER Piggott*
3 *VENUS Williams*
4 *Nick GILLINGHAM*
5 *Scott HASTINGS*
6 *RIO Ferdinand*
7 *BEN NEVIS*
8 *Dominic CORK*
9 *Justin EDINBURGH*
10 *Malcolm CROSBY*
11 *David BEDFORD*

game 22

round one
name the year
1 *1989*
2 *1986*

round two
picture board
1 *Robbie Keane of Inter Milan at a Serie A clash with Napoli in October 2000*
2 *New Zealand rugby hero Jonah Lomu chills out at a friendly vs. France in 2000*

round three
twenty sporting questions
1 *John Eales*
2 *Allan Border*
3 *American Samoa*
4 *Greg Norman*
5 *Newcastle*
6 *Middlesbrough*
7 *Pat Cash*
8 *David Campese*
9 *Mark Bosnich*
10 *Shane Warne*
11 *Perth*
12 *Australian Rules football*
13 *Debbie Flintoff-King*
14 *Ian Thorpe*
15 *Scotland*
16 *1956*
17 *Rod Laver*
18 *Mark Taylor*
19 *Karrie Webb*
20 *Leeds United*

round four
sporting links
1 *They've all won Olympic medals. Colin coxed the British eight to silver in Moscow, Prince Constantin was in the winning dragon boat in Rome and Ronaldo took bronze in Atlanta*
2 *They've all lit the Olympic flame: Ron in Melbourne in 1956, before taking bronze in Tokyo in 1964; Rafer in LA in 1984, after winning gold in Rome in 1960. Cathy uniquely did both in Sydney in 2000.*

round five
where am I?

1 Moscow
2 Glasgow

round six
what happened next?
1 b)
2 a)

round seven
home or away
1 Dean Saunders
2 Ato Boldon
3 Harvey Howard
4 Jimmy Connors

round eight
captain's away
1 True
2 True
3 True
4 False
5 False
6 True
7 True
8 False

round nine
mystery guest
1 Glenn Hoddle
2 Shane Warne

round ten
on the buzzer
1 12 yards
2 Five
3 There isn't one
4 The 100 metres hurdles
5 14
6 Snooker or billiards
7 Tennis – Wimbledon
8 Boxing (it stands for Technical Knock-Out)
9 Radios
10 Graham Gooch
11 One
12 Table tennis
13 Basketball
14 10
15 A relay baton
16 Score a goal

game 23

round one
name the year
1 1990
2 1970

round two
picture board
1 South Africa's Joost van der Westhuizen playing in a friendly against Wales in November 2000
2 New Zealand's Henry Paul passes the ball in the 2000 Rugby World Cup semi-final vs. England

round three
twenty sporting questions
1 Will Carling
2 Tony Stanger
3 Newport
4 Jean-Pierre Rives
5 Willie-John McBride
6 Auckland
7 Michael Lynagh
8 Jonah Lomu
9 Leicester Tigers
10 Japan
11 Harlequins
12 Joel Stransky
13 Garry Owen
14 Scotland
15 Australia and New Zealand
16 Hugo Porta
17 USA
18 Bridgend
19 Williams
20 Calcutta Cup

round four
sporting links
1 Ken Richmond – he banged the gong at the start of countless J. Arthur Rank films! Weissmuller was the definitive screen Tarzan; Sakata was immortalised as Oddjob
2 Devon Loch's jockey was... Dick Francis! The other two authors are Dickie Bird and Steve Bruce

round five
where am I?
1 Holland
2 Pakistan

round six
what happened next?
1 a)
2 b)

round seven
home or away
1 Bjorn Borg
2 John Daly
3 David Sales
4 Graeme Souness

round eight
captain's away
1 Michael Owen
Gary Lineker
2 Kevin Gallagher
Ally McCoist

round nine
mystery guest
1 Kenny Dalglish
2 Seve Ballesteros

round ten
on the buzzer
1 Tiger Woods
2 Steve Bull
3 Harold 'Dickie' Bird
4 Christina Boxer
5 Leeds
6 Craig Stadler
7 Derby County
8 Elliot Bunney
9 Allan Lamb
10 Sunderland
11 Phil Tufnell
12 Leicester City
13 Robbie and Henry Paul

game 24

round one
name the year
1 1996
2 1987

round two
picture board
1 Michael Schumacher fools around in a red wig after his 2000 Malaysian Grand Prix victory
2 Intense concentration from Abel Xavier of Portugal in the semi-final of Euro 2000 against France

round three
twenty sporting questions
1 Salvatore Schillaci
2 Diego Dominguez
3 Alpine ski-ing
4 Fiona May
5 Genoa
6 Tour de France
7 Dino Zoff
8 Diving
9 Alberto Ascari
10 Rowing
11 Costantino Rocca
12 AC Milan
13 Gianfranco and Lanfranco (Frankie) Dettori
14 Motor-cyling
15 Roberto di Matteo
16 Primo Camera
17 200 metres
18 Tennis – the French Open
19 Fencing
20 Turin

round four
sporting links
1 Aladar Gerevich – he was on Hungary's winning sabre team in six consecutive Games from

1932 to 1960, as well as picking up individual gold in 1948. Steven Redgrave won gold at five Games in a row. Durwood Knowles competed at eight Games, winning gold in 1964

2 Liechtenstein, thanks to downhill ski-er Hanni Wenzel winning two titles at Lake Placid in 1980 – Liechtenstein's population was estimated to be 25,000 at the time. Freestyle ski-er Lina Cheryazova took Uzbekistan's first and so far only gold in Lillehammer, but the billion-plus people of China are still waiting...

round five
where am I?

1 Plymouth
2 Ashington

round six
what happened next?

1 b)
2 a)

round seven
home or away

1 Royal Troon (eighth hole)
2 Shaun Edwards
3 Heike Drechsler – in the long-jump
4 Twelve – six stumps, four bails and two bats

round eight
captain's away

1 They all appeared in major Hollywood films. Jordan played himself alongside Bugs Bunny in Space Jam! Weissmuller played the title role in 12 Tarzan movies. Harold Sakata starred in the James Bond film Goldfinger, as Odd Job.

2 All goalkeepers. Julio was in the reserves at Real Madrid before topping the charts, David was on Coventry City's books and then played 37 times for Hereford United before becoming a TV personality and Pope John Paul II, played between the sticks as a youth in Poland

round nine
mystery guest

1 Dennis Bergkamp
2 Lester Piggott

round ten
on the buzzer

1 ALBATROSS
2 BAYERN Munich
3 Dominic CORK
4 Tony DRAGO
5 EVERTON
6 FOUR
7 GREEN Bay
8 HIGH-jump
9 Paul INCE
10 Colin JACKSON
11 Lance KLUSENER
12 LEICESTER
13 Nigel MANSELL
14 Jack NICKLAUS
15 David O'LEARY

game 25

round one
name the year

1 1990
2 1981

round two
picture board

1 A young David Coulthard karting
2 Lazio's Fabrizio Ravanelli does his trademark goal celebration in a 2000 game vs. Sparta Prague in the Champions League

round three
twenty sporting questions

1 Mansfield Town
2 Modern pentathlon
3 Miinnehoma
4 Murrayfield
5 Melbourne
6 Marsh (Rodney)
7 Martin (Todd)
8 Moroccan
9 Macclesfield Town
10 McManus (Alan)
11 Mansell (Nigel)
12 Middlesex
13 Masterkova (Svetlana)
14 Motherwell
15 Minnesota
16 Montgomerie (Colin)
17 Martin (Lee)
18 Merry (Katharine)
19 McCall (Oliver)
20 Molineux

round four
sporting links

1 They were shared. The two fastest bobsleigh crews recorded identical times, all the Five Nations won two matches each and John Francome sat out the last few days of the season once he'd equalled the injured Peter Scudamore's total of winners
2 Five foot two. That's how tall Walden and the Chair are, and it was the winning jump in Amsterdam, 1928.

round five
where am I?

1 Denmark
2 Ecuador

round six
what happened next?

1 a)
2 a)

round seven
home or away

1 David Wilkie
2 Silverstone
3 Juventus
4 Zinzan and Robin Brooke

round eight
captain's away

1 Kushti is a traditional form of wrestling in Iran where the competitors wear tight leather trousers which can be used for holds
2 Kaboom is a backward somersault in a tuck position, used in trampolining

round nine
mystery guest

1 Pat Eddery
2 Osvaldo Ardiles

round ten
on the buzzer

1 Sturm Graz
2 Rugby Union World Cup Final
3 Horse racing (home of the Prix de l'Arc de Triomphe)
4 Olympique Marseille
5 Flushing Meadow – US Open
6 Norway
7 Indoor bowls
8 Tour de France
9 Darts
10 Bury
11 Augusta National (US Masters)
12 Australia (WACA – Perth, Gabba – Brisbane, SCG – Sydney)
13 Monza
14 The Curragh

game 26

round one
name the year

1. 1999
2. 1967

round two
picture board

1. New Zealand's Robbie Paul exults after their 2000 Rugby World Cup semi-final win over England
2. Leeds United's Ian Harte is kissed by Gary Kelly after scoring in the Champions League qualifying round game vs. TSV Munich

round three
twenty sporting questions

1. Helsinki
2. Sergey Bubka
3. 200 metres
4. Merlene Ottey
5. Husband and wife (Marion Jones and C.J. Hunter)
6. Fatima Whitbread
7. Kriss Akabusi
8. Triple jump
9. Yuri Sedykh
10. Stuttgart, 1993
11. The Bahamas
12. Daley Thompson
13. They broke the pre-race world records (Sandra Farmer-Patrick and Tonja Buford)
14. Long-jump
15. New Zealand
16. Inger Miller
17. John Regis
18. Liz McColgan
19. Zambia
20. Michael Johnson

round four
sporting links

1. They all won four consecutive Olympic gold medals in an individual event
2. All have a capital city in their name. Brian LONDON, Brian LIMA and SANTIAGO Bernabeu

round five
where am I?

1. Adelaide
2. Dublin

round six
what happened next?

1. a)
2. b)

round seven
home or away

1. Ernie Els
2. Seth Johnson
3. Allan Wells
4. Azumah Nelson

round eight
captain's away

1. Real tennis
2. Baseball – Players put a doughnut-shaped piece of lead on the end of their bat to make it heavier whilst they warm up, but have to remove it before they go to the plate to bat

round nine
mystery guest

1. Jonathan Edwards
2. Damon Hill

round ten
on the buzzer

1. Lee Westwood
2. Tim Henman
3. Leon and Michael Spinks
4. Carl (and Carol) Lewis
5. Antonio and Ignacio Garrido
6. Zinzan and Robin Brooke
7. Cyrille and John Regis
8. They are the same person
9. Mark and Steve Waugh
10. West Ham – Harry Redknapp, his brother-in-law Frank Lampard Snr, and his son Frank Jnr.
11. Damon Hill
12. Gianfranco and Lanfranco Dettori
13. Italy – Cesare and Paulo Maldini
14. Liam Botham (dad is Ian)
15. Ben Cohen (uncle is George)

game 27

round one
name the year

1. 1993
2. 1971

round two
picture board

1. David Coulthard sprays champagne after his 1999 Belgian Grand Prix win
2. Tiger Woods in silhouette at the 2000 British Open at St Andrews

round three
twenty sporting questions

1. Sutton United
2. James 'Buster' Douglas
3. Kenya
4. Paul Lawrie
5. Jelena Dokic
6. Joe Johnson
7. Ieuan Evans
8. Olivier Panis
9. North Korea
10. Paraskevi Patoulidou
11. Sri Lanka
12. Foinavon
13. Salford Reds
14. Lloyd Honeyghan
15. The Soviet Union
16. John Daly
17. Cameroon
18. Western Samoa
19. Michael Chang
20. Oakland Raiders

round four
sporting links

1. All share their names with vegetables: Dottie PEPPER, Ken LEEK, Andy BEAN
2. All share their names with months: Don JANUARY, JUNE Croft, Fiona MAY

round five
where am I?

1. Budapest
2. Liverpool

round six
what happened next?

1. b)
2. a)

round seven
home or away

1. Italy
2. Jackie Stewart
3. Rob Henderson
4. Richard Dunwoody

round eight
captain's away

1. Cambridge United and Wycombe Wanderers
2. Cowdenbeath and Clydebank

round nine
mystery guest

1. Will Carling
2. Roberto Baggio

round ten
on the buzzer

1. John Daly
2. Alison Curbishley
3. John Barnes
4. John Eales
5. Muhammed Ali
6. Sue Rolph
7. Alison Nicholas

8 John Regis
9 Gymnastics
10 Jonny Wilkinson
11 Ally McLeod
12 Jean van de Velde
13 Su-baru
14 Ali Carter
15 Davor Su-ker

game 28

round one
name the year

1 1976
2 2000

round two
picture board

1 Frank Bruno poses on a Harley-Davidson before his 1996 world title fight
2 Daley Thompson in unusual garb – launching his new career as a saloon-car racing driver back in 1993

round three
twenty sporting questions

1 India
2 Richard Hadlee
3 Heath Streak
4 Glamorgan
5 India
6 David Gower
7 Mark Alleyne
8 West Indies
9 Sydney
10 Durham
11 St Helens, Swansea
12 Sachin Tendulkar
13 The Ashes
14 Graham Gooch
15 Melbourne
16 Jim Laker
17 Wasim Akram
18 Somerset
19 Zimbabwe
20 Darren Lehmann

round four
sporting links

1 They've managed two different clubs to league titles, Herbert with Huddersfield and Arsenal, Brian with Derby and Nottingham Forest and Kenny with Liverpool and Blackburn
2 They've all scored 100 runs and taken 10 wickets in the same Test match.

round five
where am I?

1 Newport
2 Seattle

round six
what happened next?

1 a)
2 b)

round seven
home or away

1 Fiona May
2 Chris Joynt
3 Ben Ainslie
4 Roy Jones Jnr

round eight
captain's away

1 True (Standish Cagney won 13 caps, Hugh de Lacy 2)
2 False (Jack Dempsey has, but no Makepeace).
3 True (for Surrey at the start of the 20th century)
4 True (during the 1960s)
5 False (No one called Starr has played)
6 True (lots of Pughs, Victor Barney played for Reading, Thomas Mulgrew played for Southampton, Ean Cuthbert for Stockport, Andy Dibble was a Welsh international 'keeper and Alan Grubb played for Spurs in the '50s.)

round nine
mystery guest

1 Ally McCoist
2 Chris Eubank

round ten
on the buzzer

1 False. Ryan was born in Cardiff, Michael in Chester
2 False – though he did go round nine holes in less than 50 strokes
3 True – ranked fourth in Europe and seventh in the world at the age of 15
4 False
5 True
6 False
7 True
8 False
9 False
10 True
11 True
12 False – Geoff got 9, but Paul got 11
13 True
14 False
15 False (Ronnie beat John Higgins)

game 29

round one
name the year

1 1988
2 1993

round two
picture board

1 Glamour girl of tennis Anna Kournikova in her game against Natasha Zvereva at the Direct Line International Championship in 2000
2 Zinzan Brooke of the Barbarians takes on the Leicester Tigers in the Scottish Amicable Trophy match in June 200

round three
twenty sporting questions

1 Alfredo di Stefano
2 Clive Lloyd
3 Maria Bueno
4 Rugby Union
5 Triple jump
6 Juan Manuel Fangio
7 Edson Arantes do Nascimento
8 Roberto di Vicenzo
9 Boxing
10 French Open
11 Emerson Fittipaldi
12 It was his first international ...and his last
13 Paraguay
14 Frederico Mendez
15 Beach volleyball
16 Ayrton Senna
17 Lance Gibbs
18 Judo
19 Chile
20 Ecuador

round four
sporting links

1 They've all played in four winning sides – 1985, 1987, 1995 and 1997. (They all also appeared in the tied competition of 1989. Seve Ballesteros played on all these teams except in 1997, when he was captain)
2 They've won all four major championships – the Olympics, the World and European Championships and the Commonwealth Games

round five
where am I?

1 Madrid
2 Gothenburg

round six
what happened next?

1 *c)*
2 *b)*

round seven
home or away
1 *Inga Tuigamala*
2 *Sonia O'Sullivan*
3 *Ian Botham (383)*
4 *Miguel Indurain*

round eight
captain's away
1 *It was the world crazy golf championships*
2 *The Wimbledon men's singles champion – the trophy is inscribed, 'The All-England Lawn Tennis Club single handed championship of the world'.*

round nine
mystery guest
1 *Greg Rusedski*
2 *Eric Cantona*

round ten
on the buzzer
1 *Ian Rush*
2 *Julius Francis*
3 *Stirling Moss*
4 *Richard Dunwoody*
5 *Colin Jackson*
6 *Mark Williams*
7 *Tony McCoy*
8 *Paul Scholes*
9 *Herbie Hide*
10 *Jane Sixsmith*
11 *Gary Lineker*
12 *Judo*
13 *Sir Steve Redgrave*
14 *Kenny Dalglish*
15 *Sandy Lyle*

game 30

round one
name the year
1 *1977*
2 *1999*

round two
picture board
1 *Gianluca Vialli succumbs to frustration after Chelsea's game against Helsingborgs in the 1998 European Cup Winners' Cup*
2 *Not a golfer, but West Indies cricketer Richie Richardson*

round three
twenty sporting questions
1 *Tottenham Hotspur*
2 *Ian Baker-Finch*
3 *Generous*
4 *Kenyan*
5 *Nigel Mansell*
6 *Crystal Palace*
7 *Michael Stich*
8 *England*
9 *Phil Simmons*
10 *Carl Lewis*
11 *Barcelona*
12 *Seagram*
13 *St Helens*
14 *Ian Woosnam*
15 *Australia*
16 *Viv Richards*
17 *Motherwell*
18 *Jimmy White*
19 *France*
20 *Alan Smith*

round four
sporting links
1 *Rain stopped play! The Test match was abandoned without a ball bowled, the Fairs Cup tie was stopped after 51 minutes and replayed the next day, while the snooker was halted temporarily due to rain leaking through the roof!*
2 *They all played internationals for more than one country – Wessels for Australia and South Africa, Tuigamala for New Zealand and Samoa and Kubala for Hungary, Czechoslovakia and Spain.*

round five
where am I?
1 *Detroit*
2 *Pittsburgh*

round six
what happened next?
1 *a)*
2 *c)*

round seven
home or away
1 *John Higgins*
2 *He was the first player to lead after the first round, but fail to make the cut after the second.*
3 *Peter Such*
4 *She beat number one seed Martina Hingis in the first round, only the third time this has happened in either men's or women's singles. Pasarell knocked out Manuel Santana; McNeil defeated Steffi Graf*

round eight
captain's away
1 *Clyde and Inverness Caledonian Thistle*
2 *Bury and Wolverhampton Wanderers*

round nine
mystery guest
1 *Ronnie O'Sullivan*
2 *Niall Quinn*

round ten
on the buzzer
1 *Scotland*
2 *Colin Montgomerie*
3 *Peter Scudamore*
4 *Stirling Moss*
5 *Steve Bruce*
6 *Ivan Lendl*
7 *Colin Jackson*
8 *Middlesbrough*
9 *Frankie Dettori*
10 *Frank Bruno*
11 *Gary Lineker*

game 31

round one
name the year
1 *1996*
2 *1972*

round two
picture board
1 *Ruby Walsh and Papillon after winning the 2000 Grand National*
2 *Denise Lewis sticks her tongue out after her third jump at the 1999 athletics world championships in Seville was declared legal*

round three
twenty sporting questions
1 *Twelve*
2 *Huddersfield Town*
3 *Peter Shilton*
4 *Liverpool*
5 *Goals scored, (Arsenal took the title when both teams finished with identical goal difference)*
6 *Jimmy Greaves*
7 *Wolverhampton Wanderers*
8 *Three points for a win, (Blackburn had one more win, but two fewer draws)*
9 *Brian Clough*
10 *They played in all 42 games*
11 *Manchester (They're now known as United and City)*
12 *John Lukic (with Leeds in 1992) Kevin Richardson (Everton in 1985)*
13 *Ipswich Town*
14 *Bill Nicholson (with Spurs)*

15 A trophy
16 Reading
17 Mark Stein
18 Arsenal
19 Alan Hansen
20 They still won the title that season!

round four
sporting links

1 Their surnames are all diminutives – Emmanuel Petit, Gladstone Small, Brian and Alan Little
2 You'll find all their surnames in the garden! Steve Stone, Andy and Grant Flower, George Bush

round five
where am I?

1 Wimbledon
2 Caesar's Palace, Las Vegas

round six
what happened next?

1 c)
2 c)

round seven
home or away

1 Matt Elliott
2 Bruny Surin
3 Emile Ntamack
4 Graeme Fowler

round eight
captain's away

1 One match was at football, the other at Rugby Union
2 Football – San Jose Clash, Tampa Bay Mutiny and New England Revolution are all Major League Soccer franchises

round nine
mystery guest

1 Jane Sixsmith
2 Frank Bruno

round ten
on the buzzer

1 Aintree – it's a Grand National fence named after Capt. Valentine
2 Love
3 Ian Harte
4 The Flowers – Andy and Grant Flower
5 Justin Rose
6 Snooker
7 Hearts
8 Lancashire and Yorkshire
9 C.J. Hunter
10 St. Mirren
11 Fred Couples
12 Gymnastics

game 32

round one
name the year

1 1974
2 1994

round two
picture board

1 Athlete Ben Challenger of Great Britain in 2000's Norwich Union Challenge against the USA
2 England's Darren Gough scuba-diving at a training camp on Lanzarote, 1997

round three
twenty sporting questions

1 1970
2 Bill Beaumont
3 Emlyn Hughes
4 David Vine (1970–78)
5 Gareth Edwards
6 Willie Carson
7 Henry Cooper
8 Ian Botham (captain on QS from 1988–96)
9 St Johnstone
10 True
11 Cliff Morgan
12 Betty Stove
13 Roger Black
14 Steve Davis (18–3)
15 Fred Trueman
16 Lucinda Green (17)
17 True
18 Bobby Moore
19 Villa Park
20 Brendan Foster (captain eight times in 1977)

round four
sporting links

1 All share their names with countries – Alan Brazil, Iran Barkley, Uruguay
2 You'll find their surnames in a pond – John Reid, Mark Fish, Dennis Lillee (sorry about the spelling!)

round five
where am I?

1 India
2 Lytham St Annes

round six
what happened next?

1 b)
2 a)

round seven
home or away

1 Finlay Calder
2 Sue O'Neill
3 Vijay Armitraj
4 Jermaine Defoe

round eight
captain's away

1 Scott Hastings of Scotland overtook his brother's haul of 61 caps. Both brothers had made their debut in 1986 against France. Scott went on to win 65 caps in total
2 Norman Conquest was in goal for Australia when they played England and was followed into the Australian team by Norman Rule. Norman Conquest's game in goal ended up in a 17–0 win for England

round nine
mystery guest

1 Frankie Dettori
2 Tiger Woods

round ten
on the buzzer

1 Zinedine Zidane
2 Yorkshire
3 Abel Xavier
4 Wentworth
5 Velodrome
6 Victor Ubogu
7 Tangerine
8 Seventeen
9 Redskins
10 Queens Park
11 Polo
12 Own goals
13 Nijinsky
14 Manchester
15 Liverpool

game 33

round one
name the year

1 1984
2 2000

round two
picture board

1 Bobby Robson in his West Bromwich Albion days – back in June 1964
2 England's Ian Wright and Paul Gascoigne grin and bear it during a training session for the 1993 World Cup qualifier against Turkey

round three
twenty sporting questions

1 *Sandy Lyle*
2 *The Claret Jug*
3 *1979*
4 *Zimbabwean*
5 *Costantino Rocca*
6 *Laura Davies*
7 *Gary Player*
8 *Walker Cup*
9 *Albatross*
10 *Greg Norman*
11 *Augusta National*
12 *Arnold Palmer*
13 *Scottish (Paul Lawrie)*
14 *Helen Alfredsson*
15 *Sergio Garcia*
16 *Roberto di Vicenzo*
17 *Ernie Els*
18 *Green*
19 *Jack Nicklaus*
20 *St Andrews*

round four
sporting links

1 *They share their names with famous operas! Mark Ring, (as in Wagner's Ring Cycle) Carmen Basilio, and Aida – a circuit in Japan*
2 *They've all been portrayed in major motion pictures. Jake LaMotta's career was the subject of Raging Bull, Bob Champion's famous win on Aldaniti was made into Champions, while Harold Abrahams and Eric Liddell were immortalised by Chariots of Fire (as were other famous athletes such as Jackson Schultz and Charley Paddock)*

round five
where am I?

1 *Canada*
2 *Norway*

round six
what happened next?

1 *b)*
2 *b)*

round seven
home or away

1 *Inger Miller*
2 *Alan Minter (in 1980)*
3 *Willie Carson*
4 *Emile Heskey – the striker won with Liverpool in 2001 and with Leicester in 1997 and 2000. He lost with Leicester in 1999*

round eight
captain's away

1 *The Moon! Shepard was an astronaut on Apollo 14 – a decade earlier he had been the first American in space*
2 *The Grand National. Held at Gatwick during the Great War, it was won by Ernie Piggott on Poethlyn*

round nine
mystery guest

1 *Eric Bristow*
2 *David Gower*

round ten
on the buzzer

1 *Andre Agassi*
2 *Bob Beamon*
3 *Chris Cowdrey*
4 *Dion Dublin*
5 *Eddie 'the Eagle' Edwards*
6 *Fred Funk*
7 *Gordon Greenidge*
8 *Heike Henkel*
9 *Innes ireland*
10 *Joe Johnson*
11 *Kevin Kilbane*
12 *Lancashire Lightning*
13 *Mike McFarlane*

game 34

round one
name the year

1 *1982*
2 *1992*

round two
picture board

1 *Leeds United's Harry Kewell is sent flying in a Premiership clash with Manchester United, 2 February 2000*
2 *Leicester's Darren Garforth having headband hassles in a 1999 Premiership scrap against Wasps*

round three
twenty sporting questions

1 *Don Budge*
2 *The Davis Cup*
3 *Virginia Wade*
4 *1968*
5 *Tim Henman, Nick Broad*
6 *Ivan Lendl*
7 *American clay*
8 *Martina Navratilova*
9 *Michael Stich*
10 *Wightman Cup*
11 *Billie Jean King*
12 *Bjorn Borg*
13 *They are the only mothers to win the tournament*
14 *Steffi Graf*
15 *Todd Woodbridge and Mark Woodforde*
16 *There were two of them – in January and December*
17 *Yannick Noah*
18 *Chris Evert*
19 *Stefan Edberg*
20 *Long trousers!*

round four
sporting links

1 *They share their names with famous authors – Gianfranco Zola (Emile Zola) Hugo Porta (Victor Hugo) and... Craig Shakespeare!*
2 *They all lost a match during the tournament*

round five
where am I?

1 *Leeds*
2 *Stockholm*

round six
what happened next?

1 *a)*
2 *c)*

round seven
home or away

1 *Austrian*
2 *David Holding*
3 *Andy Gray and Graeme Sharp*
4 *John Daly*

round eight
captain's away

1 *Fuzzy Zoeller, '84 US Open. Larry Mize, '87 Masters. Lee Janzen, '93 and '98 US Open. Paul Azinger, '93 USPGA. Jose Maria Olazabal, '94 and '99 Masters.*
2 *Rubstic, Rhyme 'n Reason, Royal Athlete, Rough Quest, Red Marauder*

round nine
mystery guest

1 *Martin Offiah*
2 *Peter Reid*

round ten
on the buzzer

1 *Dennis Wise*
2 *Keith Wood*
3 *Brian Lara*
4 *Damon Hill*
5 *Sandy Lyle*
6 *Roger Hunt*
7 *Jonah Lomu*
8 *Steve Cram*
9 *David Boon*
10 *Ian Rush*
11 *Neil Back*
12 *Steffi Graf*
13 *Allan Lamb*

game 35

round one
name the year

1 1991
2 1975

round two
picture board

1 Great Britain's 400m runner Iwan Thomas reflects on the task ahead at Seville in 1999
2 Paul Lawrie kisses the cup after winning the Open at Carnoustie in 1999

round three
twenty sporting questions

1 Aberdeen
2 Rangers
3 Steve Nicol
4 Holland
5 Clydebank
6 Brian McClair
7 Queen's Park
8 30
9 Andy Gray
10 St Mirren
11 Kilmarnock
12 Henrik Larsson
13 Real Madrid
14 Costa Rica
15 Arbroath
16 Alex Ferguson
17 Alan Hansen
18 Dunfermline Athletic
19 Don Hutchison
20 Gary McAllister

round four
sporting links

1 They were all just 14 years old at the time
2 All share their names with famous composers – Andrew Strauss, Phil Bach and Thomas Dvorak

round five
where am I?

1 Berlin
2 Amsterdam

round six
what happened next?

1 a)
2 c)

round seven
home or away

1 Steve and Mark Waugh
2 It was the first match run by three female officials
3 Leon Lloyd
4 Audley Harrison

round eight
captain's away

1 Golf – It was the venue for the 1996 US Amateur Championship (won, incidentally, by one Tiger Woods)
2 Football – home ground of Austria's Sturm Graz
3 Horse racing – One of the major Hong Kong courses
4 Greyhound racing or horse racing – it's a track in New South Wales, Australia
5 Motor racing – The venue for the Indianapolis 500
6 American football – Home to the Arizona Cardinals
7 Rugby League – Home of the Castleford Tigers
8 Football – Home of Kilmarnock

round nine
mystery guest

1 Walter Swinburn
2 Sean Long

round ten
on the buzzer

1 George Foreman
2 Sachin Tendulkar
3 Wes Brown
4 Nigel Mansell
5 Jason Leonard
6 Greg Norman
7 Ian Wright
8 Dominic Dale
9 Thomas Hearns
10 Torvill and Dean
11 Nottingham Forest
12 Rory Underwood
13 Sunil Gavaskar
14 Sergey Bubka
15 Lester Piggott
16 Rugby League

game 36

round one
name the year

1 1977
2 2000

round two
picture board

1 Ian Rush and Robbie Fowler at Liverpool's fancy dress Christmas party back in 1993
2 Dashing outlaw John Barnes at the same event in 1990

round three
twenty sporting questions

1 Red Marauder
2 Craig Brown
3 Blue
4 Llanelli
5 Black Arabs
6 Athens
7 Frimley Green
8 Toronto Blue Jays
9 Zimbabwe
10 Craig White
11 Yellow
12 Roger Black
13 Birmingham
14 Green Bay
15 Reds
16 Coventry City
17 Tanni Grey-Thompson
18 Jack Nicklaus
19 Tangerine
20 Alistair Brown

round four
sporting links

1 They share their names with days of the week! Kenneth Monday, Sunday Bada, Sheffield Wednesday
2 They were all walkovers. Spain refused to play in protest at the Soviets' support for the Republic in the Spanish Civil War, Stevenson's opponent Ion Alexe was injured in his semi-final, while all three of Halswelle's opponents withdrew after the final was ordered to be re-run

round five
where am I?

1 Poland
2 China

round six
what happened next?

1 c)
2 b)

round seven
home or away

1 Gary Lineker – who grabbed three goals against Poland in the 1986 finals in Mexico
2 Merlene Ottey
3 Diego Dominguez
4 Australian

round eight
captain's away

1 Bob Tway ('86 US PGA), Wayne Grady ('90 US PGA), John Daly ('91 US PGA and '95 Open)
2 Seve Ballesteros ('84 and '88 Open and '80 and '83

Masters), Ian Baker-Finch (1991 Open), Mark Brooks (1996 US PGA)

round nine
mystery guest

1 Ernie Els
2 Clive Woodward

round ten
on the buzzer

1 Allan Border
2 Christopher Dean
3 East Fife
4 Gerard Houllier
5 Ian Jones
6 Kuala Lumpur
7 Martina Navratilova
8 Olivier Peslier
9 Queensbury Rules
10 Sachin Tendulkar

game 37

round one
name the year

1 2000
2 1987

round two
picture board

1 Neil Jenkins of the British Lions rugby team in a game against the Gauteng Lions in 1997
2 Manchester United's Ryan Giggs in a Premiership game against Liverpool, 11 November 1999

round three
twenty sporting questions

1 Tottenham Hotspur (Cup Winners' Cup, 1963)
2 Phil Neal (Liverpool, 1977 and 1984)
3 Jimmy Rimmer (on the bench for Man Utd in 1968, then injured playing for Aston Villa in 1982)
4 Hampden Park, Glasgow
5 Billy McNeill
6 It was contested by two English teams (Spurs and Wolves)
7 Francis Lee (Manchester City)
8 Peter Osgood
9 Coventry City
10 On the toss of a coin
11 Eric Cantona
12 Dundee
13 Owen Hargreaves (for Bayern Munich)
14 Paul Lambert (Borussia Dortmund, 1997)
15 Wrexham
16 Carl Shutt (for Leeds against Stuttgart)
17 Arsenal (1980 Cup Winners' Cup, 2000 UEFA Cup)
18 Newcastle United
19 John Wark
20 Birmingham City

round four
sporting links

1 Eldrick (Tiger) Woods Adedayo Adebayo
Lomano Tresor Lua-Lua
2 Leslie Mark Hughes
Slobodan Zivojinovic
Djamolodine Abdoujaparov

round five
where am I?

1 Leicester
2 Finland

round six
what happened next?

1 b)
2 a)

round seven
home or away

1 Take four wickets in an over
2 Steve McManaman – for Real Madrid
3 Greg Searle
4 Graham Obree

round eight
captain's away

1 Aston Villa, Crewe Alexandra, Crystal Palace, Kidderminster Harriers, Leyton Orient, Nottingham Forest, Plymouth Argyle, Port Vale, Preston North End, Queens Park Rangers, Rushden & Diamonds, Sheffield Wednesday, Tottenham Hotspur

round nine
mystery guest

1 Nick Faldo
2 John McEnroe

round ten
on the buzzer

1 David Narey
2 Tony Adams
3 Paolo Maldini
4 Darren Anderton
5 David Elleray
6 Davor Suker
7 Didier Deschamps
8 Paul Ince
9 Barry Venison
10 Pegguy Arphexad
11 Marcel Desailly
The player is: DAVID SEAMAN

game 38

round one
name the year

1 1985
2 1998

round two
picture board

1 Zimbabwe's Heath Streak begs for the wicket of Mark Ramprakash on Day One of the First Test, 2000
2 Almost human: Desert Orchid in his stable, 1998

round three
twenty sporting questions

1 Kuala Lumpur, Malaysia
2 Denise Lewis
3 Wales (Cardiff)
4 Swimming
5 Judy Oakes
6 Liz McColgan (née Lynch)
7 Tony Jarrett
8 Auckland, New Zealand
9 200 metres
10 Badminton
11 Iwan Thomas
12 Audley Harrison
13 Long Jump
14 1982 (Brisbane)
15 Bob Weir
16 Trinidad and Tobago
17 True (52)
18 Barry McGuigan
19 Dalton Grant
20 Manchester

round four
sporting links

1 Downhill ski-ing – in the downhill at Val Gardena
2 Virginia Wade – in 1968
3 Neil Thomas – silver in the floor exercises in both 1993 and 1994
4 Fencing – Sheen took gold in the foil
5 Neil Adams – at half-middleweight in 1981
6 Bobsleigh – in Innsbruck

round five
where am I?

1 Calgary
2 Kansas City

round six
what happened next?

1 c)
2 a)

round seven
home or away
1 *Jan Kodes*
2 *He scored a try against champions Australia*
3 *Frank Lampard Jnr*
4 *He was an amateur – Baddeley was only 18, and the first amateur to win the tournament for 39 years*

round eight
captain's away
1 *Beach volleyball – they are the signals which the players use behind their backs to help their partners*
2 *The British Mascot Grand National – The race held at Huntingdon was won by Harry the Hornet of Watford, from Cyril the Swan and Beau Brummie. The Scunny Bunny, who was widely tipped, finished well down the field*

round nine
mystery guest
1 *David Coulthard*
2 *Richard Dunwoody*

round ten
on the buzzer
1 *Cricket*
2 *In a golf bag*
3 *Football*
4 *Rugby League*
5 *On a tennis court*
6 *High-jump*
7 *Shoes*
8 *Cricket*
9 *Snooker*
10 *Football ('juventus' means 'young men' so they're known as 'the old lady'. Fiorentina play in violet, so they're 'the viola').*
11 *Rugby Union*
12 *Hurdles*

game 39

round one
name the year
1 *1998*
2 *1989*

round two
picture board
1 *The West Indies' Courtney Walsh at a warm-up for the First Test vs. England in June of 2000*
2 *Lance Klusener of South Africa unleashes a delivery during the Group A World Cup match against Sri Lanka in May 1999*

round three
twenty sporting questions
1 *Table tennis*
2 *Thompson (Jeff)*
3 *Tranmere Rovers*
4 *Trevino (Lee)*
5 *Triathlon*
6 *Titley (Jason)*
7 *Tennis*
8 *Tottenham Hotspur*
9 *Tokyo*
10 *Turkey*
11 *Tendulkar (Sachin)*
12 *Three*
13 *Taylor (Dennis)*
14 *Tomba (Alberto)*
15 *Thorburn (Paul)*
16 *Toronto*
17 *Turnberry*
18 *Torquay United*
19 *Tyson (Mike)*
20 *Tannadice Park*

round four
sporting links
1 *They were all last minute replacements. The Danish players cut short their summer holidays to fill Yugoslavia's place at Euro '92, Austrian reserve Leonhard Stock was promoted to the team the day before the race after coming first in two training runs, and Carl Llewellyn twice took over rides from injured colleagues*
2 *They are the only gold medallists from their countries. Crawford came from Trinidad and Tobago, Nesty was born there as well but represented Surinam; Akii Bua comes from Uganda*

round five
where am I?
1 *Belgium*
2 *Morocco*

round six
what happened next?
1 *b)*
2 *c)*

round seven
home or away
1 *Bradford Bulls*
2 *Dianne Modahl*
3 *Savo Milosevic*
4 *Cal Ripken Jnr*

round eight
captain's away
1 *An ice hockey puck*
2 *He's the only left-hander to win the tournament*

round nine
mystery guest
1 *Ian Botham*
2 *Linford Christie*

round ten
on the buzzer
1 *Germany*
2 *Costa Rica*
3 *France (Paris)*
4 *Fiji*
5 *Pakistan*
6 *Jamaica*
7 *Italy*
8 *Spain (Valderrama)*
9 *Croatia*
10 *Western Samoa*
11 *Portugal*
12 *The West Indies*
13 *South Africa*
14 *Brazil*
15 *England*

game 40

round one
name the year
1 *1997*
2 *1978*

round two
picture board
1 *England captain Nasser Hussain limbers up during practice for the First Test vs. Zimbabwe in May 2000*
2 *England's Ashley Giles in action against Sri Lanka on the first day of the Third Test in Colombo in March 2001*

round three
twenty sporting questions
1 *Gary McAllister*
2 *Sir Steven Redgrave*
3 *Shot putt*
4 *Ally McCoist*
5 *41*
6 *Carl Fogarty*
7 *Neville Southall*
8 *Laura Davies*
9 *Lord's*
10 *The Australians Woodbridge and Woodforde*
11 *Ivan Lendl*
12 *Bobby Robson (aged 66)*
13 *Arnold Palmer and Jack Nicklaus*
14 *Michael Judge*

15 True
16 New Zealand
17 Sergey Bubka
18 Ian Wright
19 Jeremy Guscott
20 Grand National

round four
sporting links

1 You'll find all their surnames on a beach – Ebbe Sand, Ian Buckett, Tim Breaker
2 Their surnames sound like types of sailing vessels – Jason Gallian, (galleon) Michael Lynagh, (liner) Nwankwo Kanu (canoe)

round five
where am I?

1 St Louis
2 Cuba

round six
what happened next?

1 b)
2 a)

round seven
home or away

1 Steve Backley
2 Norman Whiteside
3 Row for both sides – Philip was with Cambridge in '82 and '83, then with Oxford in '85 and '86. Young rowed for Cambridge in '90, then switched sides to partner Matthew in the Oxford boat in '91.
4 Tony Roche

round eight
captain's away

1 Motor racing – the Argentinian Grand Prix. Jody Sheckter won it driving a Wolf Ford car
2 The Marathon. Brazilian Ronaldo da Costa (nicknamed Ronaldinho) broke the record in Berlin in only his second marathon

round nine
mystery guest

1 Chris Boardman
2 Mika Hakkinen

round ten
on the buzzer

1 Paul Ince
2 Warren Hegg
3 Cliff Thorburn
4 Craig Stadler
5 Mick Skinner
6 John Crawley
7 Eric Bristow
8 Martin Offiah
9 Ole Gunnar Solskjaer
10 John Daly
11 Darren Anderton
12 David Lloyd
13 Ray Reardon
14 Jack Nicklaus
15 Thomas Hearns
16 Peter Bonetti

game 41

round one
name the year

1 1997
2 1983

round two
picture board

1 Venus Williams during her match with Emilie Loit in the 2000 French Open
2 Arsenal goalkeeper Alex Manninger in a March 2001 Premiership game against Aston Villa

round three
twenty sporting questions

1 David Elleray
2 Dallas Cowboys
3 Graham Taylor
4 Jose-Maria Olazabal
5 Jeremy Bates
6 England
7 Parma
8 Willie Carson
9 Sergi Brugera
10 Chris Eubank
11 Devon Malcolm
12 400 metres
13 Coventry City
14 Michael Schumacher
15 Wales
16 Linford Christie
17 Dean Saunders
18 USA
19 AC Milan
20 Warwickshire

round four
sporting links

1 Their names are all related to money – Pat Cash, Vic Marks, Florin Raducioiu
2 Their names are all related to precious stones – Paul Jewell, Ruby Walsh, Rushden and Diamonds

round five
where am I?

1 Ukraine
2 Czech Republic

round six
what happened next?

1 c)
2 a)

round seven
home or away

1 John Lukic – played in goal for Arsenal against Lazio
2 The Netherlands – who beat Korea in the final
3 Stephane Diagana
4 Jack Nicklaus

round eight
captain's away

1 Coventry (Street), Oxford (Street), Leicester (Square), Liverpool (Street Station)
2 Pontefract, Doncaster, Catterick, Redcar, Cartmell, Carlisle

round nine
mystery guest

1 Graham Gooch
2 Johnny Herbert

round ten
on the buzzer

1 George Graham
2 Darren Morgan
3 Real Madrid
4 Wim Jansen
5 Clive Woodward
6 Sir Alex Ferguson
7 Roger Taylor
8 Walter Smith
9 Steve Smith
10 Harry Redknapp
11 Denver Broncos
12 Ron Noades
13 St Helens
14 Tony Jacklin
15 Mike Gatting

game 42

round one
name the year

1 1979
2 2001

round two
picture board

1 Thomas Bjorn rues his tee shot from the 4th in the Heineken Classic at Perth in February 2001
2 Manager Lawrie Sanchez exults in Wycombe Wanderers' victory in the FA Cup quarter-final against Leicester City, 10 March 2001

round three
twenty sporting questions

1 *Cricket*
2 *Martina Hingis*
3 *Brian Kidd*
4 *Swimming*
5 *Ronnie O'Sullivan*
6 *Bruce Mclaren*
7 *Boxing*
8 *Steve Smith*
9 *Johnny Wilkinson*
10 *Sergio Garcia*
11 *Football. (Juventus means 'young men'... so naturally the club are nicknamed 'the old lady'!)*
12 *Paul Newlove*
13 *Stephen Hendry*
14 *400 metres*
15 *Sachin Tendulkar*
16 *Mats Wilander*
17 *Albania*
18 *Jonah Lomu*
19 *Lester Piggott*
20 *Open Golf Championship (appropriately, Old Tom Morris is indeed the oldest!)*

round four
sporting links

1 *They've all appeared on Top of the Pops – but not singing! Kevin presented a show with Dave Lee Travis, a large picture of Jocky Wilson was erected in the studio for a performance of 'Jackie Wilson Said' by Dexy's, and Jackie Stewart was in the video for Robbie Williams' 'Love Supreme'*
2 *They were all playing on their opponents' home grounds. The West Indies beat England at Lords, Liverpool beat Roma in Rome and Europe won the Cup at Muirfield Village – a course designed by... Jack Nicklaus.*

round five
where am I?

1 *San Marino. Their Grand Prix takes place at Imola, while their historic eight-second goal came in Bologna – both in Italy*
2 *Willesden*

round six
what happened next?

1 *a)*
2 *c)*

round seven
home or away

1 *Raymond Barneveld*
2 *Terry Neill*
3 *Bob Weir, in the hammer in '82 and the discus in '98*
4 *Mark Pitman*

round eight
captain's away

1 *Rollie Fingers (ex-San Diego Padres pitcher, now in the Hall of Fame), Yogi Berra (ex-New York Yankees catcher, now in Hall of Fame), Picabo Street (1998 Olympic ski-ing champion), Randy Wolf (pitcher for the Philadelphia Phillies)*
2 *Patrick Ewing (Olympic gold medallist with USA), Don Maclean (current NBA player with Miami Heat), Joan Crawford (former US captain now in the Hall of Fame, female), Kenny Rogers (baseball pitcher for the Texas Rangers)*

round nine
mystery guest

1 *Denise Lewis*
2 *Stephen Hendry*

round ten
on the buzzer

1 *Goodison Park*
2 *London Welsh*
3 *Golf (they've both staged the USPGA)*
4 *Preston Guild Hall*
5 *Spain*
6 *Roland Garros*
7 *Shrewsbury*
8 *Cricket (both are Australian Test grounds)*
9 *The Belfry*
10 *Twickenham*
11 *Barcelona*
12 *Sunderland or Benfica*
13 *Suzuka, Japan*
14 *Doncaster*
15 *Headingley*
16 *Villa Park*

game 43

round one
name the year

1 *2001*
2 *1992*

round two
picture board

1 *Leeds United's 'keeper Nigel Martyn shouts instructions in the game against Manchester United, 3 March 2001*
2 *Pat Cash jokes around in a charity match against Lleyton Hewitt during the Australian Open at Melbourne, January 2000*

round three
twenty sporting questions

1 *Bruce Grobbelaar*
2 *Gary Kirsten*
3 *George Weah*
4 *Wayne Ferreira*
5 *Ivory Coast*
6 *Haile Gebrselassie*
7 *Gerrie Coetzee*
8 *Kyalami*
9 *Egyptian*
10 *Nigeria*
11 *Francois Pienaar*
12 *Jonty Rhodes*
13 *Swimming*
14 *Pakistan*
15 *Jody Scheckter*
16 *Gary Player*
17 *Craig Johnston*
18 *Hicham El Guerrouj*
19 *Leicester*
20 *Lance Klusener*

round four
sporting links

1 *They all won titles as amateurs and then professionals. Laver's Grand Slams were 1962 (amateur) and 1969 (professional), Doherty took the amateur title in 1989 and the professional in 1997, Whitaker was world amateur champion in 1983 and professional champion in 1989.*
2 *They all ran the teams as well as competing in them. Brabham is the only driver to win the world title in his own car, Dalglish was the first player-manager to do the 'double' while Palmer captained the US team as well as playing.*

round five
where am I?

1 *Florida*
2 *Cyprus*

round six
what happened next?

1 *c)*
2 *b)*

round seven
home or away

1 *The Refrigerator*
2 *Neil Adams*
3 *George Burley – the Ipswich*

manager who was an FA Cup winner in 1978

4 Phillipe Carbonneau – the scrum-half appeared for Toulouse in 1996 and for Brive in the next two finals

round eight
captain's away

1 Ray 'Boom Boom' Mancini – True (WBA Lightweight champion in 1982)
2 Peter 'Young Rump Steak' Crawley – True (bare-knuckle champion in the 19th century)
3 Arthur 'Rock Hands' Robson – False
4 Verno 'The Inferno' Phillips – True (former WBO junior middleweight champion)
5 'Piano Mover' Jones – True (fought during 1930s)
6 Sheila 'La Rockette' Stallone – False
7 Lyndon 'The Man of' Steele – False
8 Harry 'The Human Windmill' Greb – True (World middleweight champion in the 1920s)

round nine
mystery guest

1 Michael Schumacher
2 Steve Davis

round ten
on the buzzer

1 Muttiah Muralitharan
2 Zinedine Zidane
3 Agostino Abbagnale
4 Ernie Els
5 Bill Beaumont
6 Joe Johnson
7 Dion Dublin
8 Boris Becker
9 Graham Gooch
10 Ray Reardon
11 Steve Smith
12 Kevin Keegan
13 Andre Agassi
14 Paul Palmer

game 44

round one
name the year

1 1991
2 1973

round two
picture board

1 Australia's Ian Thorpe celebrates a gold medal and a new world record in the men's 400 metre freestyle at the Sydney Olympics
2 Fiona May of Italy receives a red flag in the long-jump at the IAAF world championships in Athens, 1997

round three
twenty sporting questions

1 Dawson (Matt)
2 Derby County
3 Dressage
4 Dortmund
5 Delgado (Pedro)
6 Dobbin (Tony)
7 Danish
8 De Goey (Ed)
9 Durban
10 Dettori (Frankie)
11 Daly (John)
12 Darts
13 Detroit
14 Kerry Dixon.
15 Dundee
16 Decathlon
17 Derbyshire
18 Douglas (James 'Buster')
19 Davis (Steve)
20 Dalglish (Kenny)

round four
sporting links

1 Their wives all won gold medals at the same games. Zatopek's wife Dana Zatopekova took javelin gold, Connolly wed discus champion Olga Fikotova after the Games, Borzov married gymnast Lyudmila Turischeva after both won more medals at the 1976 Games.
2 They all set records for low scoring. The Australians and South Africans only managed 234 runs between them, the fewest in a completed Test; Norman completed his four rounds in just 267 strokes, while Charlton became the only player not to win a frame in a match at the Crucible

round five
where am I?

1 Eastbourne
2 Belfast

round six
what happened next?

1 b)
2 b)

round seven
home or away

1 Cincinnati
2 Brendan Reilly – he jumped 2.29m to set a new Irish record; Brendan previously competed for Britain and has a personal best of 2.32m
3 David Unsworth
4 Gavin Hamilton. He played for Scotland in the World Cup, then made his England debut in the first Test in South Africa

round eight
captain's away

1 Captain Cook
2 None – they're all underneath

round nine
mystery guest

1 Michael Johnson
2 Martina Navratilova

round ten
on the buzzer

1 Jimmy Hill
2 Peter Alliss
3 David Gower
4 Glenn Hoddle
5 Martin Brundle
6 Linford Christie
7 John Motson
8 John Francome
9 Sue Barker
10 Ron Atkinson
11 John Virgo
12 Richie Benaud
13 David Ginola
14 David Coleman